A Feast of Weeds

CALIFORNIA STUDIES IN FOOD AND CULTURE

Darra Goldstein, Editor

A Feast of Weeds

A LITERARY GUIDE TO FORAGING AND COOKING WILD EDIBLE PLANTS

Luigi Ballerini

Recipes by Ada De Santis
Illustrations by Giuliano Della Casa
Translated by Gianpiero W. Doebler

UNIVERSITY OF CALIFORNIA PRESS

BERKELEY LOS ANGELES LONDON

The publisher gratefully acknowledges the generous support of the Humanities Endowment Fund of the University of California Press Foundation.

University of California Press, one of the most distinguished university presses in the United States, enriches lives around the world by advancing scholarship in the humanities, social sciences, and natural sciences. Its activities are supported by the UC Press Foundation and by philanthropic contributions from individuals and institutions. For more information, visit www.ucpress.edu.

University of California Press
Berkeley and Los Angeles, California

University of California Press, Ltd.
London, England

The translation of this work has been funded by SEPS

Via Val d'Aposa 7 - 40123 Bologna - Italy
seps@seps.it - www.seps.it

Library of Congress Cataloging-in-Publication Data

Ballerini, Luigi.
    [Erbe da mangiare. English]
    A feast of weeds : a literary guide to foraging and cooking wild edible plants / Luigi Ballerini ; recipes by Ada De Santis ; illustrations by Giuliano Della Casa ; translated by Gianpiero W. Doebler.
        p.   cm. — (California studies in food and culture ; 38)
    Translation of: Erbe da mangiare.
    Translated from Italian.
    Includes bibliographical references and index.
    ISBN 978-0-520-27034-3 (cloth : alk. paper)
    1. Wild plants, Edible.   2. Cooking (Wild foods)   3. Cooking, Italian —
Southern style.   I. Title.   II. Series: California studies in food and culture ; 38.
    QK98.5.A1B3513   2012
    581.6'32—dc23   2012013040

Manufactured in the United States of America

21   20   19   18   17   16   15   14   13   12
10   9   8   7   6   5   4   3   2   1

The paper used in this publication meets the minimum requirements of ANSI/NISO z39.48 – 1992 (R 2002) (Permanence of Paper).

CONTENTS

Preface

INSTRUCTIONS FOR USING THIS BOOK

This book is based on the assumption that you can still get just far enough away from a city to find yourself in a field, forest, or clearing that has not been completely overrun by the fumes of some stinking factory or by the gasses emitted from millions of tailpipes. This is the kind of place in which you might be able to gather dozens of edible wild greens (carefully, of course, to avoid damaging the parts of the plant that allow its regeneration). Do you go hunting for mushrooms? If so, then why not for wild greens?

Why not briefly relive the primal experience of gathering? Although inscribed in every human being's DNA, gathering is often discouraged by environmental circumstances and even more so by the laziness into which we fall from having everything we want at hand in the refrigerator or cupboard. Why not dedicate a few hours of your weekend or vacation to an activity that (in addition to getting a breath of air and enjoying the singular beauty of many grasses and flowers) lets you reacquaint yourself with tastes you have forgotten—or that you never knew?

As in many fields—and particularly in the field of nutrition—what was once scorned as belonging to the poor and rural has become fashionable. Of necessity, those cursed by lack of time obtain their food only at the supermarket. However, those who manage to give their existence a less frenetic rhythm may learn, first, to recognize edible wild plants; second, to gather their shoots, leaves, and berries; and third, to cook such dishes as blackberry risotto, mullet with wild fennel, and soup made with the leaves of the red poppy.

If you have completely forsaken foraging (or never experienced it), it is best if you are guided by an expert in the beginning, even when looking for plants that you might recognize with your eyes closed: common greens like poppy, chicory, and dandelion; fruits like blueberries, strawberries, and blackberries; and cacti like the prickly pear. You must keep in mind that the point at which a plant is best to eat may not be when it has fully matured or when it has taken on its familiar appearance. Moreover, some plants look remarkably alike, and others, although very different, go by the same name. It is a good idea, then, that your guide be a *spiertu*—a term used in Puglia that means not only "expert" but also "awake" and "quick," which he must be if he is not to pass up the most savory specimens of your object of desire, as well as to avoid picking up those that can give you a belly ache.[1]

To become a forager (and through tasting what you gather, you inevitably will), you must proceed in stages, beginning with the plants that are found most easily and moving on to those for which, to locate good ones, you must reach some rocky seaside that has not been overrun by hordes of bivouacking tourists ready to leave behind indelible traces of their brief (and often unruly) stay.

It would be ideal if every novice gatherer were also an excellent cook, capable of both translating the recipes of others into lip-smacking lunches and dinners and formulating new ones. In the meantime, we begin by offering here a good number of recipes invented or elaborated by Ada De Santis, who knows these wild plants well and has long prepared them for herself, her husband Salvatore (Toto) Villani, and for their friends and guests. We are not speaking of a restaurant, but of a farm just outside Otranto, on the Salentine peninsula in southern Puglia—the so-called heel of Italy—where the ancient law of hospitality is still deeply respected. In fact, it is embraced there with passion and a justifiable measure of pride. I have had the good fortune to number myself among the elect souls who have enjoyed meals that Ada fashioned from what she had foraged.

Ada De Santis enthusiastically agreed to divulge the secrets of her kitchen and the surprising culinary wisdom passed on to her from generations of people who had a direct relationship with the earth, people who profoundly lived the bond uniting the wild and the cultivated. Her only caution was that, once transcribed, her recipes become not standardized formulas, but conversation starters. Reading them is a bit like speaking with her in her own kitchen, listening to the answers that she often gives to her guests' many questions: Where did you get it? How do you tenderize it? For how long do you cook it? Putting her instructions into practice seemed to us the most suitable and amiable way to continue to lunch and dine *chez elle,* to taste her menu of wild plants that are both edible and good for your health.

Except for the blueberries, which Ada "imports" from northern Italy, and the pomegranate, which by now is more a plant of the garden than of the forest, all of the plants in this cookbook can be found growing wild on Puglia's Salentine peninsula. Most of them (with the exception of capers) can also be found in the United States and particularly in California, where foraging is quickly becoming a trend and, to be sure, will soon morph into a radical movement. For some perverse reason, in fact, governmental agencies such as the Food and Drug Administration, faithful to their mandate, have decided that you can legally feed your friends all manner of plastic garbage but that you must stay away from the divinely flavored wild fennel from Topanga Canyon and any other edible wild plant (including nettles) whose nutritional and dietary values have benefited humanity since time immemorial. Of course, aspiring foragers must be careful to act in good faith, to tread softly wherever they go, to obtain all the necessary permits before foraging on government property, and to avoid eating something poisonous in error.

The temptation to eliminate from the list of Ada's edible wild greens, flowers, and fruits those that may not be accessible in your immediate surroundings has been quickly vanquished. Just as a good angler never leaves home without a portable fishing rod (a good trout stream may cross your way when you least expect it), practicing foragers know, and incipient ones will soon learn, that this type of rusticating pleasure is waiting for them everywhere across the nation, north and south of its borders, and, of course, overseas in every country where a widespread curiosity in the domain of taste, and a less intrusive concern for the sanitization of the world, has fostered a whole new wave of culinary excellence.

An introductory narrative has been written for each wild green in this book. The wild plants that found their way to Ada De Santis's kitchen became starting points for discussions that can range widely from the historical to the humorous, from the ancients to the absurd, from medieval medicine to modern science. Although these examinations sometimes stray from strictly culinary considerations, they always manage to find their way back to Ada's tasty creations.

When it is cold or rainy and the country roads are reduced to swamps, or when fields, beaches, and rocky coasts are merely memories, we might draw profit from looking at what Pliny or Hildegard von Bingen said about purslane or thyme, or from reading what Castore Durante and Nicholas Culpeper said about mint. We might be tempted to ponder questions like why did the Iroquois like strawberries so much? Or, just how thrilling *was* that woman Fats Domino claims to have found on Blueberry Hill?

Gathering, cooking, and reading seems like a triad of imperatives much more appetizing than the *believing, obeying, and fighting* through which one famous twentieth-century dictator tried to reduce Italy to idiocy (largely succeeding) and the *buying, pretending not to know, and not giving a damn about others* with which his political heirs pursue that same design.

We have checked the quoted sources as carefully as possible. The books that speak of wild plants are many, and a great number of stories and opinions ricochet rather carelessly from one to another. We have also made prudent use of the Internet, a *mare magnum* of both surprising information and superlative rubbish. Admittedly, it would have been nice to get to the bottom of the legend of the Virgin Mary's milk falling onto the thistle and of Mohammed's transformation of mallow into geraniums. We are still searching, but in the meantime, *A Feast of Weeds* must go to press. If we could have gone more slowly—on the back of a mule, perhaps, on foot, or by bicycle—there might have been time to go back to the first manifestations of those fables. If a wise reader knows how to assist us in this need, we would be, as they say, eternally grateful. Even more important, if something incorrect were to be found, we would like to know. The hopes for subsequent editions are the last of the last to die.

To conclude, this book came to light with the assistance of many old and new friends, some close to the world of wild greens, others only curious. I sincerely thank Giuliano Della Casa, the great illustrator of Pellegrino Artusi's *Science in the Kitchen and the Art of Eating Well.* Recognition is also due to Pino Peluso, a most valuable adviser and guide in the fields of the Salento; to botany lover and poet Angelo Lumelli; to Gaetano Tenore, who, at the last moment, placed hours of his masterly experience at my disposal; to Antonello Tenore, poet and great connoisseur of wild greens; to Uccio Milo, delightful companion and unexpected witness to many discoveries; to nursery man Roberto De Giorgi and Professor Francesco Minonne, who pulled me from the sands of many lexicographical doubts; to Professor Gabriella Giglioni, assured guide among the thorns of ancient texts; to Doctor Raffaele De Santis, generous and elegant resolver of textual and other innumerable problems; to Valentina De Santis, scrupulous photographer; to Luigi Rizzo and Gianluca Rizzo, providers of texts and elucidators of culinary customs; to Doctor Michele Tenore, for his benevolent and entertaining assistance; to Carmelo Santoro, indispensable broadcaster; and, of course, *dulcis in fundo,* to my editors at University of California Press, Dore Brown, Kate Marshall, and especially Stanley Holwitz, who first thought of turning *Erbe da mangiare* into English, and to Gianpiero Doebler, who masterfully did so.

Introduction

EATING GREENS DOES NOT MEAN GRAZING

The first to have eaten that herb known as *eringion* was Achille Troiano of Troia di Puglia. There is a pungent herb there whose only good part is its root—which induces lust. It is eaten with cinnamon and with clove... Marina of Offlaga was the inventor of the *fiadoni* and the *raffioli* of *enola,* [and] of eating bitter greens... Melibea of Manerbio was the inventor of *casoncelli, offelle* and *salviati.* She was a very determined woman, and it is clear that she killed a bear of monstrous size with her own hands.

ORTENSIO DI LANDO[1]

THE BODY OF VENUS IS PERHAPS the sexiest pasture in the world. Not so much the Venus *genitrix* Lucretius writes about at the beginning of *De rerum natura,* but the knockout goddess described in the works of many others, William Shakespeare's in particular. In *Venus and Adonis,* the bard has the Olympian and ultra-lascivious woman say, in offering herself to Adonis (who does not even want her, taken as he is—Adonis too!—by the pleasures of hunting wild boar: a real fixation): "I'll be a park and thou shalt be my deer / Feed where thou wilt, on mountain or in dale: / Graze on my lips, and if those hills be dry, / Stray lower, where the pleasant fountains lie." These verses are at once innocent and immodest, shaded, curvilinear, soft and tender and moist, excited by the hope of a *jouissance* that, naturally, not even the goddess of love will ever experience.[2] Killed by his own prey, Adonis is transformed, for a change, into a flower.

He who divinely yearns for love can only curse it and acknowledge the incomparable and always merciless sweetness of erotic desire. That the goddess of love herself would be the one formulating this burning equation between love and pain (caused by the inevitable removal of the desired object) has given more than one psychoanalyst a run for his money, to say nothing of his patients. But it is clear that we are speaking here of mental fields. If any grass grows there, it must only be the metaphoric grass of knowledge. On the other hand, real fields—or rather, the uncultivated lands, clearings, and meadows through which we walk in search of edible greens—do not have the same color of purest ivory as the body of Venus but, *imbre iuvante,* a beautiful green color or, if the rain has been disappointing or the earth tufaceous, a color that is deceptive like gold, or hard and strong like the wind that beats against it. This is what the gardens of Eden, where men found their first sustenance, must have been like.

In Genesis 1:29–30, God confronts the problem of nutrition, assigning both greens and tree fruit to man and leaving animals only the greens: "See, I have given you every plant yielding seed that is upon the face of all the earth, and every tree with seed in its fruit; you shall have them for food. And to every beast of the earth, and to every bird of the air, and to everything that creeps on the earth, everything that has the breath of life, I have given every green plant for food."[3]

The *Hymn of Amon-Re* offers a more marked distinction between edible jurisdictions:

> Thou art the sole one, who made all that is,
> The solitary sole one, who made what exists,
> From whose eyes mankind came forth,
> And upon whose mouth the gods came into being.
> He who made herbage for the cattle,
> And the fruit tree for mankind,
> Who made that (on which) the fish in the river may live,
> And the birds soaring in the sky
> He who gives breath to that which is in the egg,
> Gives life to the son of the slug,
> And makes that on which gnats may live,
> And worms and flies in like manner;
> Who supplies the needs of the mice in their holes,
> And gives life to flying things in every tree
> Hail to thee, who did all this!
> Solitary sole one, with many hands,
> Who spends the night wakeful, while all men are asleep,
> Seeking benefit for his creatures.
> Amon, enduring in all things, Atum and Har-akhti.[4]

The biblical story later records a radical rethinking—we don't know whether by God Himself or (more plausibly) by those charged with translating His will into text. Having perhaps completely misunderstood His words, they inform us that survivors of the Flood would not only continue to eat grass but would also be able to feed on meat (if butchered according to criteria that solidified over the centuries)—something that, up until that moment, had seemed out of the question: "God blessed Noah and his sons and said to them, 'Be fruitful and multiply, and fill the earth. The fear and dread of you shall rest on every animal of the earth and on every bird of the air, on everything that creeps on the ground, and on all the fish of the sea; into your hand they are delivered. Every moving thing that lives shall be food for you; and just as I gave you the green plants, I give you everything. Only, you shall not eat flesh with its life, that is, its blood'" (Genesis 9:1–4).

This is a step forward (or backward) that, a few centuries later, may have given metaphysical legitimacy (even if, obviously, that was not required) to the assertions of Galen, one of antiquity's greatest luminaries of medical science, who said: "as we [human beings] are unable to draw any nourishment from grass, although this is possible for cattle, similarly we can derive nourishment from radishes, albeit not to the same extent as from meat; for almost the whole of the latter is mastered by our natures; it is transformed and altered and constitutes useful blood; but, in the radish, what is appropriate and capable of being altered (and that only with difficulty, and with much labour) is the very smallest part; almost the whole of it is surplus matter, and passes through the digestive organs, only a very little being taken up into the veins as blood" (*On the Natural Faculties,* Book I, x).

Plutarch, who lived during the reigns of the Emperors Trajan and Hadrian, would have dissented peremptorily. His treatise "Of Eating of Flesh" is a veritable tirade against those who "set before people courses of ghastly corpses and ghosts" and "give those parts the names of meat and delicacies that but a little before lowed, cried, moved, and lived." Plutarch's reasoning goes in the opposite direction of the Bible's author: "As for those people who first ventured upon eating of flesh, it is very probable that the whole reason of their so doing was scarcity and want of other food; for it is not likely that their living together in lawless and extravagant lusts, or their growing wanton and capricious through the excessive variety of provisions then among them, brought them to such unsociable pleasures as these, against Nature. . . . But whence is it that a certain ravenousness and frenzy drives you in these happy days to pollute yourselves with blood, since you have such an abundance of things necessary for your subsistence? . . . Why do you profane the lawgiver Ceres, and shame the mild and gentle Bacchus, as not furnishing you with sufficiency?"[5]

Documents such as this clearly tell of the quarrel between supporters of a vegetarian diet and the earliest steak grillers. In antiquity, eating meat often became an opportunity to be full of big talk: in Book VII of the *Iliad,* we see "the long savory cuts that line the backbone" of a roasted ox given to the gigantic Ajax of Telemon by Agamemnon as a sign of honor for the duel he fought with Hector that had been interrupted by nightfall.[6] But these are trifles compared to those of the superb athlete Milo of Croton (sixth century B.C.), who, after having brought down and killed an ox with his fist, hoisted it onto his shoulders, carried it home, roasted it, and then ate it whole, by himself. According to another legend, this one circulated by Pausanias, he did the same—the transport, not the lunch—with his own monument to Olympia (*Description of Greece,* Book VI, XIV, 5–9).

During the High Renaissance, Leonardo da Vinci shines in the opposite camp. His reputation as a vegetarian artist was so singular and proverbial that, in a letter written in 1516 by the Florentine explorer Andrea Corsali, the author informs us of having come across, at the mouth of the Indus River, peoples "who do not dine on anything whatsoever that has blood . . . like our Leonardo da Vinci." We must ask ourselves if the embarrassment of having to paint a supper with lamb (which he eventually omitted) on the table might not have contributed, along with the aesthetic torment, to the historical fact that completion of Leonardo's famous fresco in Santa Maria delle Grazie dragged on for a good four years (1495–98).

To Leonardo, those who dined on animal meat were the same as cannibals, and they are violently attacked as such in a text accompanying an anatomical study preserved at Windsor. With irate wonder, Leonardo asks himself: "Does not nature bring forth a sufficiency of simple things to produce satiety? Or if you cannot content yourself with simple things, can you not by blending these together make an infinite number of compounds, as did Platina and other authors who have written for epicures?"[7]

A similar bell is sounded at the end of the seventeenth century in England. John Evelyn (1620–1706), in a book dedicated entirely to salad greens (*Acetaria, a Discourse of Sallets [Salads]*), translates a quote from the Latin of a contemporary botanist, John Ray.[8] As Evelyn puts it, "The Use of Plants is all our Life long of [such] universal Importance and Concern, that we can neither live nor subsist in any Plenty with Decency or Conveniency or be said to live indeed at all without them. . . . and ah, how much more innocent, sweet and healthful is a Table cover'd with these than with all the reeking

Flesh of butcher'd and slaughter'd Animals! Certainly Man by Nature was never made to be a *Carnivorous* Creature [with all due respect to Galen!]; nor is he armed at all for Prey and Rapin, with gag'd [jagged] and pointed Teeth and crooked Claws, sharpened to rend and tear: But with gentle Hands to gather Fruit and Vegetables, and with Teeth to chew and eat them." Then, with a lashing rhetoric of great efficacy, he concludes, "Nor do we so much as read the Use of Flesh for Food, was at all permitted him [man], till after the Universal Deluge."[9]

A second conflict, much less threatening than the first, percolates through the pages of the present volume. It consists of the different judgments that writers express regarding wild plants versus those that have been cultivated. Before addressing this, it's wise to note briefly that in the Judeo-Christian context (or at least at the beginning of this very long and often infelicitous tradition), agriculture was born as the result of a curse: "Because you have listened to the voice of your wife, and have eaten of the tree about which I commanded you, 'You shall not eat of it,' cursed is the ground because of you; in toil you shall eat of it all the days of your life; thorns and thistles it shall bring forth for you; and you shall eat the plants of the field. By the sweat of your face you shall eat bread" (Genesis 3:17–19). The wrath of the Lord knows no bounds indeed: man must be demoted to the level of the beasts (thorns, thistles, field plants), from which he will be able to distinguish himself solely by putting himself to work like a beast, for a handful of ears of wheat.

However, if we can put this curse aside for a moment, we discover that in different cultural environments, the passage from gathering to cultivation is seen as a great opportunity for celebrating the acuity of the human brain. Evidence of this sort, which we could call proto-Humanistic, is not rare in the Greco-Roman world. Such pride emerges unexpectedly even in texts not specifically dedicated to agro-nutrition. In Sophocles's *Antigone,* for example, at the beginning of the second chorus, we read that one of the results of which man (that great prodigy!) may boast is having succeeded in exhausting tireless, immortal Gaia—the most ancient of the gods—by raising clods of dirt with horse-drawn plows. Centuries later, in a text less fundamental (and, perhaps because of this, even more persuasive from our point of view), at the start of his poem *Medicamina faciei femineae* (The cosmetics of women; also translated as The art of beauty), Ovid expresses his satisfaction with the cosmetic use of cultivated plants (hardly the sweat of one's brow!): "Art improves nature; 'twas by art we found / The vast advantage of the furrow'd ground; / The soil manur'd, a fruitful harvest bore, / Where thorns and hungry brambles grew before; / By art the gard'ner grafts his trees, to bear / A kinder fruit, and recompense his care."[10]

The debate over whether plants must all be considered cultivatable or not dates back at least to Theophrastus, who has a negative opinion of it (see the Capers chapter in this book) and who mentions Hipponax, a philosopher with, conversely, a positive opinion. Theophrastus takes issue with Hipponax and raises a point of capital importance for the purposes of this book: "Hippon[ax] declares that of every plant there exists both a cultivated and a wild form, and that 'cultivated' simply means that the plant has received attention, while 'wild' means that it has not; but though he is partly right, he is partly wrong. It is true that any plant deteriorates by neglect and so becomes wild; but it is not true that every plant may be improved by attention, as has been said" (*Enquiry into Plants,* III, ii, 1–2).

As far as flavors and medicinal virtues are concerned, the strength of this assertion is verifiable even (or especially) today, since cultivation predominates and is sustained by techniques so invasive and chemically evil that cases where the cultivated plant is the source of genuine biological poisonings are no longer infrequent (not unlike what has happened in the meat world among various brands of hamburger).

Here's an easy comparison: try making a salad with arugula that you have gathered yourself in a field and compare its taste with what you have made a hundred times with prewashed and sterilized arugula bought at the supermarket or even at a farmers' market. It's easy to predict the comment that will immediately come to your lips: "There is no comparison."

A source of pride, cultivation of plants and edible greens must also profess to be the result of political and economic will. This dates back to the time of Charlemagne and his immediate heir, Louis the Pious, in the *Capitulare de Villis,*[11] a collection of seventy directives for the governance and management of real estate owned by the emperor. The text is a forest of *we wish*es: "we wish our stewards [the highest authorities operating in the territory] to give a tithe of all our products to the churches," "we wish that each steward in his district have measures of the *modius,*" "we wish that every year during Lent . . . our stewards carefully render according to our instructions the money arising from the products of our land, after we know for the particular year what our income is," and so on. Extremely valuable to us is the last entry in the catalog, wherein "we wish that the stewards have all sorts of plants in the garden," followed by a list that includes (beyond the easily imaginable greens like beans and rosemary) anise, arugula, mallow, squill, chicory, mint, poppy, parsnip, and the like—but not, however, chamomile, which we are told Frankish women used to turn their hair blonde.

Reading the *Capitulare de Villis,* we learn above all that the Carolingians, whom we might be inclined to imagine as full-fledged carnivores (with the blonde emperor always on horseback behind some wild boar, like Adonis and Asterix), were involved in a kind of love affair with edible and medicinal plants. They certainly cultivated many more of them than we do, and they were pleased to watch them grow (so tender and dewy)—to the point that someone by the peculiar name of Walafrid Strabo[12] wrote very beautiful poetry about them in Latin hexameter, including an entire poem called *Hortulus* (basically, "little vegetable garden"). And it matters little that, in addition to the odor of manure (which, in the opening, the author candidly admits to handling), the inspiration came to him from Virgil's *Georgics.* In it we read astonishing words about, among other things, the poppy (see the relevant chapter in this book).

However things might have been (or are), the Carolingian idea of cultivating greens certainly had something to do not only with the idea of a nutritional regimen but also (judging by the presence of inedible plants like squill) with the renewed hope of finding remedies for the infirmities of the organism. In short, it was a question of medicine. It had virtually nothing to do with a program of gastronomic refinement (for that, we would have to wait for the Renaissance). Furthermore, the distance between wild and cultivated, with respect to both nutrition and taste, must have been much less in the time of the garden than it is in our transgenic era. Today, this distance seems insurmountable.

We have already noted Leonardo's mention of the "infinite number of compounds" that can be made following the formulas of Platina (who had decanted them from a then-unpublished manuscript of Maestro Martino)[13] in which the distinction between wild and cultivated is noticeably softened. On the other hand, writing in England in the seventeenth century, Nicholas Culpeper, a physician who did not think about cuisine, notes the different medicinal effectiveness of things that grow on their own in the field and those grown in the garden. At a gastronomic level, the ball returns to Italy, or nearly so, in the sense that it is picked up by an Italian living abroad, Giacomo Castelvetro of Modena (1546–1616), forced into exile (like his uncle Ludovico, the famous Aristotelian scholar) by "the evils and cruelties of the Roman Inquisition." In *Brieve racconto di tutte le radici, di tutte l'erbe e di tutti i frutti, che crudi o cotti in Italia si mangiano* [Brief account of all the roots, all the herbs and all the fruits that are eaten in Italy, whether raw or cooked],[14] the distance between wild and cultivated is finally mitigated in a decisively culinary manner. As the title states, emphasis is placed on that which is best served as it is, and that which it is better to blanch, boil, grate, or the like. Among other things, this means that the practice of cultivation had been adopted in the case of some species, while gathering continued to be preferred in the case of others—just as Theophrastus had wished!

Addressing his English benefactors, Castelvetro speaks of Italy with some bitterness (understandably, given his condition as an exile). Once he has vented himself, however, nostalgia takes the upper hand, and the mere memory of a flavor is enough to make him hope that his hosts might be inspired to reproduce it. A pedagogic urge, directly connected to pride in his own Italian origins, is triggered within him by the observation that despite "the variety of good things to eat which have been introduced into this noble country of yours [England] over the past fifty years," including many plants "previously considered inedible, worthless or even poisonous, . . . few of these delicious and health-giving plants are being grown to be eaten." And even when the English do plant them, they do so "less for the table than for show by those who want to boast of their exotic plants and well-stocked gardens."[15]

In the wake of this more or less plausible Italic primacy (and bearing a clear imprint of the Renaissance, which in the sixteenth century expanded its sphere of application from art, music, political science, and so on to include gastronomy as well), Castelvetro starts to expatiate on salads as the specialty where the national talent shows itself best. And here, almost without noticing, we have slipped to the third and last point that this introduction seeks to illustrate. After the carno-vegetarian conflict and the one between wild and cultivated plants, there now comes the conflict between Italy and the rest of Europe. True, Castelvetro polemicizes more with the Germans than with the English (perhaps it seemed to him to be in bad taste to criticize those who were supporting him), but he clearly appears to be addressing the latter indirectly. For example, "It is not necessary to have many good greens to ensure that the salad comes out well." Rather, what counts is the know-how, the *techné*, the mastery of the art. He continues, "It is important to know how to wash your herbs, and then how to season them. Too many housewives and foreign cooks get their green stuff all ready to wash and put it in a bucket of water, or some other pot, and slosh it about a little, and then, instead of taking it out with their hands, as they ought to do, they tip the leaves and water out together, so that all the sand and grit is poured out with them. Distinctly unpleasant to chew on . . . " Look how misplaced national pride can be!

As for seasoning, here again the operation is complex and cannot be reduced to gestures of ordinary desolation.

> I insist that first you must shake your salad really well and then dry it thoroughly. . . . Then put it into a bowl in which you have previously put some salt and stir them together, and then add the oil with a generous hand, and stir the salad again with clean fingers or a knife and fork, which is more seemly, so that each leaf is properly coated with oil. Never do as the Germans and other uncouth nations do—pile the badly washed leaves, neither shaken nor dried, up in a mound like a pyramid, then throw on a little salt, not much oil and far too much vinegar, without even stirring. And all this done to produce a decorative effect, where we Italians would much rather feast the palate than the eye.[16]

It's hard to say whether the Italian superiority of which Castelvetro boasts is plausible. In reality, we have already seen how medieval gardens were well supplied with comestible greens (and not only those that enjoyed imperial protection). We must add here that the oldest recipe for salad that comes down to us was conceived in England around 1390: "Take parsley, sage, garlic, chiboll [spring onions], onions, leeks, borage, mint, porrects [more leeks], fennel and cress, rue, rosemary, purslane. Lave [i.e., bathe] and wash them clean. Pike them [choose the best ones], pluck them small with thine hands [tear them into small pieces] and mix them well with raw oil. Lay on vinegar and salt and serve it forth." Writing this were the master cooks of Richard II (1367–1400), who, beyond his fame as a *viandier* and as a gourmet to which the recipe book *The Forme of Cury*[17] bears witness, acquired celebrity among posterity thanks to William Shakespeare, who chose the tragic incidents of that king as the subject of one of his most famous dramas.

That said, it is not unthinkable that in England table greens may have known highs and lows. They may have been appreciated in some periods and detested in others, and Castelvetro may have intervened at a moment when the winds were favorable to his assertions. In fact, the English traveler Robert Dallington, in *A Survey of the Great Duke's State of Tuscany. In the Year of our Lord 1596,* had emphatically noted this Italian predilection for salad about twenty years before Castelvetro had boasted of it: "Concerning Herbage, I shal not need to speake, but that it is the most generall food of the

Tuscan, at whose table a Sallet is as ordinarie as Salt at ours; for being eaten of all sorts of persons, and at all times of the yeare: of the rich because they love to spare; of the poore, because they cannot choose; of many Religious, because of their vow."

Perhaps an echo of this more or less Italic passion for salad[18] remains in the expression *Italian dressing*, which in the United States indicates an emulsion for salad based on water, oil, vinegar or lemon juice, salt, pepper, chopped onion, peppers, sugar (not always), garlic, oregano, fennel, and dill. Is it necessary to add that this very popular seasoning on the American side of the Atlantic is unknown in the country from which it takes its name?

Armed with these doubts, we turn back to the main thread of our discussion and happily conclude for now with two observations by Emilio Faccioli in his brief introduction to the Italian edition of Castelvetro's work:

For many, the pleasure of cultivating vegetables for consumption by one's family is still common, and although it is ever more rare, the delight of searching by walking among the greens that grow wild still exists. One can take pride in being able to recognize them and in making enviably exquisite dishes from them. . . . Greens, fruits, and roots know how to exert themselves on the heart of the man who, through the adverse events of life, has not been able to enjoy them as much as he might want. Merely naming them, seeing them again and tasting them in his imagination, he feels awakened in himself the memory of his native land and of the domestic customs to which all the sweetness of a lost time is tied.[19]

Bay Leaves

LAURUS NOBILIS; ITALIAN: *ALLORO*

THE STORY OF HOW THE LAUREL TREE and its bay leaves entered into the imaginary, symbolical, and real worlds of culture should be known to everyone. But to avoid any misunderstanding, its introduction will be reviewed briefly here, following Ovid in particular (*Metamorphoses* I, 452–567). Apollo, an expert archer, makes fun of the boy Eros fooling around with an arrow bigger than he is. Eros does not appreciate the mockery, and as soon as he returns to Parnassus, he strikes Apollo, the god of prophecy and poetry, with a dart of gold, and Daphne, the nymph, with one of lead. The result: Apollo falls hopelessly in love with Daphne at first glance, while Daphne is nauseated by him. A follower of Artemis (and, therefore, a hunter), Daphne was completely taken with the dewy pleasures of hunting in the woods and had never given much thought to nuptial pleasures. She had even sworn to herself and to her father, Peneus (who didn't much like the idea of not having grandchildren), to remain a virgin. Ignoring the amorous attention of a god, however, is not easy. It is not enough for Daphne simply to run away, since it doesn't take much for the fleet-footed Apollo to reach her. But when the girl feels his breath on her neck, she decides to take a step (that is more correctly called a transition) from which no retreat is possible. She asks for help from her father, who, instead of taking advantage of the opportunity to become a grandfather, surprisingly consents to Daphne's desire and transforms her into the beautiful laurel tree that we know and that has inspired sculptors and painters, poets, and musicians of every type, form, and age.[1]

Ovid adds two details to this tale that cause even those who are not poetically inclined to shiver. First, placing a hand on the trunk of the tree, Apollo feels Daphne's heart beating and, overcome, covers the bark with kisses. Second, to his request to possess her (if not in flesh and bone, at least as a symbolic tree), Daphne beautifully responds yes in the only way she can: she shakes her thick mass of leaves. (Alas, you can't have everything.) His kisses rebuffed, Apollo—the god who strikes from afar, the deity who knows the mind of Zeus—ends up making Daphne a proposal that she cannot refuse. He will turn her leaves into the symbol of victory over enemies, rivals, victims, and—since all victories need to be celebrated—poetry, at least of the epic sort, particularly if it describes the endeavors of ancient Romans. To inscribe the virtues of lyric poetry under the heading of "laurel," however, we must wait until Petrarch in the fourteenth century.[2]

Behind this tender and subtly ambiguous story hides a cult that is rather violent and difficult to reconstruct. It would be a pity, however, not to go a few steps down that path. I don't mean to pursue it to the story's origins (which are ultimately lost in the night of the human soul), but only to the point where narrated facts become clues to hidden (but not undiscoverable) material truths. At a minimum, these truths confound the values deposited moralistically in the more codified and superficial version of the myth.

The presence of Peneus (father and river) permits us to transfer the action to the Vale of Tempe, in Thessaly, where Apollo, in service to King Admetus, had gone to purify himself after the assassination of the Delphic she-dragon and the usurpation of her sanctuary. Here, the stories branch out and fragment beyond all possibility of reducing them to a diagram. Refusing categorically to enter that hornet's nest, I suggest that the courageous reader turn to the pages of Karl Kerény (*The Gods of the Greeks*) and of Jacques Brosse (*Mythologie des arbres*) and to the sources to which those authors refer.[3] For now, we must be satisfied with the discovery that the Thessalian (and pre-Hellenic) Daphne—before being sweetened in the verses of some Greek mythographer and, finally, in Ovid's texts—must have been a ("red-purple," "blood red") priestess of Mother Earth, the ruler of an orgiastic cult practiced by "laurel-dependent" maenads. At Delphi (where Apollo may have returned with the tree dedicated to him), the chewing of laurel leaves would become the principal exercise through which Pythia (and only she, because a specific prohibition was in force for everyone else) reached the state of excitement that allowed her to pronounce oracles. This does not exactly mean that there cannot be an oracle without an orgy, but certainly that there is no oracle without a transformation, and that excitement can mean the integration of an enigma with the experience of knowledge.

In this inhospitable and fearsome Thessaly (and more widely, in regions in northern Greece), what happened to Apollo seems to function as a type of "tablecloth" over the underlying, preexisting story that trembled and pounded to make itself known. Even the story that has Apollo arriving in Thessaly from Delphi is suspect, acceptable only in a narration told from the perspective of what happened at Delphi. It is known that the deity of the bow and the kithara had loved other nymphs before Daphne, including Aria, also called Dione, and consecrated to the pre-Hellenic cult of the oracular oak of Dodona. There is a strong temptation to read in these loves a conquest by invading gods (the Hellenics in particular, who came form the north, the land of the Hyperboreans) and previous sieges (first prehistoric and then Pelasgian). Is it not of supreme importance that oak-leaf garlands were replaced by the laurel leaves with which we crown the foreheads of caesars and poets?[4] Is it not extraordinary that the Delphi deity's message was entrusted to the rustling of laurel leaves in the wind and that this repeats—exactly— what happened (but with oak) at Dodona? And is it not equally extraordinary that the same thing occurs, this time without interpretive mediation by some mumbling Pythia, in the text of the Ovidian *Metamorphoses*?

In the first century of the Common Era, Tibullus (in Elegy V of his second book of poetry) captures well the sense of peace, civility, and gentleness of which the laurel would subsequently become a metaphorical symbol (and of which Apollo becomes the guarantor). He recalls prophetesses who "prophesied of omens dire, / The comet's monitory fire, / Stones raining down, and tumult in the sky / Of trumpets, swords, and routed chivalry; / The very forests whispered fear, / And through the stormful year / Tears, burning tears, from marble altars ran; / Dumb beast took voice to tell the fate of man; / The Sun himself in light did fail / As if he yoked his car to horses mortal-pale." But at the same time, the poet is happy to announce that "Such was the olden time. O Phoebus [Apollo], now / Of mild, benignant brow, / Let those portents buried be / In the wild, unfathomed sea! / Now let thy laurel loudly flame / On altars to thy gracious name, / And give good omen of a fruitful year / Crackling laurel if the rustic hear, / He knows his granary shall bursting be, / And sweet new wine flow free," and so on.[5]

Yes, because the laurel always speaks, either with its crown when the wind blows or as leaves placed on a roaring fire in a chimney, particularly if there is no wind. The poet Angelo Lumelli swears that where he comes from (the hills of Alexandria, where the regions of Liguria, Lombardy, and Piedmont meet), people still hear omens in the rustling of laurel leaves, or they did until recently.

But it's time to delve into the great miracle that is Petrarch's *Canzoniere,* which would extract from the *lauro* (but in Latin, where plants are feminine, from *Laura*) shades of meaning that literally changed the course of poetry and of the thought that subtends it. Poetry would have to wait for Rimbaud, more than four and a half centuries later, before it would experience an earthquake of similar magnitude.

That the myth of Apollo and Daphne may lend itself to the multiple aims of Petrarchan poetic reasoning is well known by everybody (except Harold Bloom, who did not think to place Petrarch in the canon of Western poetry), but not everyone may realize what a stroke of genius it was to have captured the alluvial malleability of its essence. In other words, Petrarch chose, as the propulsive muscle of his writing, the harmonious encounter of two contradictions: one creature who concedes when she can no longer concede, and a pursuer who does not give up pursuing, with the full knowledge that his pursuit will not be fruitful. Through this inexhaustible plot, Petrarch restores to the world the sense of a truth that does not need to prove itself (what Nietzsche would have described as a truth in an extra moral sense). The metamorphosis in Petrarch's poetry, as Elémire Zolla observed with great acumen, is the transformation of an inert material, the silvery lead that the Athenians extracted from Laurium (the mine that made Athens rich), into a Laura who is "the aura [*l'aura*] or the air [*l'aria*], the spirit of knowledge; it is gold [*l'auro*] the solar metal or finally the laurel [*lauro*] . . . the plant of prophecy, of virginity, of genius or angelic guardianship. Finally, Petrarch added a puzzle to the puns: she is the golden mane [*l'aureo crine*], symbol of the ether that envelops the sky like hair envelops the head. . . . The tormenting melody of the Petrarchan verse shows that these games are the only way of speaking about the unspeakable. These vertiginous and almost mad exchanges are narrated with the most intense, the most sweetly anxious voice that you could hear, with the most intimate and truthful seriousness. Laura is, therefore, the air: *l'aura che 'l verde lauro e l'aureo crine / soavemente sospirando move / fa con sue viste leggiadrette e nove / l'anime da lor corpi pellegrine.*"[6]

It is strange, though not unimaginable, that a poet who raised the most sublime (and tormented) paean to the unattainability of permanent truth, to its manifestation as aspiration, to its being (like love) a thrust that does not produce equal and opposite motions, would let a crown of laurel be placed on his head (in Rome, on the Capitoline Hill)—perhaps by the hairy hands of the Orso (Bear) of Anguillara, one of two senators charged with the governance of Rome at the time (the Pope was in Avignon when Petrarch wrote). Yet it was only April 8, 1431, and Petrarch was a mere *adulescentulus* (as the forty-year-old Cicero would have said). The crown of laurel declared him *magnum poetam et historicum*. It conferred to him all the privileges enjoyed by professors of the noble and liberal arts and by those with Roman citizenship (a crown that one could carry wherever he wanted).

It might seem tragicomic to pass from the Capitoline Hill (even in turbulent years like those of the Avignon captivity) to the kitchen of our own house, but we must do so just the same. With Petrarch behind us, we find Alain Denis, who remarks: "The bay leaf is part of the aromatic bundle at the base of marinades, gravies and sauces in every kitchen—used almost as frequently as parsley . . . . Bay leaves surround the figs to be dried, the steaks to be roasted, skewers, livers, and many other foods. The English boil it in the milk used to prepare *crème brûlée*. It is better to use the mature and dry leaves rather than the young and fresh ones, which give a bitter tone to sauces and a flavor that is too intense. At any rate, it must be used sparingly."[7]

Nor will we forget the great English physician and astrologer Nicholas Culpeper (1616–54) and his renowned *Complete Herbal* (1653), according to which the laurel, the tree of the sun, is very potent, especially when the stars are in the constellation of Leo: "Neither witch nor devil, thunder nor lightning, will hurt a man in the place where a Bay-tree is."[8]

BAY LEAF GRAPPA

Makes about 1 pint (500 ml)

35 fresh bay leaves
2 cups (500 ml) unflavored grappa
2½ tablespoons (30 g) sugar

Wash the bay leaves carefully and dry them. Make 2 or 3 incisions in each leaf (it is enough to bend them a little with your hands or use your fingernails). This facilitates the flow of the sap, which will give the grappa the characteristic taste of the laurel. Put the leaves in a 1-quart (1-l) glass container with an airtight cap. Pour in the grappa, add the sugar, and stir until the sugar dissolves. Cap and leave in the open for 8 days (and nights). Filter through a tight-weave strainer and store in a capped bottle. This is an excellent after-dinner drink.

BAY LEAF INFUSION

Serves 1

5 fresh bay leaves
Sugar, to taste
Zest of 1 untreated (unwaxed) lemon, in strips

Harvest the bay leaves and let them dry for 8 days in a shallow dish. Once dried, place them in a glass jar with an airtight cap until you are ready to make the infusion. For the infusion, proceed in this simple fashion: pour ⅔ cup (150 ml) water into a 1-quart (1-l) saucepan, cover, place over medium heat, and bring to a boil. When the water boils, crumble in the bay leaves. Re-cover and let boil for another 10 minutes.

Filter the infusion through a tight-weave strainer into a cup and add the sugar and lemon zest. This infusion is both a digestif and a disinfectant and must be drunk hot.

BAY LEAF LIQUEUR

Makes about 2 cups (500 ml)

40 fresh bay leaves
¼ cup (50 g) sugar
1⅔ cups (400 ml) pure alcohol (95 percent)

Wash the bay leaves carefully and dry them. Make 2 or 3 incisions in each leaf (it is enough to bend them a little with your hands or use your fingernails).

This facilitates the flow of the sap, which will give the liqueur the characteristic taste of the laurel. Put the leaves in a 1-quart (1-l) glass container with an airtight cap. Pour in 6½ tablespoons (100 ml) water, add the sugar, and mix with a spoon until the sugar has dissolved. Add the alcohol and continue to mix for a few minutes. Cap and leave the infused mixture in a cool, dark place for 15 days.

Filter through a tight-weave strainer and store in a capped bottle.

ANCHOVY PIE WITH BAY LEAVES

Serves 4

14 ounces (400 g) medium-size anchovies
¾ teaspoon (5 g) fine salt
30 Belgian endive leaves
2 tablespoons (20 g) dried bread crumbs
  Scant 2 tablespoons (15 g) capers in brine, rinsed
2 cloves garlic, minced
2 tomatoes, finely chopped
4 teaspoons (5 g) minced fresh parsley
2 teaspoons (2 g) ground dried oregano
¼ cup (60 ml) extra-virgin olive oil
18 fresh bay leaves

Remove the heads from the anchovies, then rinse the fish carefully. Slit each anchovy along its belly, open it, being careful not to separate the halves, and remove the backbone. Rinse the fish again carefully and dry them, again making sure not to separate the halves.

In a 1½-quart (1.5-l) saucepan, combine 1 cup (240 ml) water and ½ teaspoon (3 g) of the salt and bring to a boil. Add the endive leaves, blanch for 1 minute, drain, and dry.

Preheat the oven to 400°F (200°C). In a medium-size bowl, combine the bread crumbs, capers, garlic, tomatoes, parsley, and the remaining ¼ teaspoon (2 g) salt. Mix everything well and divide into two equal portions. Oil the bottom and sides of a 12-by-7-inch (30-by-18-cm) baking dish with 4 teaspoons (20 ml) of the oil. Spread half of the bay leaves on the bottom of the dish and top with half of the anchovies, flesh side up. Spread one portion of the bread-crumb mixture evenly on top of the anchovies. Arrange half of the endive leaves on the crumb mixture and sprinkle the surface with 4 teaspoons (20 ml) of the oil. Repeat the layers, ending with the endive leaves and the remaining oil.

Place the dish in the oven and bake until hot, about 10 minutes. The pie may be eaten hot or cold.

Blackberries

IN ITALIAN, BOTH BLACKBERRIES AND MULBERRIES are called *more*. It's a shame, however, that blackberries, which grow on a bush, have nothing at all to do with the berries that ripen on the mulberry tree, "adorned [like a fig tree] with gemmules of gold," that the showers of March "strike with silver"[1] (according to what Angiolo Silvio Novaro, 1866–1938, tells us), just as it strikes the "old tiles of the roof" and "the dried motes of the garden." If our berries were mulberries, we would not have to be surreptitious (as we must be here) in plunging into the wonderful story of contested and final love (he kills himself believing she is dead, then she kills herself seeing him dead) between Pyramus and Thisbe as told by Ovid (*Metamorphoses* IV, 55 et seq.) and reprised in a farcical manner by William Shakespeare in *A Midsummer Night's Dream*, his comic masterwork.

A mulberry tree plays a central role in the Ovidian fable. The two lovers should have met under it; instead, it becomes the silent witness to their death. The blood sprays (he kills himself with a sword) from the body of Pyramus "just as when a water pipe bursts, if there is some flaw in the lead, and through the narrow hissing crack a long stream of water shoots out, and beats on the air. The fruits of the tree were sprinkled with his blood, and changed to a dark purple hue." A few minutes later, it is Thisbe's turn, and her prayer (fulfilled by the gods) is that the tree "bear forever the marks of our death: always have a fruit of a dark and mournful hue, to make men remember the blood we two have shed!"[2]

Even the humble blackberries from a bush, however, can give great satisfaction, both on a gastronomic level and with regard to stories. More than one hundred species of forest blackberries exist.[3] They hybridize easily among themselves (rendering it difficult to catalog them) and are excellent plants to counter the temptations of the flesh in front of which even Saint Francis— he who domesticated wolves and did not mince words when speaking with popes—seems to have had a moment of hesitation. There are many accounts of supposed events in which the saint throws himself naked (in the depths of winter) among the thorns, which may have been those of a bed of roses (same family, after all). A bramble bush still exists at the sanctuary of Porziuncola, where Saint Francis's brotherhood began. In fact, it appears that it is all that remains of the thick forest to which Francis and his first followers withdrew after having renounced lay life. According to some, Francis thought up this system of throwing oneself among the thorns not only to remove the body from the temptations of the flesh but to counter any doubt regarding the sanctity of the Franciscan order that one had joined.

Of these two motives, that of lust is the dominant one, and it is the easiest to illustrate without resorting to allegories that are difficult to decode. In 1655, the brothers Carlo Francesco and Giuseppe Nuvolone happily demonstrated this when painting the fresco on the vault of Chapel X of the Sacro Monte di Orta, next to the eponymous lake in the province of Novara. The statuary group that occupies the floor of the chapel shows, in addition to Saint Francis (nude, naturally, but with an angel ready to cover him with a cloak), defeated demons in flight, one of them with pendulous breasts and satyrlike hooves, "for the purpose," says the guidebook, of showing "to the faithful sexual temptation in all its gravity." But to realize fully what's behind all that you must raise your eyes (not all tourists do so) and admire the painted features of a "courtesan of Frederick II who, crouching by a bed," continues the guide, "invites Francis and tries to ensnare him. In the distance, some dignitaries secretly watch the situation unfold. A man of fiery temperament and sensitive to beauty, Francis remains with the courtesan . . . but resists the sexual attraction!"[4]

And so legend is added to legend, diegetic confidence to petty amusement, and we get farther and farther from blackberries, which have worked hard across the centuries to attain the recognition and respect that the modern era has granted them. The writer, musician, cosmologist, dramaturge, philosopher, political adviser, prophet, and naturalist Hildegard von Bingen (born in 1098, a year before the Crusaders conquered Jerusalem) largely avoids blackberries, limiting herself to assuring that "the dewberry fruit that grows on the bramble harms neither a healthy nor a sick person and is easily digested, although medicine is not found in it." The bramble itself, however, is a different matter: "If someone's tongue either swells up or has ulcers, he should use a bramble, or a small lancet, to cut his tongue, so that the mucus breaks through. If he has a toothache, he should do the same thing to his gums, and he will be better. If worms eat a person or animal, pulverize bramble and place the powder on the flesh where the worms are eating. The worms will die, and the person will be healed. If someone's lungs are ailing and he has a chest cough, he should take feverfew, and a little less bramble, even less hyssop, and a smaller amount of oregano. He should boil this in good wine with honey, then strain it through a cloth and drink a little after eating moderately. Later he may drink more of it, after a full meal. If he does this regularly, his lungs will recuperate and the mucus will be carried away" (*Physica,* CLXIX).[5]

The reputation of both bush and berries gets noticeably worse with Michele Savonarola (1385–1468), who writes in his *Libreto:* "The edible blackberries are bad for the stomach and rot quickly, particularly the sweet ones, and their rotting is very bad and very harmful. Yet, although acidic, it does not harm the choleric, hot stomach, and so does not cause decay. . . . The large and black ones are among the best. They should be eaten on an empty stomach; taken in advance they will help digest the food and thus increase appetite. They lubricate the food and descend from the stomach soon but delay its exit from the intestines. But eaten after a meal, they are cold foods in the stomach and cause harmful putrefaction, and this is what Galen says."[6]

Much different is the attitude of the ancients with regard to blackberries. As an example, we must turn to Gaius Pliny the Second (also known as Pliny the Elder and, hereafter, as Pliny). You will not find a better supporter in the centuries-long procession of blackberry lovers. The only danger is that he can exaggerate every so often and may end up being counterproductive. Here, in its entirety, is Pliny's valuable testimony—his paean—from his *Naturalis historia,* regarding the edible and medicinal blackberry: "Not even brambles did Nature create for harmful purposes only, and so she has given them their blackberries, that are food even for men. They have a drying and astringent property [*idem* in Dioscorides, *De materia medica*, IV, 37], being very good for gums, tonsils and genitals. They counteract the venom of the most vicious serpents, such as the haemorrhois and prester; the bloom or the berry counteracts that of scorpions. They close wounds without any danger of gatherings. Their stalks are diuretic, being pounded when young and the juice extracted, which is then condensed in the sun to the thickness of honey, and is considered to be, whether taken by the mouth or used as ointment, a specific for affections of the mouth or eyes, for spitting of blood, quinsy, troubles of the uterus or anus, and for celiac affections. For affections of the mouth, indeed, even the chewed leaves are efficacious and they are used as ointment for running sores, or for any kind of sore on the head. Even prepared thus without other ingredient they are applied near the left breast for heart-burn, also to the stomach for stomach-ache, and to the eyes for procidence. The juice of them is also dropped into the ears. Added to rose wax-salve it heals condylomata. A decoction in wine of its tender shoots is a quick remedy for affections of the uvula.[7] The same shoots, eaten by themselves like cabbage sprouts, or a decoction of them in a dry wine, strengthen loose teeth. They check looseness of the bowels and discharges of blood, and are good for dysentery. They are dried in the shade and then burnt so that the ash may reduce a relaxed uvula. The leaves also dried and crushed are said to be useful for sores on draught animals. The blackberries which grow on them can furnish a better mouth-medicine than even the cultivated mulberry. Made up on the same prescription or with hypocisthis and honey only, they are taken in drink for cholera, for heart-burn, and for the stings of spiders. Among the medicines that are called styptics, there is none more effective than the root of a bramble bearing blackberries boiled down in wine to one third, so that sores in the mouth and the anus may be rinsed with the decoction and fomented; so powerful is it that the very sponges used become hard as stone" (*Naturalis historia*, XXIV, 73, 117).[8]

The enthusiasm for blackberries turns up again in England, a bit more soberly, in Nicholas Culpeper (who largely summarizes the medical qualities that the ancients attributed to the fruit, leaves, and roots of the bush but adds, maliciously, that if someone were to ask why the blackberry, which is under the influence of Venus, is so thorny, you could respond that it is also under the influence of Mars). In the symbolic repertory of the lake poets, the blackberry bush expresses an uncontrollable and nonetheless elegant desire for a return to nature. Musing on the ruins of an uncompleted dwelling invaded by brambles, William Wordsworth (1770–1850) has a suggestion for anyone who, disturbed by the structure's incompleteness, might threaten to complete it. The poet recommends leaving the fragments to the brambles and roses so that the legless lizard will have a place to stretch in the winter sun and the robin can jump from one stone to another ("Lines Written with a Slate Pencil on a Stone").

The blackberry bush, which often grows at the edges of dirt roads, is nowadays frequently covered by the dust raised by the cars that it would be best not to allow on such roads. Fortunately, it also grows in the middle of forests, thickets, and untilled fields. It really seems to grow everywhere, and the story that Aesop tells about a fox who, wanting to jump a hedge, got a bad start and slipped, is hardly surprising. In order not to fall, the fox grabbed onto a bramble. "But why," he asked the bramble when, in total pain, he noticed the mess he was in and the blood coming from his paws, "when I turned to you for help, do you do me more harm than good?" "It's hardly my fault," responded the bramble. "It's you who should not have grabbed onto me, I who was born to grab onto others." And that's where the story ends, leaving a final (though perhaps obvious) admonition unstated.

In spring and summer the blackberry bush bears white flowers. The fruit (which can be gathered from July to September) is formed in tiny drupes, first green, then red, and then, when they are finally ripe, black black black.

BLACKBERRY GRAPPA

Makes about 1 pint (500 ml)

⅔ cup (100 g) blackberries
1⅔ cups (400 ml) unflavored grappa
1½ tablespoons (20 g) sugar

Make sure that the blackberries that you have gathered are ripe (black) and firm. Wash carefully, let them drain in a tight-weave strainer, and then place them on paper towels to dry. Put the berries in a 1-quart (1-l) glass container with an airtight cap. Pour in the grappa, add the sugar, and mix well with a spoon until the sugar dissolves. Cap and leave in the open for 8 days (and nights). Filter through a tight-weave strainer and store in a capped bottle.

CREAM PIE WITH BLACKBERRIES
Serves 6

FOR THE CRUST

2 cups plus 2 tablespoons (265 g) all-purpose or
   type oo flour
½ cup (100 g) sugar
¼ teaspoon (2 g) fine salt
⅔ cup (135 g) cold butter, cut into cubes
1 egg
4 teaspoons (20 ml) sparkling mineral water, ice-cold
   Butter and flour for preparing the pan
¾ cup (150 g) dried cannellini beans

FOR THE CREAM

3 egg yolks
½ cup (100 g) sugar
½ cup (70 g) all-purpose flour
2 cups plus 2 tablespoons (500 ml) whole milk
   Zest of 1 untreated (unwaxed) lemon, in strips

FOR THE TOPPING

2 cups (300 g) blackberries, washed and well dried

To prepare the crust: In a bowl, combine 2 cups (250 g) of the flour, the sugar, the salt, the butter, and the egg. Mix everything while gradually adding the sparkling water, mixing just until the ingredients come together in a rough mass. Shape the dough into a ball, flatten it into a disk, put it in a covered bowl, and then in the refrigerator for 2 hours.

Preheat the oven to 350°F (180°C). Remove the dough from the refrigerator. Sprinkle some of the remaining 2 tablespoons (15 g) flour on a marble or wood work surface and set the dough on the surface. Sprinkle the remaining flour on top of the dough. With a rolling pin, roll out the dough into a circle 11 inches (28 cm) in diameter. If the dough begins to tear, press it together with your hands. Butter a 9-inch (23-cm) round pan with 1¼-inch (3-cm) sides. Then, with a swirling motion, add the remaining flour to the pan so that it sticks well everywhere, tapping out the excess. Line the pan with the dough circle, pressing it against the bottom and sides of the pan. Cut a sheet of parchment paper into a 9-inch (23-cm) circle, place it on top of the dough, and spill the beans onto the paper. This will keep the dough from swelling in the oven.

Bake the crust until you see that it has a nice golden color, about 30 minutes. Remove from the oven, scoop out the beans and lift out the parchment, and let the crust cool on a wire rack. Now invert a flat 10-inch (25-cm) plate on top of the pan and turn the pan and plate together so the crust falls onto the plate. Turn the crust over again onto a second plate of the same size.

To prepare the cream: Place the egg yolks and the sugar in a bowl and stir with a wooden spoon to combine. Add the flour little by little while stirring constantly to prevent lumps from forming. Add the milk, always pouring it slowly and without ever ceasing to stir. Pass the mixture through a tight-weave strainer into a 3-quart (3-l) saucepan and add the lemon zest. Place the pan over medium heat and continue to stir, always in the same direction, for 30 minutes (be careful not to let the mixture start to boil). Then reduce the heat to very low and cook for another 5 minutes, continuing to stir (otherwise the cream will stick to the bottom). Remove the pan from the heat, remove and discard the lemon zest, and continue to stir the cream often as it cools.

Pour the cooled cream into the crust and arrange the blackberries on top.

BLACKBERRY SHOOT SALAD

Serves 4

1⅓ cups (200 g) blackberry shoots
Juice of 1 lemon
Pinch of fine salt
Extra-virgin olive oil, to taste

Gather the blackberry shoots, which are the tender part of the plant that produces the berries. Wash them carefully, let them drain well in a colander, and then place them on paper towels to dry. Make sure that they are completely dry and then put them in a bowl. Put the lemon juice and salt into another, smaller bowl and add the olive oil. Beat with a fork for about 1 minute to emulsify. Just before serving, pour the dressing onto the shoots and toss well with a spoon and fork.

BLACKBERRY RISOTTO

Serves 4

⅔ cup (100 g) blackberries
6½ cups (1.5 l) vegetable broth
    Coarse salt
¼ cup (60 ml) extra-virgin olive oil
1 onion, finely chopped
1¾ cups (350 g) Arborio or Vialone Nano rice
¼ cup (60 ml) dry white wine
4 teaspoons (20 g) butter
⅓ cup (40 g) grated Parmesan cheese

Make sure that the blackberries you have gathered are ripe (black) and firm. Wash them, let them drain well in a colander, and then place them on paper towels to dry. Pour the broth into a 3-quart (3-l) pot, place over medium-high heat, and bring to a boil. Season to taste with the salt. The rice will be cooked in this broth, which must be kept at a simmer. Meanwhile, pour the oil into a 4-quart (4-l) pot and place over very low heat. Add the onion and cook for about 3 minutes. Take care that the onion does not burn. Raise the heat to medium, add the rice, and stir with a wooden spoon for a good 5 minutes to toast it. Pour in the white wine and continue to stir until it has evaporated.

Now begin to add the broth, a little at a time, stirring after each addition and allowing it to evaporate before adding more. After 15 minutes of cooking, add the blackberries and stir for another 5 minutes. At this point the rice should be tender but still slightly firm at the center of each grain. Turn off the heat, add the butter and Parmesan, and stir until everything is well mixed. Let rest for 5 minutes before serving.

BLACKBERRY SEMIFREDDO
Serves 4

⅔ cup (100 g) blackberries
Scant 3 cups (700 ml) whole milk
6½ tablespoons (80 g) sugar
⅛ teaspoon (1 g) salt
1 vanilla bean
1 cup (180 g) Arborio or Vialone Nano rice
1 whole egg
2 egg yolks

Make sure that the blackberries you have gathered are ripe (black) and firm. Wash them, let them drain well in a colander, and then place them on paper towels to dry. In a 2½-quart (2.5-l) pot, combine the milk, sugar, salt, and vanilla bean. Stir everything together with a wooden spoon and place over medium heat. As soon as the milk begins to boil, add the rice and continue stirring. When the mixture starts to boil again, lower the heat to the lowest possible setting and cook for 50 minutes. Stir often, particularly near the end of cooking, to prevent the mixture from sticking to the pot. Remove from the heat and let cool.

Put the whole egg and egg yolks in a large bowl and beat them with a fork until blended. Then add the cooled rice and continue to stir until everything is mixed together perfectly. Finally, add the blackberries and stir well a little bit more.

Cut a sheet of parchment paper large enough to line the bottom and sides of a container about 6 inches (15 cm) wide and 3½ inches (9 cm) deep. Dampen the paper, wring it out, and line the container (lining the container this way will make unmolding the *semifreddo* easier). Spoon the rice mixture into the lined mold and refrigerate for at least 3 hours.

Just before serving, invert a serving plate on top of the mold and invert the mold and plate together so the *semifreddo* falls onto the plate. Lift off the mold, peel away the parchment, and serve cold.

Blueberries

VACCINIUM SPP.; ITALIAN: *MIRTILLI*

IN THE RECENT HISTORY of the United States, there are two Fats. One is Minnesota Fats, a wizard of billiards and a character in the novel *The Hustler* by Walter Trevis (1928–84), adapted for the eponymous film with Paul Newman and Jackie Gleason. The other one, which interests us here, is Fats Domino,[1] the singer who, in 1956, brought worldwide popularity to "Blueberry Hill," a song composed in 1940 and previously recorded success-fully by Gene Autry (for the film *The Singing Hill*) and Glenn Miller, among others.

Reading the lyrics without the music in which they are set, and without the vibrato of Fats Domino's voice, you might ask yourself what is so special about them. "Little or nothing," you are likely to say, even if it did take two people to write them: Al Lewis and Larry Stock. The music, however, is by Vincent Rose, a musician born in Palermo in 1880, and who, in 1920, after having written "Avalon" (words by Al Jolson) was sued, along with every-one who had had something to do with the song, by the recording label G. Ricordi. According to Ricordi, the song's opening melody was too similar to "E lucevan le stelle." The verdict went in favor of Puccini (and his heirs).

Here, however, are the words of "Blueberry Hill," minus the repeated lines: "I found my thrill / on Blueberry Hill / . . . / when I found you. / The moon stood still / on Blueberry Hill / and lingered until / My dream came true. / Though we're apart / You're part of me still / for you were my thrill / on Blueberry Hill." And after a series of repetitions: "The wind in the willow played / Love's sweet melody / But all of those vows we made / were never to be." Then, once again: "I found my thrill . . ." until the end.

But a closer look reveals it to be a text of considerable sophistication. The rhyme is nearly unequivocal (*hill, still, thrill*, etc.) The rare interruptions of the rhymed couplets (*you/true, played/made* and *melody/be*), plus the hapax legomenon of *apart,* magnifies, if anything, the obsessive regularity with which Fats molds it with a teleological hold. It's a small, Metastasian aria fallen into a barrel of rum and subjected to electroshock, to distortions of awesome exactitude, a rhythm-and-blues beat deliberately kept on a leash and then allowed to explode with flourishes (we are still talking about the execution) postponed by a breath, just enough to confound all promises, prognostications, and bets.

After Fats Domino, "Blueberry Hill" was recorded by Louis Armstrong in Stockholm, in 1962. The two productions could not be more different. Fats, stupendously serious, even grave, does not bat an eye, exhibiting a masterful touch of refined stolidity, accompanied only by the piano. Satchmo, carefree as a witch, elegant, ironic, and embellished, standing in front of his band, toward which he turns once in awhile, joking, as if he were part of his own audience. He sings and comments. Fats is essential and Doric, like Sophocles; Satchmo, sarcastic like Euripides.

For Italians who have only seen blueberries at the supermarket (in plastic containers) or in some mountain forest, dewy and hanging from (beautiful) small plants no more than six inches tall, it is difficult to imagine them big, fat, and richly displayed on the American bushes that go from a few inches to thirteen feet in height—bushes that do not bring to mind the landscape of the South where jazz and rock and roll (and their above-mentioned interpreters) originated. But this, as they say, is nobody's fault. Unlike the symbolic world, the world of the imagination knows no bounds.

The blueberry, both the version found in Italy (*Vaccinium myrtillus*) and the overbearing kind found in America (various species of *Vaccinium,* also known by the section name *Cyannococcus*), loves water and cold . . . and, in America, the mud of marshlands. It is enough to skim the pages that Henry David Thoreau dedicates to blueberries and other edible berries in *Wild Fruits* (an "incomplete" work published for the first time only in 2000) to feel burdened by wet clothes, soggy feet, and muddy shoes. It's not that the brush and the slopes of Italian mountains are not wet, but the idea of mud does not come to the mind of any Italian blueberry gatherer. In Thoreau, on the other hand, the mud, the marsh, and the stagnant pond fill the blueberry with a difficult, inaccessible taste, a *nescio quid* that is hostile and unredeemed, not softened even by the meticulous love in which the author wraps his own naturalistic universe. Of course, there is a rather marked temporal gap between the forests of a modern Sunday stroll in Italy and those in which Henry David Thoreau obstinately made his way in nineteenth-century New England, where it was still possible to reach, not far from Concord, "a long, narrow, and winding blueberry swamp which I did not know existed there. A deep, withdrawn meadow sunk low amid the forest, filled with green waving sedge three feet high, . . . for the most part dry to the feet then, though with a bottom of unfathomed mud, not penetrable except in midsummer or midwinter, and with no print of man or beast in it that I could detect. . . . Great blueberries, as big as old-fashioned bullets."[2]

And now, putting aside the mud and the uninviting allusions to the discharge of musketry, *procedamus* anew *ad myrtillum,* whose name, as we read in the *Dizionario etimologico* of Cortellazzo and Zolli, is a rather improper denomination, deriving from myrtle, a plant unknown in the Alps! But proper or improper though the name may be, the term *mirtillo* has by now driven out, in ordinary Italian, the numerous other popular denominations, with the exception perhaps of *bàgiole,* which persists in Tuscany. It is also curious that, for wild berries, Italian employs names that are distinct and phonetically unrelated, even in part: *lampone* (raspberry), *fragola* (strawberry), *mirtillo* (blueberry), and so on. English, on the other hand, follows a completely different strategy, having an index of specifications (*blue-, straw-, rasp-, elder-,* and the like) that precede the generic ending *-berry.* The variety of berries is truly amazing and a lifetime is barely enough to examine some of the etymological derivations and for someone to compare the resulting terms. Among the latter, it would be sufficient to establish with certainty whether cranberry (which produces a deliciously acidic juice very useful for combating cystitis) is or is not the same as the "red blueberry" (*V. vitis idaea*) that grows in the same environments as blackberries and blueberries, but which many people do not gather, believing it to be an immature blueberry. Phytotherapeutic medicine holds that blueberries may act effectively in treating ophthalmic diseases, ulcers, and sclerosis. We will not have to wait long to discover other benefits.

The period for harvesting of the leaves (from which, when dried, infusions and decoctions are made) includes all of June and July. The fruit is gathered when it is ripe—for the most part in August.

BLUEBERRY GRAPPA

Makes 1 pint (500 ml)

1 cup (150 g) blueberries
2 cups (500 ml) unflavored grappa
Scant ¼ cup (40 g) sugar

Wash the blueberries carefully, let them drain in a tight-weave strainer, and then place them on paper towels to dry. Put the berries in a 1-quart (1-l) glass container with an airtight cap. Pour in the grappa, add the sugar, and mix well with a spoon until the sugar dissolves. Cap and leave in the open for 8 days (and nights). Filter through a tight-weave strainer and store in a capped bottle.

Borage

BORAGO OFFICINALIS; ITALIAN: BORRAGINE

SOME SAY THAT THE NAME *BORAGE* derives from *borra* (or *burra*), which in turn goes back to the Late Latin *borrago*. Since *borra* means the shearing of cloth, wool, waste used for felt or stuffing, or rough fabrics, the connection between *borra* and *borrago* may have been proposed by someone who rapidly drew conclusions from having felt the hairy surface of borage leaves. The etymologists of both the *Oxford English Dictionary* and the *Grande dizionario della lingua italiana* (better known as "Il Battaglia") subscribe to this erroneous origin. Less easily satisfied, but certainly more reliable, Manlio Cortellazzo and Paolo Zolli, in their *Dizionario etimologico della lingua italiana,* tie *borragine(m)* to the Arabic *abū'arak,* which means "sweat producer" (literally, "father of sweat") and therefore, "plant that makes you sweat." Finally, there are also those who suggest that the term *borage* comes from the Celtic *borrach,* which means "courage."

We have, then, three proposed etymologies, each with an experiential basis. The experience of touching borage is open to everyone, and doing so does not cause any problems. As for the second experience, anyone can verify the effects of borage with impunity: it either makes you sweat or it doesn't (and in any case, sweating is good for you). With the third connection, however, some caution is in order. Courage, in itself, is a good thing, but it can be misplaced and can lead to dangerous adventures. As Alain Denis writes in his *Erbe spezie condimenti*,[1] those who vouch for "drinking a cup of liquor in which a few borage petals are floating" are not likely to find enough of it (courage, that is) to convince themselves to depart for the Holy Land. It seems to have worked for some Crusaders, however, who were hesitant about the journey at first, but then, after having drunk their borage-enhanced beverage, set off with much conviction.

Be that as it may, in Italian, borage is also called *borrana* and (in both ancient times and those that today we call protomodern) *buglossa*, in other words, ox tongue, which it somewhat resembles, aside from its color. There are also those who treat borage and *buglossa* as two distinct plants, however, even if they say almost the same things about both, as Burton does (Robert Burton [1577–1640], not the twentieth-century Richard, who was more involved in cinematic-matrimonial matters) in his always surprising *Anatomy of Melancholy*, published in 1621.[2]

In the third subsection of the first part of the fourth section of the second part of Burton's extra-voluminous contribution to medical science, the author writes that borage and *buglossa* can aspire to advanced positions with respect to their substance in general and, in particular, to their sap, roots, seeds, flowers, and leaves when transformed into decoctions, distillations, extracts, oils, and the like. *Buglossa* is moist and warm, notes Burton, and thus can be numbered among those greens that drive out melancholy and gladden the heart. After a long list of ancient authors on whose authority Burton establishes the correctness of his own knowledge (including the usual suspects Galen, Dioscorides, Pliny, Plutarch, Diodorus, and Caelius), he informs us that *buglossa* (or borage) is the very same nepenthe that Homer writes about in Book IV of the *Odyssey* (v. 243 et seq.). There, Helen slips nepenthe into the wine that her guests drink to put an end to the endless whining of her husband, Menelaus (a noble laden with much glory and other, less glorious protuberances). Homer recites that it was a drug with "magic to make us all forget our pains . . . / No one who drank it deeply, mulled in wine, / could let a tear roll down his cheeks that day, / not even if his mother should die, his father die, / not even if right before his eyes some enemy brought down / a brother or darling son with a sharp bronze blade."[3] And Homer reveals that he is speaking of a wild green when he informs us that "So cunning the drugs that Zeus's daughter plied, / potent gifts from Polydamna the wife of Thon, / a woman of Egypt, land where the teeming soil / bears the richest yield of herbs in all the world: / many health itself when mixed in the wine, / and many deadly poison."[4]

Burton's special esteem for borage comes through in the figures illustrating the frontispiece of his magnum opus. The eighth figure is dedicated to borage and, together with the ninth (dedicated to hellebore), is the object of the following elegy in eight-syllable rhyme: "Borage and Hellebor fill two scenes / Soveraign [sic] plants to purge the veins / Of Melancholy, and chear the heart, / Of those black fumes which make it smart; / To clear the Brain of misty fogs, / Which dull our senses, and Soul clogs." Burton concludes that it is: "The best medicine that ere God made / For this malady, if well assaid."[5]

Borage's effectiveness in curing sadness had already been noted (in fact, shouted) by Jacques Ferrand in his fundamental text, *Mélancolie érotique* (1610). To drive the "humor" that lies at the base of this affliction from the most problematic of human orifices, the French physician (and pettifogger) had proposed, following the elimination of excrement from the first region of the body (by means of an enema), the (presumably) oral taking of "a syrup or concoction like the following: a large handful of buglossa and one of borage, along with the roots of chicory, endive, sorrel, pimpernel, and ceterach. Add to this half a handful of hops and betony and half an ounce of polypody. Then add three drams of clean raisins and currants and three sweet prunes. Combine 1½ drams of melon, pumpkin, and cucumber seeds; 1 dram of verbena and anise seeds; and a small handful of thyme, hellweed, and cordial of three flowers. Make two pounds of the decoction. Then add . . . " But really, we need not add anything else here. Rather, any reader who might still be erotically melancholy (and wants to try to cure himself in the manner described by Ferrand) is advised to consult page 365 of the newest version of the book edited by Donald Beecher and Massimo Ciavolella.[6]

Continuing in a less truculent manner along the medical path and leaping back about six hundred years, the imperturbable Hildegard von Bingen asserts things with respect to borage that are no less amazing. For example, if your eyesight is failing, to recover clarity of vision all you have to do is mince some borage, reduce it to a batter, spread it on a red silk cloth, and then place it over your eyes and leave it there all night. Once is not enough, however. To get good results, you must repeat the application often. If this borage pomade manages to get on the inside of your eyelids as well, all the better. But if the silk is green or white instead of red, the borage—no longer reduced to a pomade but in liquid form—may be employed to cure other annoyances, including whistling in one's ears. Here's how: soak some cloth in borage juice and cover the neck of the sufferer up to the ears, which must remain uncovered. Once again, *repetita juvant* and your ears will stop whistling. Mixed with bran and warmed, then spread on one's belly—particularly in the umbilical zone—the same juice cures intestinal ulcers (*Physica,* CCI, II, 72).

The surprises that borage holds, finally, are not limited to sweat, courage, or even to its effectiveness as redress for blue moods. Its reputation as a plant capable of raising morale and even rendering one euphoric has been widely documented since antiquity. In *The Herball or Generall Historie of Plantes,* dating to the last decade of the sixteenth century, John Gerard (1545–1612) asserts that Pliny wanted to give borage (which he labels *buglossa*) the name *euphrosynum,*[7] precisely because of its quality to make men "merry and joy-full," and he does not hesitate to bring up that which everyone had brought up for centuries, and which they would continue to bring up for centuries to come: the Latin adage *Ego borago gaudia semper ago.*[8]

If courage (sweaty or not) fails, and if sadness does not show itself to the door, we can still hope that borage at least puts us in a good mood, as suggested by the name given to the herb by the inhabitants of Wales (famous throughout the world for their garrulous lightheartedness), *llawenlys,* which means "herb of happiness, of joy." But if, by chance, the exhilarating effects of borage in Wales were not recorded, a sip of borage juice had a decidedly good result in the Land of Oz, where it seems that happiness succeeded in combining with a discrete dose of courage in the chest of he who needed it most: the Cowardly Lion, who converses with his traveling companions as follows:

DOROTHY: Your majesty, if you were King, you wouldn't be afraid of anything?
LION: Not nobody, not nohow!
TIN MAN: Not even a rhinoceros?
LION: Imposserous!
DOROTHY: How about a hippopotamus?
LION: Why, I'd thrash him from top to bottomus!
DOROTHY: Supposin' you met an elephant?
LION: I'd wrap him up in cellophant!
SCARECROW: What if it were a brontosaurus?
LION: I'd show him who was King of the Fores'.
ALL: And how?
LION: How? . . . Borage![9]

Some suspect that it is not so much the borage itself that produces these exhilarating effects as it is the consistent consumption of the liquors to which refined connoisseurs of mixed beverages have added it for centuries. Among these is Charles Dickens, who, judging from his vast amount of published work, must have passed more time writing novels than drinking borage cocktails. Nonetheless, it seems he had a true predilection for them. The formula that commonly goes by the name Charles Dickens punch is composed of 2 cups boiling water, ½ cup sugar, 2 tablespoons lemon peel, ¼ cup borage flowers, 2 cups sherry, 1 cup brandy, and 4 cups cider. Boil the sugar, lemon peel, and borage flowers in the water for about fifteen minutes. Filter through a tight-weave strainer, then add the sherry, brandy and cider. *Salute!*[10]

Borage (which appears to be originally from Syria) is found everywhere in the Mediterranean zone: at the edge of paths (particularly if they are near a watercourse), in both cultivated and uncultivated places, and even among ruins. Its taste is somewhat similar to that of cucumber. The leaves and flowers are most commonly eaten, but the stalk is edible as well if cooked beforehand. The fresh leaves are good in every type of mixture. They can also be fried in a skillet, breaded, or boiled to make stuffing for ravioli or tortelloni. They are excellent in vegetable soups or added to long drinks in place of mint. Like nasturtiums, borage flowers combine well with lettuce salads or can be fried like zucchini flowers.

The period for collecting borage flowers is whenever there are any; for the leaves, when they are tender—that is, from April to September.

———————

STUFFED SHELLS WITH RICOTTA AND BORAGE

Serves 6

- 1 pound (450 g) borage tops and leaves (about 5 cups)
- 4½ tablespoons (60 g) coarse salt
- 6 tablespoons (85 g) butter, plus 1 teaspoon (5 g) for preparing the pan
- Freshly grated nutmeg, to taste
- Ground black pepper
- 1¾ cups (450 g) sheep's milk ricotta cheese, well drained in a cheesecloth-lined tight-weave strainer
- 1 egg
- ¼ cup (30 g) grated Parmesan cheese, plus some to sprinkle over the béchamel before baking
- 2 cups (500 ml) whole milk

¼ cup (35 g) all-purpose flour
½ teaspoon (3 g) fine salt
35 large pasta shells

To prepare the stuffing: Use only the most tender borage tops and leaves. Don kitchen gloves to handle them, washing them carefully to make sure that no dirt remains. Then pour 2½ quarts (2.5 l) water into a large pot and place over high heat. When the water starts to boil, add 2 tablespoons (30 g) of the coarse salt. Then, when the water starts to boil again, drop in the borage and let it cook for 3 minutes. Remove the borage from the water with a wire skimmer and drain well, then mince with kitchen shears or a knife.

Place a 9-inch (23-cm) skillet over medium heat and add 2 tablespoons (30 g) of the butter. After 1 minute, add the borage, season with nutmeg and pepper, and cook, stirring occasionally, for 5 minutes to blend the flavors. Turn off the heat and let the mixture cool.

Put the drained ricotta in a bowl and break it up with a metal spoon or fork. Add the egg and mix well. Add the cooled borage and the Parmesan and mix again, stirring vigorously.

To prepare the béchamel: Pour the milk into a small saucepan, place over medium heat, and heat until scalded, about 5 minutes. Meanwhile, in a 2½-quart (2.5-l) saucepan, melt the remaining 4 tablespoons (55 g) butter over medium-low heat for about 3 minutes. Now add the flour and whisk constantly and with extreme care for 2 minutes, making sure no clumps form. Add the hot milk and fine salt and continue to stir constantly for 5 minutes. The flour must be completely dissolved and the béchamel must be creamy but not dense. Turn off the heat. Stir the béchamel occasionally so that a skin does not form on top.

To assemble the dish: Pour 3 quarts (3 l) water into a 5-quart (5-l) pot and place over high heat. When it begins to boil, add the remaining 2 tablespoons (30 g) coarse salt. When the water starts to boil again, add the shells. Then, counting from when the water begins to boil once again, cook the shells for 10 minutes; they should be just al dente. Drain the shells well in a colander and transfer them to a plate. Stuff them with the filling, using a small spoon or a pastry bag fitted with a plain tip.

Preheat the oven to 400°F (200°C). Grease the bottom and sides of an 11-by-7-inch (33-by-20-cm) baking dish with butter. Arrange the stuffed shells in the prepared dish. Pour the béchamel over the shells, and then sprinkle some Parmesan over the béchamel. Bake until the béchamel is bubbling and the shells are heated through, 15 to 20 minutes. Remove immediately from the oven and serve.

The dish can be baked the previous day and kept in the refrigerator. Before serving, reheat in a 350°F (180°C) oven for about 15 minutes until piping hot.

BORAGE LEAVES MILANESE

Serves 4

10 borage leaves, each about 4½ inches (11 cm) long and
    3½ inches (9 cm) wide
2 eggs
3⅔ cups (400 g) dried bread crumbs
1⅔ cups (400 ml) extra-virgin olive oil
¾ teaspoon (5 g) fine salt

Don kitchen gloves and wash the borage leaves thoroughly but carefully, taking care not to damage or tear them. Dry the leaves well with paper towels. Break the egg into a bowl and beat with a fork for about 2 minutes. Put the bread crumbs in a second bowl.

One at a time, immerse the leaves in the beaten egg, making sure it covers both sides well, then coat with the bread crumbs. Set aside on a large, flat plate. Pour the oil into a 9-inch (23-cm) skillet and place over medium heat. Line a large plate with paper towels.

When the oil begins to bubble but before it starts to smoke, lay 2 or 3 borage leaves in the oil and fry for 2 minutes. Turn the leaves over and fry for another 2 minutes. They should be golden on both sides. With a fork or a wire skimmer, lift the leaves out of the oil and place on the towel-lined plate. Repeat with the remaining leaves. Sprinkle with the salt and serve hot.

BORAGE FRITTATA

Serves 4

½ pound (250 g) borage leaves (about 2¾ cups)
4 teaspoons (25 g) coarse salt
5 eggs

¼ teaspoon (2 g) fine salt
½ teaspoon (1 g) ground black pepper
Rounded ¼ teaspoon (1 g) ground red pepper
5 teaspoons (10 g) grated pecorino or Parmesan cheese
¾ cup (180 ml) extra-virgin olive oil

Don kitchen gloves and wash the borage leaves thoroughly, making sure that no dirt remains. Pour 3 quarts (3 l) water into a 5½-quart (5-l) pot and place over high heat. When the water begins to boil, add the coarse salt and the borage leaves and cook for 5 minutes, timing from when the water begins to boil again. Remove the leaves from the water with a wire skimmer and squeeze them well to release all of the water. Cut the leaves into pieces about 1¼ inches (3 cm) long.

In a bowl, beat the eggs with a fork for about 1 minute. Add the fine salt, black pepper, red pepper, and pecorino and mix together well, then stir in the borage.

Pour the oil into a 9-inch (23-cm) nonstick skillet and place over medium-low heat. After about 1 minute, add the contents of the bowl. Cover the skillet and cook over very low heat for about 10 minutes. Then remove the skillet from the heat, uncover, and, with a wooden spatula, check that the edges and the center of the frittata did not stick. Invert a plate slightly larger than the skillet on top of the pan and turn the skillet and plate together so the frittata falls onto the plate. Slide the frittata, browned side up, back into the skillet and cook, uncovered, over very low heat for 15 minutes longer. Turn off the heat and slide the frittata onto a plate. The frittata may be eaten hot or cold.

BORAGE FRITTERS

Serves 4

20 borage leaves, each about 3½ inches (9 cm) long and
    2½ inches (6 cm) wide
¾ cup (100 g) all-purpose flour
½ cup (120 ml) sparkling mineral water, ice-cold
1¼ teaspoons (5 g) active dry yeast
½ teaspoon (3 g) fine salt
1⅔ cups (400 ml) extra-virgin olive oil

Don kitchen gloves and wash the borage leaves thoroughly but carefully, taking care not to damage or tear them. Dry the leaves well with paper towels. Put the flour in a bowl and dilute it with the ice-cold water, pouring it in slowly, a little at a time, and whisking until a light, uniform batter forms. Add the yeast and ⅛ teaspoon (1 g) of the salt and continue to stir for several minutes. Line a large plate with paper towels.

Pour the oil into a pan about 7 inches (18 cm) in diameter and 3¼ inches (8 cm) deep and place over medium heat. When the oil begins to bubble but before it starts to smoke, dip 3 leaves into the batter, lay them in the oil, and fry for 2 minutes. Then turn the leaves over and fry for another 2 minutes. They should be golden on both sides. With a fork or a wire skimmer, lift the fritters out of the oil and place on the towel-lined plate. Repeat with the remaining leaves. Sprinkle the fritters with the remaining salt and serve hot.

POTATO AND BORAGE GNOCCHI

Serves 4

1⅓ pounds (600 g) borage tops and leaves (about 6¾ cups)
4 tablespoons (80 g) coarse salt
⅓ cup (70 ml) extra-virgin olive oil
1¾ teaspoons (4 g) ground black pepper
2¼ pounds (1 kg) yellow-fleshed potatoes, of uniform size
2⅓ cups (300 g) all-purpose flour, plus more for sprinkling
⅓ cup (80 g) butter
4 or 5 fresh sage leaves
¾ cup (80 g) grated Parmesan cheese

To prepare the borage: Use only the most tender borage tops and leaves. Don kitchen gloves to handle them, washing them carefully to make sure that no dirt remains. Pour 3 quarts (3 l) water into an 8-quart (8-l) pot, cover, and place over high heat. When the water begins to boil, add 2 tablespoons (40 g) of the coarse salt. When the water begins to boil again, drop in the borage and cook for 3 minutes. Remove the borage from the water with a wire skimmer and drain well, then shred with kitchen shears or a knife.

Pour the oil into a 9-inch (23-cm) skillet and place over medium heat. After 1 minute or so, add the borage and cook, stirring occasionally, for 5 minutes to season. Add half of the pepper, stir everything again, and turn off the heat. Leave the borage in the pan.

To prepare the gnocchi: Put the potatoes in the same pan in which you boiled the borage, add water to cover by at least 2 inches (5 cm), and place over medium heat. After the water reaches a boil, lower the heat and let the potatoes simmer until tender, about 30 minutes. Drain in a colander. While the potatoes are still hot, peel them and pass them through a potato ricer into a bowl, then let cool.

Add the flour, a little at a time, to the potatoes and mix until the dough holds together. Now take part of the mixture, place it on a floured work surface, and roll it back and forth under your palm to form a cylinder 10 to 12 inches (25 to 30 cm) long and ⅔ inch (1.5 cm) in diameter. The dough is easier to work with if you sprinkle a little flour on top every now and again. Repeat until all of the dough has been formed into cylinders. Then, using a knife, cut each cylinder into 1¼-inch (3-cm) pieces and place the pieces (that is, the gnocchi) on plates that have been sprinkled with flour.

To cook the gnocchi: Pour about 4 quarts (4 l) water into the same pan in which you cooked the potatoes and place over high heat. When the water begins to boil, add the remaining 2 tablespoons (40 g) salt. When the water begins to boil again, lower one plate of the gnocchi into the water. As soon as the gnocchi begin to float, take them out with a wire skimmer, drain well, and slide them onto a warmed shallow serving platter or into a rectangular baking dish. Repeat until you have cooked all of the gnocchi, without giving into the temptation to add salt.

To finish: While the gnocchi are cooking, return the skillet with the borage to low heat to warm gently. When all of the gnocchi are cooked, check to see if there is a little bit of water at the bottom of the platter or dish. If there is no water (and there should be some), pour 6 tablespoons (90 ml) of the water in which you cooked the gnocchi into the pan with the borage. Stir the borage with a wooden spoon, then combine it with the gnocchi and stir vigorously to mix. Place the butter in a small saucepan and let it melt over medium-low heat (this will take about 2 minutes). Add the sage leaves to the pan, heat for about 1 minute, and then pour the melted butter and leaves onto the gnocchi and mix carefully. Add the Parmesan and the remaining pepper, stir one last time to ensure that everything is mixed together well, and serve.

BORAGE FLOWERS FRIED IN BATTER

Serves 4

15 bunches borage flowers
2⅓ cups (300 g) all-purpose flour
¼ teaspoon (2 g) fine salt
2 cups (500 ml) plus 2 teaspoons (10 ml) extra-virgin olive oil
⅔ cup (150 ml) sparkling mineral water, ice-cold

Beautiful and delicate, borage flowers, which can be blue or white, are open during the day and closed at night. Wear kitchen gloves to harvest the flowers and then wash the bunches carefully, dipping them in at least 5 inches (13 cm) of water; otherwise, the flowers will fall off immediately. Drain well, placing the bunches first in a colander and then on paper towels. Put the flour, salt, and 2 teaspoons (10 ml) of the oil in a bowl 8 inches (20 cm) in diameter at the top, 4 inches (10 cm) deep, and 4 inches (10 cm) wide at the base, or of similar size, and mix together. Add the water and whisk until a smooth batter with no lumps forms. Line a large plate with paper towels.

Pour the remaining 2 cups (500 ml) oil into a pan 8 inches (20 cm) in diameter and 3½ inches (9 cm) deep and place over medium heat. When the oil begins to bubble but before it starts to smoke, dip 3 or 4 flower bunches into the batter, making sure they are covered completely, and then lay them in the oil and fry for 2 minutes. Turn the bunches over and fry for another 2 minutes. They should be crispy and golden. With a wire skimmer, lift the bunches out of the oil and place on the towel-lined plate. Repeat with the remaining bunches. Serve hot, preferably in a wicker basket lined with paper towels.

POLENTA WITH BORAGE

Serves 4

1¾ pounds (800 g) borage leaves (about 9 cups)
⅔ cup (150 ml) extra-virgin olive oil
⅔ cup (70 g) finely chopped spring onions (white part only) or white onion

1 tablespoon (15 g) coarse salt

1¼ teaspoons (3 g) ground black pepper

2 cups (300 g) stone-ground cornmeal

⅓ cup (40 g) grated Parmesan cheese

Don kitchen gloves and wash the borage leaves thoroughly, making sure that no dirt remains. Chop the leaves roughly and set aside.

Pour the oil into a 5-quart (5-l) saucepan place over low heat, and heat for 1 minute. Add the onions and cook until lightly browned, about 15 minutes. Take care that they do not burn. Add the borage and stir well with a spoon and fork until the borage and onions are well mixed and the flavors have blended. Raise the heat, add one-third of the salt, and stir again. Repeat with the remaining salt in two additions, stirring after each addition. When the borage seems properly "bruised," add the pepper, cover the pan, and cook for 2 to 3 minutes.

Uncover, stir, add 6½ cups (1.5 l) water, cover again, and bring to a boil. While the water is heating, put the cornmeal on a plate, which will make it easier to add to the pan. When the water begins to boil, uncover the pan and pour in the cornmeal, letting it rain down very slowly while whisking vigorously to make sure that no lumps form. Everything must be mixed together perfectly. Reduce the heat to medium-low and cook for 50 minutes, never forgetting to stir. The polenta is ready when it pulls away from the sides of the pan and no longer tastes grainy. Turn off the heat, sprinkle the polenta with the Parmesan, stir in the cheese, and serve.

BORAGE RISOTTO

Serves 4

1½ pounds (700 g) borage tops and leaves (about 7¾ cups)

5 teaspoons (30 g) coarse salt, plus more as needed

4¼ cups (1 l) vegetable broth

½ cup (120 ml) extra-virgin olive oil

About 1¼ cups (120 g) finely chopped spring onions or white onion

2 cups (400 g) Arborio or Vialone Nano rice

⅓ cup (40 g) grated Parmesan cheese

2 tablespoons (30 g) butter

Use only the most tender borage tops and leaves. Don kitchen gloves to handle them, washing them carefully to make sure that no dirt remains. Then pour 3 quarts (3 l) water into a 5½-quart (5.5-l) pot and place over high heat. When the water begins to boil, add the salt. When the water begins to boil again, drop in the borage and cook for about 5 minutes. Remove the borage from the water with a wire skimmer and drain well, then cut into pieces about 1¼ inches (3 cm) long with kitchen shears.

Pour the broth into a 3-quart (3-l) pot, place over medium-high heat, and bring to a boil. Season to taste with salt. The rice will be cooked in this broth, which must be kept at a simmer. Meanwhile, pour the oil into a 4-quart (4-l) pot and place over very low heat. Add the onions and cook until golden, about 5 minutes. Take care that the onions do not burn. Add the borage and cook, stirring continuously, for about 5 minutes to blend the flavors. Raise the heat to medium, add the rice, and stir with a wooden spoon for a good 5 minutes to toast it.

Now begin to add the broth, a little at a time, stirring after each addition and allowing it to evaporate before adding more. After 15 to 20 minutes of cooking, turn off the heat. At this point the rice should be tender but still slightly firm at the center of each grain. Add the Parmesan and butter and stir so everything is well mixed. Let rest for 5 minutes before serving.

BORAGE FLOWER RISOTTO

Serves 4

⅓ pound (150 g) borage flowers (about 1⅔ cups)
2½ teaspoons (15 g) coarse salt
1¾ cups (350 g) Arborio or Vialone Nano rice
¼ cup (60 ml) extra-virgin olive oil
¼ cup (30 g) grated Parmesan cheese
1¼ teaspoons (3 g) ground black pepper

Wear kitchen gloves to harvest the most tender stems of borage in bloom. Then, with kitchen shears, remove the flowers at the base of the stalk and wash the blooms carefully.

Pour 6½ cups (1.5 l) water into 3-quart (3-l) pot, place over medium-high heat, and bring to a boil, then add the salt. The rice will be cooked in this water, which must be kept at a simmer. Meanwhile, pour the oil into a 4-quart (4-l) pan, place over medium heat, and heat for about 1 minute. Place the borage flowers in the oil and stir for no less than 2 minutes. Then add the rice and stir with a wooden spoon for a good 5 minutes to toast it.

Now begin to add the water, a little at a time, stirring after each addition and allowing it to evaporate before adding more. After 15 to 20 minutes, turn off the heat. At this point the rice should be tender but still slightly firm at the center of each grain. Add the Parmesan and pepper and stir so that everything mixes together well. Let rest for about 5 minutes before serving.

BORAGE AND RICOTTA PIE

Serves 6

FOR THE CRUST
2⅓ cups (300 g) all-purpose flour, plus more for sprinkling
1 teaspoon (6 g) fine salt
2 egg yolks
2 teaspoons (10 g) butter, cut into cubes
⅓ cup (80 ml) warm water

FOR THE FILLING
14 ounces (400 g) borage tops and leaves (about 4½ cups)
2¼ teaspoons (10 g) coarse salt
1¼ cups (300 g) sheep's milk ricotta cheese, well drained in a cheesecloth-lined tight-weave strainer
1 egg
⅓ cup (40 g) grated Parmesan cheese
Freshly grated nutmeg

TO ASSEMBLE
2 teaspoons (10 ml) extra-virgin olive oil
1 egg

To prepare the crust: Mound the flour on a work surface, make a well in the center, and add the salt and egg yolks to the well. Bury the butter pieces in the flour, then pour in the warm water, a little at a time, and mix everything together well. Work the dough with your hands until it becomes soft and compact. Let the dough rest under a bowl for about 1 hour.

To prepare the filling: Use only the most tender borage tops and leaves. Don kitchen gloves to handle them, washing them carefully to make sure that no dirt remains. Pour 3 quarts (3 l) water into an 8-quart (8-l) pot and place over high heat. When the water begins to boil, add the coarse salt. When the water begins to boil again, add the borage and cook for about 5 minutes. Remove the borage from the water with a wire skimmer and drain well, pressing to remove as much water as possible. Cut the borage into pieces about 1¼ (3 cm) long with kitchen shears or a knife.

Place the ricotta in a wide bowl and break it up with a fork. In a cup or small bowl, beat the egg for about 1 minute. Add the beaten egg to the ricotta and mix together. Then add the borage, Parmesan, and a few gratings of nutmeg and mix well.

To assemble the pie: Sprinkle a little flour on a marble or wood work surface. Divide the dough in half and shape each half into a ball. Place a ball on the work surface and flatten with your palm. With a rolling pin, roll out the dough into a circle about 14 inches (35 cm) in diameter. Repeat with the second ball of dough.

Preheat the oven to 400° F (200° C). Grease the bottom and sides of a pie pan 12 inches (30 cm) in diameter and 1¾ inches (4 cm) deep with the oil. Line the pan with a dough circle, pressing it against the bottom and sides and allowing it to extend slightly beyond the rim of the pan. Spoon the filling into the pan, spreading it evenly over the crust. Top the filling with the second dough circle and press along the edge of the pan with a fork to join the top and bottom crusts together well. In a cup or small bowl, beat the remaining egg until blended. With a pastry brush, brush the beaten egg evenly over the top and edge of the pie. With the fork, make a pair of small holes in the top crust to vent the steam as the pie bakes.

Bake the pie until the crust is golden brown, about 40 minutes. It is good hot, cold, or reheated.

Capers

CAPPARIS SPINOSA; ITALIAN: CAPPERI

IN ITALY, IT'S COMMON KNOWLEDGE that the best capers are from Lipari and Pantelleria. But they grow anywhere there is a cliff or a place that is arid and sunny. They even emerge from the cracks in the walls (Cyclopean, Roman, medieval, Spanish, and so on) of who knows how many Italian cities and who knows how many other more or less sovereign nations. In Lugo, in a town in the region of Emilia-Romagna, they have literally invaded the fortress (*rocca*) for hundreds of years and today are the subject of discussion and amazement. In a locally published tourist guide to the fortress, we read, "Capers have been present [at the fortress] for centuries, as attested . . . by reliable documents in the city archives, where we find specific reference to the capers at the fortress in the municipal budgets since the nineteenth century . . . . Since the postwar period, harvest of the fortress capers has been done by the civic employees who maintain the city's gardens and green spaces. They also prune the caper bushes until late winter and do the subsequent selection and thinning of the flowers, obviously with the assistance of ladders. The floral gems they collect . . . are placed in brine in little jars that the municipal administration offers free to guests of the city. Because the gardeners harvest only the highest-quality capers and not the entire crop, in recent years the administration has 'liberalized' the harvest of the remaining capers, instituting what could be called the 'right of capering,' in which 'fans' of capers ... can gather what they can reach from the ground. . . . A number of years ago, the worldwide fame of the ... capers of Lugo was tested directly in London, when cute (and miniscule) jars of Italian capers bearing the label 'Capers of the Rocca of Lugo' were sold in Harrods department store, but those certainly had never flowered on the walls of our Rocca."[1] *Sic transit gloria mundi.*

It is the bud of the caper flower that is used, but the stem (if tender) can also be pickled. It has always been used in the kitchen, and the entire aristocracy of naturalists, physicians, and gourmets speaks of it widely. Theophrastus, who we have already encountered in the Introduction to this volume and who worked hard to distinguish plants that can be cultivated from those that cannot (arguing against those who held that all plants were cultivable),[2] lists capers among the latter.[3] Almost as if to soften his antisocial character, however, he notes that the "caper ... flowers in summer and the leaf remains green till the rising of the Pleiades. It rejoices in sandy light soils, ... near towns."[4]

Columella, a contemporary of Nero, writes in complete contradiction to Theophrastus, however: "The *caper-bulb*, in many provinces, grows of its own accord in fallow lands, but where there is a scarcity of it, if it must be sown, it will require a dry place, and that ought to be surrounded with a small ditch beforehand, which may be filled with stones and lime or Carthaginian clay, so that it may be a type of entrenchment that the stalks of the aforesaid seed may not be able to break through. These commonly spread themselves over the whole land, unless they are hindered by some fence or mound. This, however, is not in itself as great an inconvenience (for they may be rooted out from time to time) as is the fact that they contain a hurtful poison that can make the ground barren. . . . It is sown at the time of both equinoxes."[5]

Quoted by Athenaeus of Naucratis (last half of the second to the beginning of the third century A.D.) in Book XIII of his *Deipnosophistae*, the satirical poet Timocles relates (in his *Neaira*) that Phryne, before becoming the most famous courtesan of her time (and before facing the trial that she would succeed in winning, showing everyone her naked and unequaled beauty), earned her living through capers: "But I, unhappy man, who first loved Phryne / When she was but a gatherer of capers, / And was not quite as rich as now she is,— / I who such sums of money spent upon her, / Am now excluded from her doors," inveighs one character.[6]

Pliny did not much trust these "berries well-known in the field of food." More specifically, he is geographically cautious. He likes Egyptian capers, but warns that "its foreign varieties should be avoided, inasmuch as the Arabian kind is poisonous and the African injures the gums, and those from Marmarica are injurious to the womb. Also, the Apulian caper-tree produces vomiting and diarrhoea by causing flatulence in all the organs" (*Naturalis historia*, XIII, 44, 127). A real catastrophe, as anyone can see. However, when speaking of its curative profile (*Naturalis historia*, XX, 59, 165–67), the list that Pliny draws up of the benefits attributed to the capers action is no less brief than it is surprising. Cooked in water, instilled in oil, ground, combined with barley flour, and so on, capers prevent paralysis; heal the spleen, the liver, and the bladder; and are an excellent remedy for toothache, otitis, ulcers of the mouth, and scrofula. "Authorities agree," Pliny concludes with admirable caution, "that the caper is harmful to the stomach." Even according to Michele Savonarola, capers "are bad nourishment, because they generate melancholic blood and choleric humors." Further, they are "hard to digest" and *incredibile dictu*, "they are not so beautiful to look at." Nevertheless, "they may be prepared with oil, salt, cinnamon, and vinegar. They provoke the appetite, cleanse the stomach, and do not harm it much. They induce the operation of the liver and even more of the spleen, and they are a true medicine for that. And Serapion says that whoever has tooth pain and eats and chews their root will be relieved from the pain" (*Libreto*, 79).

Nowadays, capers are not at all disparaged in the kitchen. In fact, such a shower of uses is recorded that capers are almost as frequently used as parsley. They are used in the white sauces of Piedmont, in Neapolitan *tielle* (savory pies), and on pizzas. They marry magnificently with a number of meats, fish, and vegetables (from tripe to lamb, from calamari to mullet, from peppers to tomatoes). Caper and anchovy sauce is also loudly praised by the immortal Artusi: "This sauce is rather hard on delicate stomachs. It is ordinarily used with steak. Take a pinch of sweetened capers, squeeze out the brine, and finely chop with a *mezzaluna* along with an anchovy from which you have removed the scales and spine. Heat this in olive oil and pour it over a beef steak that you have grilled and then seasoned with salt and pepper and some butter. Use the butter sparingly, however, otherwise it will clash, in the stomach, with the vinegar from the capers."[7]

The flower is eaten before it blooms. In a single season, a dozen or so harvests can be made every ten to twelve days in the period that runs from April to July.

LAMB STEW WITH CAPERS

Serves 4

½ cup (120 ml) plus 2 tablespoons (30 ml) dry white wine
1⅓ pounds (600 g) boneless lamb (shoulder, leg, or loin),
     cut into about 12 pieces
⅓ cup (75 ml) extra-virgin olive oil
⅓ cup (40 g) finely chopped spring onions
1 rosemary sprig
1 teaspoon (2 g) ground black pepper
¼ teaspoon (2 g) coarse salt
5 teaspoons (15 g) capers in brine, rinsed
⅓ cup (75 ml) extra-virgin olive oil

In a 2½-quart (2.5-l) bowl, combine ⅓ cup (75 ml) water and ½ cup (120 ml) of the wine. Immerse the lamb in the liquid and let it marinate for 5 minutes. Remove the pieces and dry well with paper towels. Discard the marinade.

Pour the oil into a pan about 9 inches (23 cm) in diameter and 3½ inches (9 cm) deep, place over medium heat, and warm for about 2 minutes. Add the lamb and brown well, about 3 minutes on each side. Add the onions, rosemary, and pepper and stir continuously for 5 minutes. Add the salt and continue to stir for another 5 minutes. Add the capers and the remaining 2 tablespoons (30 ml) wine and cook until the wine evaporates. At this point, pour in 1¼ cups (300 ml) water and wait for it to begin to boil. Then reduce the heat to the lowest setting, cover, and simmer for about 2½ hours. The lamb is ready when about 6½ tablespoons (100 ml) of sauce remains in the pot. Remove from the heat and leave covered for 10 minutes before serving.

BAKED ANCHOVIES WITH CAPERS

Serves 4

25 medium-size anchovies
8 teaspoons (40 ml) extra-virgin olive oil
3 tablespoons (20 g) dried bread crumbs
3 ripe tomatoes, chopped

3½ teaspoons (10 g) capers in brine, rinsed
2 cloves garlic, minced
4 teaspoons (5 g) chopped fresh parsley
2 teaspoons (2 g) minced fresh oregano
½ teaspoon (3 g) fine salt

Remove the head from each anchovy, then rinse the anchovies. With a sharp knife, slit each anchovy along its belly and carefully remove the backbone without separating the fillets. Rinse the anchovies again, being careful to keep the fillets attached, and pat dry.

Preheat the oven to 400°F (200°C). Grease the bottom and sides of a shallow 12-by-8-inch (30-by-20-cm) baking dish with 4 teaspoons (20 ml) of the oil. Layer half of the anchovies in a single layer on the bottom the dish, top evenly with half of the bread crumbs, and then with half each of the tomatoes, capers, garlic, parsley, oregano, and salt. Drizzle 2 teaspoons (10 ml) of the remaining oil over the top. Repeat the layering once, starting with the remaining anchovies. Place in the oven for 5 minutes.

SALTED CAPERS

Makes 1¾ cups (250 g)

1¾ cups (250 g) capers
3 tablespoons (50 g) coarse salt

Use only the smallest capers. In a glass container with a capacity of about 1¼ cups (300 ml), make a layer of capers 1¼ to 1½ inches (3 to 4 cm) thick. Sprinkle about 2 teaspoons (10 g) of the salt on the capers. Let stand at room temperature for 2 to 3 days, stirring the capers and salt a couple of times each day. Then, add the same amount of capers and salt and let stand for another 2 to 3 days, again making sure you stir the capers and salt a couple of times each day. Repeat, adding the remaining capers and salt in three equal additions, letting each addition stand for 2 to 3 days before adding the next batch and always stirring a couple times each day. Once the last addition of capers and salt is in the container, continue to stir the mixture a couple of times each day. The capers are ready when all of the salt has melted, usually after about 2 months.

SPAGHETTI ALLA CRUDAIOLA WITH
TUNA AND CAPERS

Serves 4

  1 can (½ pound/250 g) tuna in olive oil, drained
6½ tablespoons (100 ml) extra-virgin olive oil
  1 clove garlic
  7 teaspoons (20 g) salted capers, rinsed
  2 tablespoons (40 g) coarse salt
14 ounces (400 g) spaghetti
  1 teaspoon (2 g) ground black pepper
  4 teaspoons (5 g) chopped fresh parsley

Put the tuna in a large bowl and crush it with a fork. In a small skillet, heat the oil over medium heat, add the garlic clove, and cook until it browns, then let the oil cool. Remove and discard the garlic clove from the oil and add the oil and the capers to the tuna and stir together well.

Pour 4 quarts (4 l) water into a 6-quart (6-l) pot, cover, and bring to a boil over high heat. As soon as the water begins to boil, add the salt. When the water returns to a boil, toss in the spaghetti and cook for 7 minutes, timing from when the water begins to boil again. Drain the spaghetti and add it to the bowl holding the tuna and the capers. Mix carefully (it is best to use a metal spoon and fork), then add the pepper and parsley, mix again, and serve.

Chamomile

MATRICARIA CHAMOMILLA; ITALIAN: *CAMOMILLA*

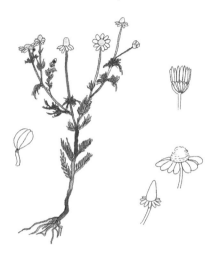

LET THOSE WHO NEVER EXPERIENCED the torment of a chamomile enema as children cast the first stone—or no, let them thank God that they were born in an era in which purges, emetics, and laxatives no longer obsessively worry the minds of grandmothers, nannies, busybody aunts, putative fathers, ogres, and black dwarves. But those who did not have this good fortune can let themselves go, mentally leave their domestic walls, and return to the new yet already dilapidated streets of some postwar suburban Italian neighborhood, with the sidewalk paved on one side and still weedy on the other, at the edge of a vegetable garden or a wheat field smack in the middle of a jumble of apartment blocks, a little past the last tram stop.

In this area, after the mower's blades had passed in June, you could glean (that is, collect) the ears of wheat that miraculously remained upright or that escaped other gatherers who, with careless speed and skill, collected the "sawed off" ears into bundles and threw them onto a cart (drawn by horses, naturally) to bring them to Cassina del Campazz or Campazzin, on the southern outskirts of Milan. Today, a different generation of children goes to that same spot on field trips to see cows and chickens that they find more exotic than the giraffes and boa constrictors of American films.

In addition to the ears of wheat, you might collect flowering stalks of chamomile. Originally from Southeast Asia, it is a plant that would need to be invented if it did not already exist. It has, thank goodness, naturalized itself throughout the world and grows at will among grains (but it is also found at the side of every road). Its full name is *Matricaria chamomilla.*[1] The first part of the name derives from *mater,* and according to the *Royal Horticultural Society Dictionary of Gardening,* it must have been given to the plant by herbalists of antiquity (including Pedanius Dioscorides, a Greek physician practicing in Nero's Rome), who used it to cure uterine disease. The second part of the name travels a more complex path. We start from the Late Latin (*chamomilla*) and go back to the Greek *chamáimelon,* a combination of *chamaí,* which means "low," and *melon,* which means "apple." Thus, we find ourselves before a "low apple" or (perhaps more plausibly) an apple fallen low (that is, on the ground). For those who may ask in amazement what chamomile might have to do with apples, the answer is nothing. The only thing is that those with a good sense of smell—for example, Castore Durante in his *Herbario novo* (1585)—hold that the scent of chamomile flowers is similar to that of some apples. But Galen had already sensed that.

Michele Savonarola describes it as the "Herb of Saint Mary, called *arcemisia* and also *matricaria*" and defines it as warm and moist (following what Avicenna, Serapion, and others had said about it). He adds that "it is used to make *tortelli* on the Feast of Saint Mary [which one?]" and explains that he "wanted to mention it because it is the herb of women, very useful for the uterus, and that is why it is called *matricaria.*"[2] Then, in a crescendo of involuntary cheerfulness and precious little political correctness, he comments: "It is good in the food of fat women and not thin, such that many women of Ferrara [his own town] will not be able to use it. And it is better fresh than dried, it comforts the cold and moist stomach, and it makes you thinner. Thus, your Lordship [that is, Borso d'Este, for whom he was writing] may make good use of it because eaten in this way it comforts the heart, opens the pathways for urine, and breaks kidney stones" (*Libreto,* 75).

Today, two of Savonarola's affirmations sound very strange: first, that fresh chamomile is better than dry, and second, that it may be eaten at all. (It is not clear whether Savonarola was implying that fat women should partake of it or whether he meant the duke, who perhaps was not so thin himself.) These assertions are not necessarily odd because they are not truthful, but simply because no one speaks of chamomile in these terms any longer. On the contrary, it is recommended that the flowers (it is best if they have just emerged) be neatly detached from the stems and dried in cool and airy places, sheltered from light and moisture. As far as gastronomic uses, chamomile is included as an ingredient in the composition of some aromatic wines and liqueurs, including sherry.[3] Not even Maria Treben (1907–91), who, in her most famous book, *Health Through God's Pharmacy*, praises chamomile exceedingly, departs from the curative sphere. Beyond the chamomile herbal tea universally known for its sedative effects, the very popular phytotherapist teaches how to prepare a poultice, an herb sachet ("a linen bag is filled with loosely dried Camomile flowers and stitched up; warmed in a dry pan and used"), and an oil ("a small bottle is filled loosely with fresh Camomile flowers picked in the sun and cold-pressed olive-oil is poured in until it covers the flowers; the bottle, well stoppered, is kept in the sun for fourteen days"). She also describes how to prepare an ointment whose preparation is worth quoting almost in its entirety: "250 gm. of lard are heated, one heaped double handful of fresh Camomile flowers are added; as it foams it is stirred, removed from the stove, covered and kept in a cool place overnight. Next day it is warmed and pressed . . . place a sieve with a piece of linen inside over a jug or pot with a spout. . . . [The result is put] into clean glass jars or pots."[4]

We learn from Treben that such a cream is an excellent preventative for hemorrhoids, that a rubbing of the oil treats neuralgia and joint pain,[5] and that chamomile in general cures fevers, cramps, flatulence, sprains, rashes, ocular inflammations, diarrhea, and hundreds of other annoyances. In her pages, we also meet the legendary Johann Künzle (1857–1945), *Kräuter-Pfarres* (shepherd herbalist) and Catholic priest of San Gallo, Switzerland, in whose book, *Chrut and Uuchrut* (Grasses and Weeds), first published in 1911, we read things regarding chamomile that are truly amazing. One (presumably) kind woman nicknamed "the Magician of Chamomile" allegedly restored hearing to five deaf people by frying one bulb of *urginea* (i.e., the squill mentioned in the present volume under the chapter dedicated to cipollini) in chamomile oil and placing several drops of the oil into the ears of each one. And that's not all: she restored movement to paralyzed limbs by rubbing them with chamomile oil; she cured conjunctivitis with compresses of chamomile flowers boiled in milk; and with two glasses of chamomile wine, one in the evening and one in the morning, she eliminated the most stubborn diuresis. The reputation of Don Künzle in the medical community was not always clear. Many considered him a charlatan, a profession that obviously depends on smooth patter and great powers of persuasion. To others, he was a wonderful philanthropic spirit. What was true for Künzle obviously also applied to the magician he describes.

Without promising results this astonishing, Nicholas Culpeper had already shown great confidence in the virtues of chamomile, but you never know whether to appreciate more the scientific scrupulousness by which he was animated or the causticity of the style with which he derides prejudices and lashes out at customs. He writes: "According to Nechessor, the Egyptians dedicated it [chamomile] to the Sun, because it cured agues, and they were like[ly] enough to do it, for they were the arrantest of apes in their religion that I ever read of.[6] . . . Also this is certain, that it most wonderfully breaks the [kidney] stone: Some take it in syrup or decoction, others inject the juice of it into the bladder with a syringe. My opinion is, that the salt of it, taken half a dram in the morning in a little white or Rhenish wine, is better than either; that it is excellent for the stone appears by this, which I have seen tried, viz, that a stone that has been taken out of the body of a man being wrapped in Camomile will in time dissolve, and in a little time too" (*Complete Herbal,* 39).

But we cannot conclude with chamomile without noting that De Gubernatis, in the few lines dedicated to it in his *Mythologie des plantes,*[7] finds a way to quote the herbalist Odo de Meung, better known as Macer Floridus (tenth century), who, in his poem in Latin hexameter, *De viribus herbarum* (On the virtues of plants), published in 1477, states that a little chamomile mixed with wine, taken orally, is also very good against the bite of poisonous snakes.

Chamomile grows as a most welcome weed (poor men used its dried flowers as pipe tobacco and poor women bleached their hair with the water in which they boiled it) in the plains and in the mountains up to about three thousand feet. The period of flowering and gathering stretches from the end of April to the end of June.

DECOCTION OF CHAMOMILE

Serves 3

1¼ cups (40 g) chamomile flowers
4¾ teaspoons (20 g) sugar
　Zest of 1 untreated (unwaxed) lemon, in strips

Gather the flowers and let them "bruise" for 2 days—that is, let them dry on a plate placed in an airy, cool place. Don't put them right in the sun or they will wither and become dark, and they must remain light. Once dried, you can expose them to the sun for 4 to 5 days. Although the flowers are dried, keep them in a closed glass jar.

For the decoction, proceed in this simple manner. Pour 2 cups (500 ml) water into a small saucepan, place over medium heat, cover, and bring to a boil. When the water begins to boil, add the chamomile flowers, re-cover, and let boil for at least 10 minutes. Filter the decoction through a tight-weave strainer into a teapot and add the sugar and lemon zest. Drunk hot, this decoction calms the nerves, helps you sleep, and is also used for stomachaches. Cold, it is excellent for vaginal washing and for relieving reddened eyes.

Cipollini

YOU WILL FIND *LAMPASCIONI* (cipollini) in every village in Puglia and the Salento (and in the regions of Basilicata, Calabria, and Sicily). Or rather, the cipollini will find you, though they might go by different names. Here is a list (certainly incomplete) of what they are popularly called in Italian alone: *lampagione, lampasione, agghioru neru, cipolla canina, cipolla selvatica, cipolla di serpe, cipollaccio, ciopollaccio col fiocco, cipollina, cipollone, cipuddazzu, giacinto selvatico, giacinto col fiocco, muscari, muscaro, muschino, pampagione, pampascione, pan del cucco, purrazzu.* Fortunately, there exists a common denominator: the plant's scientific name, *Muscari comosum* (from *móschos,* which means "moss," and *kòme* which means "head of hair," and from which the word *comet* [star with hair] also derives). It is uncertain why it was given this name, but some assert that it's because of the scent—one variety of cipollini (*M. muscarini*) does, in fact, smell like moss. The idea of hair, on the other hand, may come from the shape of its flower clusters.

Wisely, the *Royal Horticultural Society Dictionary of Gardening* (vol. III, 269) translates it as "tuft." Baptizing it as such was Carolus Clusius, née Charles de L'Écluse (1526–1609), an illustrious professor of botany at the

University of Leiden, where he participated in the creation of the Hortus botanicus, one of the oldest botanical gardens in Europe. He was also a great expert on tulips and was among the first to bring them to Holland. Author of fundamental works on the flora of Spain and Portugal and of Austria and Hungary (he was called to Vienna by Maximilian II, Holy Roman emperor from 1564 until his death in 1576), Clusius supposedly obtained the first bulb of the fragrant species of cipollini from a garden in Constantinople.[1]

It grows wild in the regions mentioned above and throughout the Mediterranean basin, particularly in untilled grasslands and pastures, but it is also widespread in the warm regions of central Europe. Only in Puglia, however, is it universally known not only as an edible plant but also as a true delicacy (and a bit in Basilicata and Calabria as well). The name *lampascione,* which by now identifies the plant throughout all of Italy, is a word from the Puglian dialect.

It is the bulb of the *M. comosum* that is eaten. It grows six to eight inches below ground and has a slightly bitter taste that causes many to recommend soaking it in cold water until it becomes more pleasurable to the palate (a couple of days, changing the water twice a day) before cooking it. In the uplands of the Murgia plateau in Puglia, some locals swear that the best way to cook it is beneath hot ashes.

As you might have guessed, the bulb is a type of wild onion and thus consists of many layers and many overlapping tunicates (from which, among other things, the leaves develop directly). The external layers must be removed, preferably after cooking. First, however, the bulb must be scrubbed well but delicately to eliminate the soil that inevitably adheres to it because of its viscosity.

Nowadays, cipollini can also be bought at the market (in Italy, these are probably cultivated bulbs imported from Morocco). Buying them at the market, however, is a bit like fishing for trout in the pools in which they are farmed using worms as bait. (This is a sport that has nothing sportlike about it—that's not fishing; it's a massacre.) Therefore, purists and the pure of heart will seek them in the fields, carefully avoiding the maritime squill (also called *cipadduzzu*), which is ten times larger, grows just touching the surface, and produces beautiful white flowers at the top of a much taller stem (florists sell them), but is also rich in poisonous glycosides, so keep away! (The bulb's scales, however, have cardiotonic properties.)

Massimo Vaglio writes, "In the Salento, the cipollini is associated with the *pampasciunaru,* a character now on its way to extinction. As free as he is an outcast, this person devotes himself only sporadically to employment as a farmworker and lives principally on what the uncultivated land, forests, and scrub offer him: mushrooms, snails, wild vegetables, asparagus, sow thistles, and the like."[2] In the past, when cultivated lands were turned by plows pulled by oxen (and pushed by man), you could find a good number of cipollini among the overturned clods, but today destructive machinery is employed, and this sort of facilitated harvest is unimaginable.

Not all cipollini can be prepared in the same way. Those that grow in very calcareous soil (the *cutrei,* as Vaglio suggests calling them) are "averse to cooking, such that they should first be boiled in rainwater."[3] Once upon a time, every rural dwelling had a cistern for collecting water whose potability was "guaranteed" by a type of eel that, swimming back and forth and feeding on the insects that would fall inside, kept the water moving and purified it. No one ever commented on the residue of the eels' digestion, which must have ended up somewhere. This water, however, is very difficult to find,[4] so in a pinch, you can add a little bicarbonate of soda to cooking water drawn from the faucet. We will take a last bit of valuable advice from Vaglio's small volume, *sin verguenza*: the boiling of the cipollini must not be "tumultuous"—that is, the heat must be kept rather low.

We find this trick already noted by Apicius in Book VII, Chapter XIV of *De re coquinaria,* which, it is worth noting, is dedicated to luxury foods (cow teats, tripe, uterus, foie gras, stomach, testicles, and kidneys). In the second of the four recipes dedicated to cipollini, the most famous gastronome of ancient Rome writes: "Soak the bulbs and parboil them in water; thereupon fry them in oil. The dressing make thus: take thyme, flea-bane, pepper, origany, honey, vinegar, reduced wine, date wine, if you like broth and a little oil. Sprinkle with pepper and serve."[5] But the most interesting recipe is the one into which Apicius injects, among the mechanical minimalist monotony that his formulas normally have, a pair of observations that are brief but, for us, interesting (and immediately bring to mind an interpolation). Referring to Varro ("Varro says of the bulbs" is the title of the recipe),[6] Apicius affirms that when cooked in water (but also "seasoned with pignolia [pine] nut or with the juice of colewort, or mustard, and pepper"), the cipollini urge the search for the mouth of Venus (*ostium Veneris*), and because of this, the bulbs are served at matrimonial feasts. That cipollini were an aphrodisiac was a superstition confirmed by Columella. According to him, "From Megaris now let the genial seeds / Of bulbs be brought, which sharpen men's desires, / And put young modest ladies on their guard. / And such as Sicca gathers, and finds hid / Below Getulian clods; and rocket sown / Near to Priapus, crown'd with ears of corn, / That slow and drowsy husbands may it rouse" (*Of Husbandry*, X, vv. 161–7). Martial also confirms this when he writes, "*Cum sit anus coniunx et sint tibi mortua membra, / nil aliud bulbis quam satur esse potes*" (*Epigrams*, XIII, 34), which, respecting the mocking tone that distinguishes this author, we would suggest translating like this: "Given that your wife is old and that your member is lacking in life, / there is nothing left for you but to sate yourself with cipollini."

Nor could Ovid be kept away from this noble flower of flowers (*Ars amatoria*, II, vv. 415–24). Generally averse to the use of herbal stimulants, he nonetheless makes an exception for cipollini: "There are some who would recommend you to use injurious herbs, such as savory; in my opinion they are so many poisons. Or else, they mingle pepper with the seed of the stinging nettle; and the yellow chamomile pounded in old wine. But the Goddess, whom the lofty Eryx receives beneath his shady hill, does not allow us to be impelled in such manner to her delights. The white onion [cipollini] which is sent from the Pelasgian city of Alcathoüs, and the salacious herbs which come out of the gardens, and eggs may be eaten; the honey of Hymettus may be eaten, and the nuts which the pine-tree with its sharp leaves produces."[7]

Yet even cipollini, which, following the best tradition (Theophrastus, Pliny, and the like), even Ovid calls by the generic name *bulbus*, falls into disgrace in *Remedia amoris* (vv. 795–800), where it is described as highly harmful, identical in this to all herbs that push one toward Venus. "And then, as [for] the medicinal properties of foods—we shall speak of those that are to be avoided and those that are instead to be ingested. The bulbs, those that are Daunian [an area in Puglia], those that are Libyan, and those that come from Megara [in Greece], are to be avoided always. Similarly, stay away from pungent arugula and from everything that may have the power to strengthen the body toward amorous ends."

In spite of Ovidian warnings under Article 8 of Italian law (Decreto Legge) number 173 of April 30, 1998, cipollini were declared a traditional agricultural food product.

On March 18 (the eve of the feast of Saint Joseph), particularly in Giurdignano but also in other villages in the Salento—a table is set and the door is left open for the "wayfarer." Whoever is passing in front of the house is invited to enter and to taste whatever the knowing hands of naturally refined cooks have prepared, following the dictates of ancient recipes: fish, sweets, vegetables, and, to drink, a good glass of Primitivo and Negroamaro. The menu is not fixed, in the sense that everyone prepares what they want, but a bowl of cipollini is de rigueur.

The harvest period for cipollini is from January to May. If possible, gather the bulbs before the first flowers form so that they are still rich in mineral salts and nutrients.

LAMB STEW WITH CIPOLLINI

Serves 4

⅔ pound (300 g) cipollini
½ cup plus 2 tablespoons (150 ml) dry white wine
1½ pounds (700 g) boneless lamb (shoulder, leg, or loin), cut into pieces
⅓ cup (75 ml) extra-virgin olive oil
1 clove garlic
⅓ cup (40 g) chopped spring onions
5 thyme sprigs
1½ teaspoons (3 g) ground black pepper
¾ teaspoon (5 g) coarse salt

Clean the cipollini well, peeling the skin, trimming off the root hairs, and cutting the stem very close to the bulb. Pour ⅓ cup (75 ml) water and ½ cup (120 ml) of the wine into a wide 3-quart (3-l) bowl. Immerse the lamb in the liquid and let it marinate for 5 minutes. Remove the lamb from the bowl and dry well with paper towels. Discard the marinade.

Pour the oil into a shallow 4 quart (4-l) pot, place over medium heat, and warm for about 2 minutes. Add the lamb and brown well, about 3 minutes on each side. Add the cipollini, garlic clove, spring onions, thyme, and pepper and stir everything for a good 5 minutes. Add the salt and stir for another 5 minutes. Then add the remaining 2 tablespoons (30 ml) wine and allow it to evaporate. At this point, pour in 1¼ cups (300 ml) water and wait for it to begin to boil. When it begins, reduce the heat to the lowest setting, cover, and simmer for about 2½ hours. The lamb is ready when about 6½ tablespoons (100 ml) of sauce remains in the pot. Remove from the heat and leave covered for 10 minutes before serving.

CIPOLLINI WITH OIL AND VINEGAR

Serves 4

1 pound (500 g) cipollini
3¼ teaspoons (20 g) coarse salt
    White wine vinegar, to taste
    Extra-virgin olive oil, to taste

Clean the cipollini well, peeling the skin, trimming off the root hairs, and cutting the stem very close to the bulb. Pour 2 quarts (2 l) water into a 4-quart (4-l) pot, cover, and place over high heat. When the water begins to boil, add the salt and immediately drop in the cipollini. Cover the pot and cook for about 20 minutes, timing from when the water starts to boil again.

Remove the cipollini from the pot with a wire skimmer and immerse in a container filled with cold water. Remove any surface skin that has peeled off, then drain in a colander. Place in a bowl and season to taste with vinegar and oil.

SWEET-AND-SOUR CIPOLLINI

Serves 4

1 pound (500 g) cipollini
3¼ teaspoons (20 g) coarse salt
    Scant ½ pound (200 g) spring onions (white part only), sliced
6½ tablespoons (100 ml) extra-virgin olive oil
    Scant 5 teaspoons (20 g) sugar
1 tablespoon (15 ml) white wine vinegar

Clean the cipollini well, peeling the skin, trimming off the root hairs, and cutting the stem very close to the bulb. Pour 2 quarts (2 l) water into a 4-quart

(4-l) pot, cover, and place over high heat. When the water begins to boil, add the salt and immediately drop in the cipollini. Cover the pot and cook for about 15 minutes, timing from when the water starts to boil again. Remove the cipollini from the pot with a wire skimmer and drain well.

Pour the oil into a shallow 2½-quart (2.5-l) pot and place over low heat. Add the spring onions and cook, stirring occasionally, for 10 minutes. Then add the cipollini and let cook for 15 minutes. Stir in the sugar and stir everything for about 4 minutes to blend the flavors. Finally, add the vinegar and cook for about 3 minutes longer, stirring continuously. The cipollini are good hot or cold.

PANFRIED CIPOLLINI

Serves 4

- 1 pound (500 g) cipollini
- 3¼ teaspoons (20 g) coarse salt
- 6½ tablespoons (100 ml) extra-virgin olive oil
- 1 large or 2 medium white onions, thinly sliced
- 1 bay leaf
- 6½ tablespooons (100 ml) red wine
- 1½ teaspoons (3 g) ground black pepper

Clean the cipollini well, peeling the skin, trimming off the root hairs, and cutting the stem very close to the bulb. Pour 2 quarts (2 l) water into a 4-quart (4-l) pot, cover, and place over high heat. When the water begins to boil, add the salt and immediately drop in the cipollini. Cover the pot and cook for about 15 minutes, timing from when the water starts to boil again. Remove the cipollini from the pot with a wire skimmer and drain well.

Pour the oil into a shallow 2½-quart (2.5-l) pot and place over low heat. Add the onions and cook, stirring occasionally, for 10 minutes. Add the bay leaf, still being careful not to let the onions burn. Then add the cipollini, raise the heat to medium, and cook, stirring often, for 10 minutes. Pour in the red wine, raise the heat to high, and cook until the wine evaporates. Sprinkle with the pepper, stir again, and remove from the heat. The cipollini are good hot or cold.

PICKLED CIPOLLINI

Makes 1 quart (1 l)

  1 pound (500 g) cipollini
  4 teaspoons (25 g) coarse salt
  4 cups (1 l) white wine vinegar
 10 black peppercorns

Clean the cipollini well, peeling the skin, trimming off the root hairs, and cutting the stem very close to the bulb. Pour 2 quarts (2 l) water into a 4-quart (4-l) pot, cover, and place over high heat. When the water begins to boil, add the salt. When the water begins to boil again, drop in the cipollini, cover the pot, and cook for 5 minutes, timing from when the water starts to boil again. Remove the cipollini from the pot with a wire skimmer and immerse in a bowl filled with cold water. Let the cipollini soak for 24 hours, changing the water three or four times to remove the bitterness.

Drain the cipollini well in a colander and set them on a kitchen towel or paper towels to dry. Finally, place them in a 1-quart (1-l) glass jar with an airtight lid and pour in the vinegar. Add the peppercorns and screw on the lid. Store the jar in a cool, dark place. The cipollini are ready to eat after 40 days and will keep for up to about 1 year.

STEWED CIPOLLINI

Serves 4

  1 pound (500 g) cipollini
 3¼ teaspoons (20 g) coarse salt
 6½ tablespoons (100 ml) extra-virgin olive oil
  1 or 2 white onions, thinly sliced
  8 cherry tomatoes, each cut into 2 or 3 pieces
  ½ teaspoon (3 g) fine salt

Clean the cipollini well, peeling the skin, trimming off the root hairs, and cutting the stem very close to the bulb. Pour 2 quarts (2 l) water into a 4-quart (4-l) pot, cover, and place over high heat. When the water begins to boil, add the coarse salt. When the water begins to boil again, drop in the cipollini, cover the pot, and cook for 15 minutes, timing from when the water starts to boil again. Remove the cipollini from the pot with a wire skimmer and drain well.

Pour the oil into a shallow 2½-quart (2.5-l) pot and place over low heat. Add the onions and cook, stirring occasionally, for 10 minutes. Be careful they do not burn. Add the cipollini and continue to cook over low heat, stirring often, for 10 minutes. Now add the tomatoes and the fine salt, raise the heat, and cook for 5 minutes, never neglecting to stir. Remove from the heat and serve hot or cold.

Crested Wartycabbage

BUNIAS ERUCAGO; ITALIAN: *RAPESTA*

"TO CURE CHILBLAIN," we read in *Grandmother's Remedies: Herbs, Stones, and Animals in the Popular Medicine of the Salento* by Antonio Costantini and Marosa Marcucci, "it was enough to immerse the extremities in water in which leaves [of crested wartycabbage] had been boiled."[1] "Was" says a lot about the remedy's effectiveness. Thank goodness (it further comes to mind) that in the Salento, the temperature does not often fall below freezing, and thus, among the calamities that once afflicted the poor, chilblain must not have been the principal one. Among the latter, however, we should place hunger, to whose demands crested wartycabbage did respond (to use some humor that may not be black, but merely dark gray): An uncle of mine who was born and undernourished in Solofra (in the province of Avellino) would sing dejectedly, "On Sunday, I want you to eat bread and crested wartycabbage [*rapesta*]." If my memory is not playing tricks, this meant that after having eaten wartycabbage every day of the week, on Sunday—as a consolation prize for the meagerness of the weekday diet—fate would place on the table a nice plate of wartycabbage.

This negative judgment that weighed on crested wartycabbage ended up making it synonymous with disgrace, nasty business, or grave difficulty, as evidenced in the expression *Ha' ccappàtu 'na rapesta* (I came across a warty-cabbage). The saying, which was recorded by Ada Nucita and is widespread throughout villages in the province of Lecce, refers to someone who incurs an injury or finds himself in an ugly situation.[2] And the expression that circulates in Basilicata, *Po' ballamme cu 'na rapesta* (Then I'll dance with a wartycabbage) does not foretell of great happiness, although at first glance a wartycabbage might seem better than a broom handle. In Basilicata, the word for *rapesta* can also be used as an adjective in the sense of "like a pest."

Heartbroken by so much fatalistic humiliation, we too are assailed by the sudden and inexplicable desire to exclaim, *O mangi 'sta rapesta o salti da 'sta fenesta* (Either eat this wartycabbage or jump from the window).

Nonetheless, the gray mood is tinged with a more rosy coloring in the verses of the Neapolitan poet Giulio Cesare Cortese (1570–1640) who, in the heroi-comic poem *La vaiasseide* (published in its entirety in 1615), places on the scene and (good-naturedly?) exposes to ridicule a group of *vaiasse*, that is, Neapolitan women usually employed as servants. "Looking at the *vaiasselle* closely / they are tender and white like *rapesta* / with a roasted pink coloring (of their cheeks) / and more flavorful than the juice of unripe grapes: / Whether it is January or August, / a work day or a day of rest, / they are always more decked out and sparkling / than the garments worn on the feast of Saint Anthony."[3]

As anyone can see, there are three good comparative references here of a loutish-gastronomic flavor, roast meat, juice of unripe grapes, and, most of all, the wartycabbage, which can be called tender and white if gathered before its yellow flowers emerge and cooked in the simplest way: divide the cluster in four (leaving a little bit of the root), boil it, sprinkle it with oil, and then put a little salt on top. Such edible compliments are typical of a baroque poet who looks down at the poor from on high and supposes that, eating as rarely as they do, the poor dream of nothing other than pigging out prodigiously: mountains of polenta, hedges of sausage, rivers of Malvasia wine, and so on—in other words, the foods and banquets of the rich. This is why wartycabbage never entered into the literary *topos* of the poor man's paradise (the Land of Cockaygne and the like). In this sense, then, Cortese's mention of *rapesta* is exceptional. Today, eating crested wartycabbage is no longer an indicator of indigence, because the rich are now discovering how refined the tastes of the poor were.

Although it does not disdain poor soils (derelict, uncultivated, grassy), crested wartycabbage nonetheless needs water to grow. In fact, nobody can find any of it in summer, unless his name is Gaetano Tenore of Otranto, who, as familiar with the fields of the Salento as he is with his own pockets, knows where irrigation substitutes for the rain. On August 24, he rustled up, as proof, two exquisite seedlings. Chewing crested wartycabbage slowly does not neutralize the flavor of its oil but brings it out. Because of this, you will want to use very fine oil, pure salt, and bread of the highest quality—all things that are now absent from the tables of the poor (alas) and from the Johnny Easymeals of the world (their loss).

Michele Savonarola declares himself uncertain whether to call it a root or an herb and settles the question with a judgment that would have done honor to Buridan's ass, which, as is well known, died of hunger not knowing how to decide whether to eat straw or hay: "Although *rapesta* is not called a proper root but a green, it can nonetheless be counted among them [that is, roots], since it lies below the earth like a root, but its leaves could be called a green." The initial ambiguity is not at all redeemed in the subsequent lines, which present wartycabbage as "very nutritious, as can clearly be seen in the way that it fattens animals." Then, after having instructed that wartycabbage "produces flatulence [and] excites coitus," the taxonomic torment returns: being "difficult to digest, ... it must be cooked well. And the root is even more difficult to digest than the leaves, whose appearance, as I said, allows us to call it both herb and green." A final uncertainty arises after trying to assure us (with too much hesitation to succeed) that "its harmfulness [presumably inherent in its difficult assimilation] is removed if it is boiled twice and cooked well a third time with very fatty meat, so that it both nourishes and is *saltem medium inter bonum et malum* [at least somewhere between good and bad]." Savonarola concludes, however, that "it is better [when] roasted well," and he adds, a little devilishly, "There is more to speculate about it, but we will leave that at present in order to be brief" (*Libreto*, 103–104).

Although we too would like to finish in the interest of brevity, we must confess that there are longstanding terminological and referential difficulties regarding crested wartycabbage. Columella distinguished wild radish from wartycabbage proper, although nowadays the two signifiers tend to overlap. The best strategy could be to take refuge in the scientific term, *Bunias erucago,* or use the English name, crested wartycabbage—so-called probably because raised white spots can be found on the leaves.

The gathering period for crested wartycabbage runs from October until April.

CRESTED WARTYCABBAGE FRITTATA

Serves 4

1 pound (500 g) crested wartycabbage
5 teaspoons (30 g) coarse salt
5 eggs
5 teaspoons (15 g) dried bread crumbs
3 tablespoons (20 g) grated pecorino cheese
⅛ teaspoon (1 g) fine salt
½ teaspoon (1 g) ground black pepper
4 teaspoons (20 ml) extra-virgin olive oil

Wash the wartycabbage carefully. Pour 3 quarts (3 l) water into a 5½-quart (5.5-l) pot, place over high heat, cover, and bring to a boil. When the water begins to boil, add the coarse salt. As soon as the water begins to boil again, add the wartycabbage and cook for about 5 minutes, timing from when the water returned to a boil. Remove the wartycabbage from the water with a wire skimmer, draining well. Cut into pieces about 1¼ inches (3 cm) long.

In a bowl, beat the eggs with a fork for at least 1 minute. Add the bread crumbs, cheese, fine salt, pepper, and wartycabbage and mix together well, diluting the mixture with a little water.

Pour the oil into a nonstick 9-inch (23-cm) skillet and place over low heat. After about 1 minute, add the contents of the bowl. Cover the skillet and cook over very low heat for about 15 minutes. Then remove the skillet from the heat, uncover, and, with a wooden spatula, check that the edges and the center of the frittata did not stick. Invert a plate slightly larger than the skillet on top of the pan. Turn the skillet and plate together so the frittata falls onto the plate. Slide the frittata, browned side up, back into the skillet and cook, uncovered, over very low heat for 15 minutes. Remove from the heat and slide the frittata onto a plate. The frittata may be eaten hot or cold.

SPAGHETTI WITH CRESTED WARTYCABBAGE
Serves 4

1¾ pounds (800 g) wartycabbage
5 teaspoons (30 g) coarse salt
6½ tablespoons (100 ml) extra-virgin olive oil
⅓ cup (40 g) finely chopped spring onions
¾ teaspoon (2 g) ground red pepper
¾ pound (350 g) spaghetti

Wash the wartycabbage carefully. Pour 3½ quarts (3.5 l) water into a 5½-quart (5.5-l) pot, place over high heat, cover, and bring to a boil. When the water begins to boil, add the coarse salt. As soon as the water begins to boil again, add the wartycabbage and cook for about 5 minutes, timing from when the water returned to a boil. Remove the wartycabbage from the pot with a wire skimmer, draining well. Leave the water in the pot. Cut into pieces about 1¼ inches (3 cm) long.

Pour the oil into a 12-inch (30-cm) skillet and place over low heat. Add the onions and red pepper and cook until the onions are lightly golden, about 10 minutes. Add the wartycabbage and cook for another 4 minutes, stirring with a wooden spoon to blend the flavors.

Meanwhile, return the wartycabbage cooking water to a boil. Toss in the spaghetti and cook for about 6 minutes, timing from when the water begins to boil again. Just before draining, scoop out 5 tablespoons (75 ml) of the cooking water and add to the skillet. Then drain the spaghetti, add it to the skillet, and cook over low heat, stirring with a wooden spoon, for 5 minutes. Serve hot.

Daisy

IN OLD ITALIAN, THE NOUN *MARGHERITA* had a meaning identical to the Latin word *margarita,* that is to say "pearl," as pointed out by Dante Alighieri, among others. In his *Il convivio* (The banquet), Dante writes that "in every species of being we see nobility and baseness exemplified, as indicated by our speaking of a noble or base horse, a noble or base falcon, a noble or base *margherita*" (IV, XIV, 9).[1] We find it again in Franco Sacchetti, the last of the Italian writers of the fourteenth century and author of *Trecentonovelle* (Three hundred stories), who says, "Heliotrope is an expensive *margherita* that is found in Cyprus and in Africa" and not "in the dry bed of the Mugnone [River] that passes through Florence, where Boccaccio's Calandrino looked for it."[2]

Whether noble or vile, a pearly *margherita* would be of little interest to a chicken searching for a something to eat. He might ask, *Cui prodest?* (What good is it to me?) and rightly so. But now let us move from chickens to pigs, which are no less wise in being able to recognize *margherite,* as we are reminded by the evangelist Matthew. His divine protagonist says in fact (7:6), "Do not give what is holy to dogs, and do not throw your pearls before swine [*margaritas vestras ante porcos*] or they will trample them under foot and turn and maul you."

This sentence, which has become a proverb, is used by each of us several times a day (particularly when a good idea that we propose as the solution to a very complicated problem is rejected by our immediate superior) but rarely with the acumen of the Dominican Girolamo Savonarola (1452–98), grandson of the physician who, elsewhere in these pages, demonstrates how hard it is to digest certain greens. Referring to readers of sacred texts, Girolamo thunders: "To all those who begin to study this Scripture with carnal sins or with arrogance, it will seem the opposite of what it seems to others [the pure, the humble—in short, the well disposed], and it will seem to them that the Holy Scripture is base speech by great men. Look what a remarkable thing this is—that the same writing seems to be made in two different ways. And this is what God did through his divine wisdom, to give no bread to dogs, nor throw pearls [*margherite*] before swine who are not worthy of them."[3]

The charlatan evangelicals who infest half of the world's television channels should meditate long and hard on these words and ask themselves honestly whether, carnal sins aside (their wives or husbands will see to these directly), the total lack of critical scrupulousness, let alone the interpretative naïveté to which they subject the biblical texts, should perhaps itself be listed under the arrogance that Savonarola describes.

The word *margherita* was sometimes also used to indicate a type of torture carried out with rope (perhaps by means of a knotted cord that mariners use, also called *margarita*). There is a nice example in *Morgante* by Luigi Pulci, where, "When our Rinaldo leapt into the fight, / he seemed to be with cherubs up in heaven, / 'mid caroling and singing and delight." And this produces such confusion among the ranks of the enemy, led by Marsilio, "They'll sing good alto, say, to their soprano, / and to the French will teach romances too– / even the sol-fa [notes] of the final rope [*margherita*] / in which their lives will altogether stop" (XXVI, octaves 126 and 127).[4]

For the word *margherita* to make its debut in the field of flowers, we will have to wait until the sixteenth century—more precisely until the publication of *La coltivazione* (On cultivation), a didactic poem (six books of unrhymed hendecasyllables) by Luigi Alamanni (1495–1528), an exile in France (he was hated by the Medici) at the court of Francis I (to whom the work, printed in Florence in 1546, is dedicated). Here, the *margherita* is welcomed into the list of those flowers that ". . . without scent make beautiful the mantle / Of sweetest April, laughing in crocus, / The immortal amaranth, the beautiful narcissus, / And the one to whom the proud lion shows its tooth / Angry and ready to wound the plant that resembles it [i.e., the dandelion]. / Then its mane painted with milk and with purple / The pious daisies that arouse envy / from the most prized flower of the name that only / today has Sena and Hera filled with honor. / A thousand lustful herbs" (vv. 605–12).[5] From its beginnings, then, the *Bellis perennis*[6] (as the common daisy has ended up being called in botanical manuals) was invested with a very specific symbolic value: it represents humility, humble pride, and restrained grace that dislikes all vulgar desire to be the center of attention. It does not, however, fear comparison with flowers that are more showy (or aggressive, like the *taraxacum*—also known as the enraged lion's tooth, or dandelion).

Giovanni Pascoli, the singer of all that is humble and proud, tender and veiled in the countryside of Tuscany and Romagna, directs his discourse on daisies (by now called *pratoline* and *margheritine,* to distinguish them from those called *margheritone,* which are larger, have a much taller stem, and belong to the chrysanthemum family) toward more intimate (and metaphysical) tones. We come across them in his *Nuovi poemetti* in, "Who ever sees the little daisies blooming? / And one day the daisies in flower / fill the meadows and cover the rocks with stars. // Who knew about you, o white flower of love / closed in your heart? And everything, suddenly, / the black earth changed color. // There are thoughts, already unknown, that remain / now in your face, whether you stay or go; born like that, in the shadow of a star's / smile or from a drop of dew . . . " (*Bellis perennis,* vv. 1–10).

When the word *love* is joined with the word *daisy*, there is no one whose mind does not turn to a gesture, repeated a thousand times, that consists of the removal of the flower's petals, one by one, reciting alternate questions of the sort "s/he loves me, s/he loves me not," until obtaining a response corresponding to the last petal removed. The answer is no less truthful than those proffered by the Oracle of Delphi, but in this case, since it is easy to make a mistake in counting, you can always start over until you get the desired result.

Like nearly all plants, the daisy, too, has medicinal qualities. According to Nicholas Culpeper, a decoction made from its leaves works well in the care of wounds that occur in the chest cavity (whatever that might be). He repeats it twice, advancing as proof the fact that the daisy is a plant "at the sign of Cancer and under the influence of Venus" (*Complete Herbal,* 61).

The compendium of esteem and elegance that has accumulated around the word *daisy* has ensured that the term has come to mean "a woman who excels in the rarity of her qualities," according to the *Vocabolario degli accademici della Crusca*. The journey from a common name—that woman is a real daisy—to a proper name—that woman is Daisy—seems painless at first. But it remains so only until we come across some of the characters to whom the name has been given. Perhaps the most famous Daisy (Gretchen) is the woman to whom Goethe's Dr. Faust takes a fancy and, with the help of Mephistopheles, succeeds in seducing and abandoning (despite his remorse and hesitations). The poor woman, who drowned the son that she had by him, is condemned to death and, wanting to expiate her own guilt, refuses the freedom that her seducer offers her, with the unwavering complicity of the devil. Once her persecutors are gone, however, a voice from heaven assures us of her redemption.

Among the romantic heroines that bear the name Daisy we cannot forget *La dame aux camelias* (The lady of the camellias), a novel (1848) and theatrical work in which Alexandre Dumas fils describes the unhappy and contested love (contested in the name of the rules of the petit bourgeois that prohibit a good man from sharing his life with a formerly kept woman) between Daisy (Marguerite) Gauthier and Armando Duval. On the stage, and later in film, this Daisy has been interpreted by immensely famous actresses, including Sarah Bernhardt, Eleonora Duse, Lillian Gish, Greta Garbo, and Isabelle Huppert. Amusingly, thanks to the music of Giuseppe Verdi (*La Traviata*, which premiered at La Fenice in Venice in 1853), its fame would be perpetuated by a small but significant floral change in the dramatis personae: the daisy becomes a violet—that is, Violetta Valery, to whom the sublime Maria Callas, among others, lent her voice.

And now, passing from the sublime to the ridiculous, let us remember that a Daisy is numbered among the animated cartoon characters of Walt Disney: Daisy Duck, the fiancée of Donald Duck, born in 1940. As for how the flower got its English name, the hypothesis has been advanced that daisy is a contraction of *Day's eye,* based on the characteristic that the flowers have of closing at sunset and reopening at daybreak. It may not be true, but it's a nice story all the same.

Beyond that, *margherita* is also a type of pizza whose colors repeat those of the Italian flag, and is so-named because its creator, Raffaele Esposito (fame contested),[7] wanted to dedicate it, in 1889, to the queen of Italy, Margherita of Savoy, a woman who even managed to enchant the national bard, Giosuè Carducci. Margherita was also the name of a political coalition of which little memory remains, although it has only recently disappeared, that merged with the Italian Democratic Party. It is an embroidery stitch in knitting; a cake of not very complicated preparation (so say I, who cannot even fry eggs in butter); and finally, a wonderful tequila-based cocktail (this, however, I do know how to mix) whose paternity is contested by three fathers (Danny Negrete, 1936; Francisco "Pancho" Morales, 1942; and Carlos "Danny" Herrera, 1947–48) and . . . a mother (Margaret—but of course!—Sames, 1948). In the pages of William Grimes's *Straight Up or On the Rocks: The Story of the American Cocktail,* however, you meet people who swear that they drank them as far back as the 1930s. Everyone's an expert!

The meadow daisy, originally from Europe and the Caucasus, now grows everywhere (just cast your eyes on any field or even on the gardens of Italian railway stations, where you are advised not to pick them), from the plains up to an altitude of nearly sixty-five-hundred feet. The part that is used is the basal rosette (before the plant flowers) or the flower itself.

Daisies may be gathered nearly all year (provided you are not as unlucky as Donald Duck).

DAISY RISOTTO

Serves 4

 2 tomatoes, halved and seeded
 1 celery stalk, cut into pieces
 1 carrot, cut into pieces
 2 onions, 1 halved and 1 finely chopped
   A few parsley sprigs, tied with kitchen string
 2⅛ teaspoons (13 g) coarse salt
 110 daisy flowers
 2½ tablespoons (40 ml) extra-virgin olive oil
 3½ tablespoons (50 g) butter
 1¾ cups (350 g) Arborio or Vialone Nano rice
   Scant ¼ cup (50 ml) dry white wine
 ⅓ cup (40 g) grated Parmesan cheese

To prepare a vegetable broth: In a 3-quart (3-l) pot, combine the tomatoes, celery, carrot, the halved onion, the parsley, and the salt. Pour in 2 quarts (2 l) water, place over medium heat, and bring to a simmer. Cook at a gentle simmer for 80 minutes. Remove from the heat and remove and discard the vegetables with a wire skimmer. Leave the broth in the pot, return the pot to medium-high heat, and bring to a simmer. The rice will be cooked in this broth, which must be kept at a simmer.

To cook the risotto: Rinse the daisies well in a basin of water, then remove the petals and set aside. Pour the oil into a second 3-quart (3-l) pot, add half of the butter, and place over very low heat. When the butter melts, add the chopped onion and cook, stirring occasionally, for 5 minutes. Take care that the onion does not burn. Raise the heat to medium, add the rice, and stir with a wooden spoon for a good 5 minutes to toast it. Pour in the wine and continue to stir until it has evaporated.

Now begin to add the broth, a little at a time, stirring after each addition and allowing it to evaporate before adding more. After 15 minutes of cooking, add the daisy petals and stir for another 3 minutes. At this point the rice should be tender but still slightly firm at the center of each grain. Turn off the heat, add the remaining butter and the Parmesan, and stir so that everything is well mixed. Let rest for about 5 minutes before serving.

False Acacia

ROBINIA PSEUDOACACIA; ITALIAN: *ACACIA*

THE PLANT WE ARE TALKING ABOUT HERE is not really an acacia, but rather a false acacia. True acacias are what are commonly called mimosas, plants that have little to do with our tree, apart from the fact that they both belong to the Leguminosae family. It was the great naturalist Carl Nilsson Linnaeus (1707–78) who decreed that it was an acacia in false clothing. Having become a nobleman for his scientific merits, he would have liked to be called Carl von Linné, but instead passed into history simply as Linnaeus. His *Species plantarum* (The form of plants), published for the first time in 1753, is a formidable example of what Roland Barthes would call taxonomic madness. The name of every plant is really a synthetic description of its characteristics with the addition of a nickname: the tomato, for example, was called *Solanum caule intermi herbaceo foliis pinnatis incises, racemis simplicibus,* nicknamed *lycopersicum.* This would be like saying that a woman was called "Slender with red hair and a freckled face and almond eyes, known as Little Turtle." Now it's enough to say *Slender Little Turtle* (or *Solanum lycopersicum*) for everyone, particularly the local grocer, to know exactly who or what is being talked about . . . or maybe not. In any case, the first term is the generic one for individuals who share some principal characteristics; the second indicates what distinguishes them.

As far as what is commonly called acacia in Italy, Linnaeus decided that it would be called *Robinia faux-acacia,* in honor of the herbalist and "simplicitist" Jean Robin, the grower of medicinal plants for Henry IV, king of France (and Navarre), born in 1553 and assassinated in 1610, despite the good sentiments that animated him and that earned him the nickname Good King Henry. It was he who said, among other things, that Paris was worth a mass, having had to convert to Catholicism (from the Huguenot that he was) in order to place the crown of the Valois on his head. He became sterile (but not through the fault of Catherine de' Medici, whose daughter, the notorious Margaret of Valois, he had married before moving on to greener pastures), giving rise to the Bourbon dynasty.

According to Jacques Brosse, in his *Les arbres de France: Histoire et legends,*[1] Jean Robin, using seeds imported from North America (its original habitat extended from Pennsylvania and Georgia to Arkansas), succeeded in making a few seedlings of false acacia grow in his own garden and then planted one of these at Place Dauphine in Paris, shortly before 1600. All of the false acacias in Europe derive from those of Jean Robin, thanks particularly to the work of his son Vespasien, who planted one in 1636 in what was then the Jardin du roi and is now the Jardin des plantes, where it can still be admired. The first time the acacia was seen in Italy was in the Botanical Garden of Padua, in 1662.

In *Osservazioni sui vegitali più utili* (Observations on the most useful vegetables), in which the enlightened patrician Luigi Castiglioni (1756–1832) concludes his report on his American journey (during which he encountered such personalities as George Washington and Benjamin Franklin), the *Robinia pseudoacacia* occupies a position of great importance. Castiglioni provides us with some valuable observations, such as the fact that the wood "is quite soft when it is green. As it dries, it becomes hard and is used for the construction of ships, fences, carriage axles and many other things, making it among the most favorable trees of North America."[2]

In America, the false acacia is often called the black locust tree. If Harriet Keeler, author of the rigorous and valuable *Our Native Trees and How to Identify Them,*[3] is right, this is the result of the fantasy of some Jesuit missionaries who confused this tree with the one with which Saint John (the Baptist, not the Evangelist) fed himself in the desert. The only problem is that the false acacia is a New World plant.[4]

Nowadays, those who love the false acacia prize its beauty and, above all, its capacity to consolidate vulnerable and unstable terrain, and give life to those desert soils (by enriching them with nitrogen) where it seems to be the only plant capable of surviving—if we believe the Botswana-set police thrillers of Alexander McCall Smith, whose protagonist, Mma Precious Ramotswe of the No. 1 Ladies' Detective Agency, has all the numbers to outclass the by now embalmed Hercule Poirot.

On the other hand, those who hate the false acacia emphasize the fact that its thick roots often suffocate native species (such as the *Quercia tartufigena,* or truffle oak, in Italy) that have the bad luck of finding themselves in its vicinity, with the result that the landscape becomes overrun with false acacia, and truffles, ever more rare, increase in price.

Bees go wild for the nectar of the bunched white flowers that appear in spring. Human beings, in addition to licking their chops after eating the honey that the bees make, lick them after eating the fritters or marmalade that they make on their own with the same flowers, with no little scorn of the danger. You must lean a ladder against the trunk of the tree, climb while making a show of dexterity, not be overcome with vertigo, cut as many bunches of flowers with garden shears as are needed to satisfy your own frittering desires, and, above all, avoid sticking yourself with the thorns that are found everywhere on the trunk and the branches. Having returned to earth, you must remove the stalk from the bunches and very carefully clean the flowers (which, being highly fragrant and sweet, attract no end of insects). From there, it's all downhill.

The harvest period for false acacia runs from early March to the end of June.

FALSE ACACIA FLOWER FRITTERS

Serves 4

2 ounces (50 g) false acacia flowers (about 1½ cups)
¼ cup (60 ml) sweet liqueur such as *rosolio* (optional)
3 egg yolks
½ cup (100 g) sugar
2 cups (480 ml) extra-virgin olive oil
2 cups (250 g) all-purpose flour
2 tablespoons (30 ml) sweet wine such as Marsala or Port
4¼ cups (1 l) whole milk

¾ teaspoon (3 g) baking powder
⅛ teaspoon (1 g) fine salt
    Honey, maple syrup, or superfine sugar, for serving

Remove the stems from the clusters of flowers and rinse the clusters carefully (because the flowers are very fragrant and sweet, they attract insects). Let the flowers soak for 30 minutes in the *rosolio* (or even just in water perfumed with gin or vodka). Drain well and pat dry.

While the flowers are soaking, in a bowl, beat the egg yolks with the sugar until well blended, then beat in 1 tablespoon (30 ml) of the oil. Very slowly pour in the flour while stirring continuously with a wooden spoon to prevent lumps from forming. Finally, add the sweet wine (some people instead prefer good grappa), milk, baking powder, and salt and mix well. Let the batter rest for 15 to 20 minutes.

Line a large plate with paper towels. Pour the remaining oil into a pan about 10½ inches (26 cm) in diameter and 4 inches (10 cm) deep and place over medium-high heat. Pass the flower clusters through the batter, coating them evenly and allowing the excess batter to drip off. When the oil is hot, working in batches, add the flowers and fry until well colored. Using a wire skimmer, lift the fritters out of the oil and place on the towel-lined plate. Repeat with the remaining flower clusters. Serve the fritters warm topped with the honey, maple syrup, or superfine sugar. If instead of entire clusters, you prefer to use individual petals, pick the petals from the flowers, stir them into the batter, and fry heaping spoonfuls of the batter in the hot oil.

FALSE ACACIA FLOWER AND APPLE MARMALADE

Makes about two 1-pint (500-ml) jars

3½ ounces (100 g) false acacia flowers (about 3 cups)
2 apples, cored and thinly sliced
    Juice of 1 lemon
3½ cups (700 g) sugar

Remove the stems from the clusters of flowers and rinse the flowers carefully, then pat dry. In a large pot, combine the apples, lemon juice, and 2 cups (500 ml) water and place over medium heat. Bring to a simmer and cook for 15 to 20 minutes, gradually adding the sugar and stirring often and briskly with a wooden spoon so the sugar dissolves completely. Add the flowers and continue to cook, stirring often, particularly once the mixture starts to thicken. To test if the marmalade is ready, drop a spoonful onto a plate and make an X in the pool; if the "wound" does not heal, the marmalade is ready. Turn off the heat and ladle the hot marmalade into sterilized glass canning jars, filling to within ¼ (6 mm) of the rim. Wipe the rim clean and immediately screw on the lids.

Place a rack in the bottom of a large pot, and place the filled jars on the rack. Add water to cover the jars by 2 inches (5 cm), place over high heat, and bring to a rapid boil. Adjust the heat to maintain a steady boil and boil for 15 minutes. Turn off the heat, let the jars cool in the water, then remove the jars from the water. Dry well and store in a cool, dark place. Once a jar has been opened, store in the refrigerator.

Mallow

WE HAD HOPED TO BEGIN by saying that with mallow (as with Mama), there is only one, except we can't because there are at least two kinds of mallow: one that stands straight and one that creeps, one with big leaves and one with small, one that is cultivated and one that grows wild. Two is also the number of opinions regarding how it should be eaten: cooked or raw. Theophrastus, for example, expressly says that mallow "needs the action of fire," so to eat it raw would be pernicious (*Enquiry into Plants,* VII, VII). This opinion was reaffirmed centuries later by Hildegard von Bingen, who came to believe that no one should ever eat mallow raw because it would be like ingesting poison (*Physica,* XCVII).

In reality, there are many more than two kinds.[1] Gerard, in *The Herball,* describes four: dwarf, crinkled (also called French), verbena, and annual. He warns that the third type does not really grow everywhere, and then he informs us of some places where he saw it with his own eyes: along the ditches to the left of the execution site that Londoners called Tyburn; in a field near Bushey, a village fourteen miles from London, behind the house of Mr. Robert Wilbraham; and among the hedges and bushes that line the street that leads from London to Old Foorde, where people go to bathe and engage in other activities. Shakespeare, a contemporary of Gerard, could have drawn inspiration from it for a drama called *Much Precision about Nothing*.

In Palestine, according to Job (30:1–4), feeding on mallow, whether raw or cooked, was a sign that you had reached the bottom of the abyss of poverty and desperation: "But now they make sport of me, / those who are younger than I, / whose fathers I would have disdained / to set with the dogs of my flock. / What could I gain from the strength of their hands? / All their vigor is gone. / Through want and hard hunger / they gnaw the dry and desolate ground, / they pick mallow and the leaves of bushes."[2]

Even John Evelyn, who knew something about salads, having written an entire book about them, recommends going slowly, asserting that mallow has, above all, a medicinal function (it is indeed an excellent laxative). Nevertheless, if the tops are boiled, he continues, they may "be admitted, and the rest (tho' out of use at present) was [used] by the Poets[3] for all Sallets in general" (*Acetaria,* 35).

As you might suspect just from these few citations, the history of mallow is complex and contradictory, rich in illustrious testimony but, given its effects, not always very noble. In his *Banquet of the Seven Wise Men* (157 d–e), Plutarch attributes to Hesiod the birth of a legend in which Epimenides of Crete—protophilosopher, sleepyhead,[4] and theorist of lying[5]—supposedly ate mallow and asphodel exclusively.[6] In fact, concludes Plutarch, "the chewing of mallows is very wholesome, and the stalk of asphodel is very luscious; but this 'expeller of hunger and thirst' I take to be rather physic than natural food, consisting of honey and I know not what barbarian cheese . . ."[7]

More cautiously, in his *Lives and Opinions of Eminent Philosophers,* Diogenes Laertius (end of the second century and first half of the third A.D.) does not specify the nutriment of Epimenides, but limits himself to bringing up an extremely reserved Demetrius, who, in turn, defers responsibility for the story to an unspecified "some" who report "that [Epimenides] used to receive food from the nymphs and keep it in a bullock's hoof; and that ingesting it in small quantities he never required any evacuations, and was never seen eating." (I, x, 114).

But things "brighten immensely" with Iamblichus Chalcidensis (245–325) who, in his *Life of Pythagoras* (24, 109) remarks how the teacher instructed his followers "to abstain from mallows because this plant is the first messenger and signal of the sympathy [between] celestial [and] terrestrial natures." In a more pedestrian fashion, Columella confirms this attraction of the plant to the stars: "the mallow shoots, / . . . follow with their bending heads the Sun" (*Of Husbandry*, X, vv. 380–381).

Among the ancients, those who did not mention the legend of Epimenides, the medicinal effects of mallow, or even the simple munch-munch of the plant can go to hell. An incomplete list of those who discuss it, each in his own way, includes Plato (but in a very fleeting way, in Book III of the *Laws*), Dioscorides, Martial, Horace, Pliny, and Cassianus Bassus. For Dioscorides, mallow is a true cure-all: It loosens the intestines and is good for the bladder (but not for the stomach). If chewed raw with a little salt, the leaves treat "lachrymal fistulas." To make them heal over properly, however, you need to omit the salt. Further, mallow is fantastic against the sting of wasps and bees. If one daubs himself everywhere with crushed mallow leaves and olive oil, there is no further danger that those pests will come to torment him. Substitute urine for the oil and apply abundantly to cure dandruff and other undesirable exfoliations. Against burns and erysipelas, nothing is better than an application of boiled leaves (once again, with the addition of olive oil). A decoction of mallow refreshes the uterus and, administered as an enema, is excellent for alleviating intestinal, uterine, and anal distress. Drink a broth of mallow leaves and roots and you will have a good probability of neutralizing the deleterious effects of the bites of even the most poisonous snakes and spiders (*De materia medica,* II, 118).

More glibly, Martial (who was not a physician, but a lawyer and, in particular, "protégé" of rich families) ascribes to mallow (which was offered to him by a peasant woman when he was in the country with friends, along with beautiful greens like lettuce and leeks, "ructatrix"[8] mint, and arugula) a unique and easily imaginable benefit: the relaxation of the intestinal muscular cavities and the consequent advancement of their contents (*Epigrams,* X, 48). Before him, Horace had exalted mallow, "which is so good for the body," coupling it with other products of the field (olives, lamb, goat "rescued from the mouth of the wolf"), swearing that he felt them descend in his belly with the same bliss that he felt with the most refined and exotic delicacies (clams from Lucrino, turbot, parrotfish, African birds, Ionic francolins).

But when it comes to talking about mallow, the lion's share (just as it is for a load of other things) goes to Pliny and his *Naturalis historia.* According to this author, mallow's marvels are many, "the most wonderful being that whoever swallows half a *cyathus*[9] of the juice of any one of them will be immune to all diseases." (Little wonder that it came to someone's mind to coin, for mallow, the antiphrastic synonym *omnimorbia*—that is, "all diseases"). Pliny then gives a long list of surprising observations from which we will extract a few that seemed to us a little over the top: "With the root of the single-stem [mallow] plant they stab around an aching tooth until the pain ceases. . . . The root attached as an amulet in dark wool stays troubles of the breasts; boiled in milk and taken like broth it relieves a cough in five days. . . . The Theban lady Olympias [a Greek midwife of the first century] [says] that with goose-grease they cause abortion . . . . It is agreed at any rate that women in labour are more quickly delivered if mallow leaves are spread under them, but they must be withdrawn immediately after delivery for fear of prolapsus of the womb." And again: mallow is "so aphrodisiac that Xenocrates maintains that the seeds of the single-stem mallow, sprinkled for the treatment of women, stimulate their sexual desire to an infinite degree" (*Naturalis historia*, XX, 84, 222–230).

Even more fantastically, and in clear contrast with Dioscorides, Hildegard von Bingen recommends it for the weak of stomach (especially if gathered at the beginning of its growth, reduced to a purée, and combined with lard), but she prohibits it in the most absolute terms to those who are well. Moreover, used externally, it would resolve two types of diseases: melancholy and cloudy vision. In the first case, one must proceed as follows: Crush some mallow and some sage (twice as much sage as mallow) in a mortar. Sprinkle with olive oil (extra virgin?), and finally apply the plaster to the head (from the forehead to the nape of the neck), holding it in situ by means of a tied cloth. The treatment lasts three days, and at night it is necessary to refresh the plaster by adding oil (but vinegar also works). More delicate is the cure for cloudy vision, which involves collection of the dew that forms on mallow leaves on nights that are clear, bright, and . . . without wind: it is not enough that they be moist. The eyelids are bathed with this dew and you "sleep with it."

How can we exclude from this frenetic crescendo the booklet *De secretis mulierum,* attributed to Albertus Magnus, which holds (as Angelo De Gubernatis reports) that mallow is an excellent means for judging whether a girl is still a virgin or not: "Have her urinate in the morning on a certain herb that carries that name *mallow.* If it withers, then [sorry, but] *est corrupta*" (*Mythologie,* vol. II, 222).

Dulcis in fundo—and in the cause of peace among peoples—there is an Islamic legend that many cite without indicating the sources. We have been won over by what could be called this story's Franciscan flavor (perhaps at the risk of making enemies in the crowded sphere of at least two of the three monotheistic religions). It seems that one day, Mohammed, having washed a shirt while traveling, stretched it out to dry on top of a mallow bush. When he removed it from the bush to put it on, the plant, instead of the usual flowers with five violet-pink petals that everyone knows, was covered with red flowers. Mohammed had miraculously caused the birth of the first geranium. There are those who have taken advantage of this story to invent a beverage. Assemble four cups of apple juice, one of sugar, six geranium sepals, four sliced green lemons, five drops of coloring (yellow or pink carnation), and, for decoration, six apple leaves and geranium petals. Let the apple juice, sugar, and geranium sepals boil for about five minutes. Add the lemon slices. Pass through a sieve, then add the coloring. Serve "on the rocks," embellished with apple leaves and geranium petals.[10]

The period for harvesting the tops of the mallow plant runs from November to May.

CREAMED MALLOW

Serves 4

½ pound (250 g) mallow leaves
8 potatoes
3 carrots
2 onions
1½ teaspoons (10 g) coarse salt
  Grated Parmesan cheese, to taste
  Extra-virgin olive oil, to taste

Eliminate any mallow leaves that have turned yellow, then wash the remaining leaves well. Cut the potatoes, carrots, and onions into large pieces and place them and the mallow leaves in a saucepan about 10 inches (25 cm) in diameter and 4 inches (10 cm) deep. Pour in 2 cups (500 ml) water and sprinkle with the salt. Cover, place over medium heat, and cook until the vegetables are tender, about 30 minutes.

Remove from the heat and pass the contents of the pan through a food mill or purée in a blender. Spoon the purée into a bowl and season at the table with the Parmesan and oil. Creamed mallow has the special characteristic of being absolutely "unclogging"—to be eaten after an enormous dinner.

DECOCTION OF MALLOW

Serves 2

1¾ ounces (50 g) mallow leaves
Sugar, to taste
Zest of 1 untreated (unwaxed) lemon, in thin strips

Eliminate any mallow leaves that have turned yellow, then wash the remaining leaves well. Pour a scant 1 cup (200 ml) water into a 1½-quart (1.5-l) saucepan, cover, place over medium heat, and bring to a boil. Add the mallow leaves, turn off the heat, and let them rest in the pan, uncovered, for 10 minutes.

Line a tight-weave strainer with cheesecloth, then filter the decoction through the strainer and pour into teacups. Sweeten each cup with sugar and add the lemon zest

This decoction, applied directly to the skin, facilitates the healing of pimples and is effective against the sting of insects and formation of pus. It is also useful for gargling and for relief in cases of gingivitis and inflammations of the mouth.

Rubbing a few mallow leaves on the teeth and gums is good for their health. It also results in a pleasant breath. This decoction is more of a medicine than a drink, but it is also good as a drink.

MALLOW FRITTATA

Serves 4

Scant ½ pound (200 g) mallow leaves
3¼ teaspoons (20 g) coarse salt
4 eggs
5 teaspoons (10 g) grated pecorino or Parmesan cheese
½ teaspoon (1 g) ground black pepper
¼ teaspoon (2 g) fine salt
4 teaspoons (20 ml) extra-virgin olive oil

Eliminate any mallow leaves that have turned yellow, then wash the remaining leaves well. Pour 2½ quarts (2.5 l) water into a 5½-quart (5.5-l) pot, cover, and place over high heat. When the water begins to boil, add the coarse salt and the mallow and boil for 5 minutes, timing from when the water begins to boil again. Remove the mallow from the water with a wire skimmer. Squeeze the leaves to remove as much water as possible, then cut into small pieces.

In a bowl, beat the eggs with a fork for at least 1 minute. Add the cheese, pepper, and fine salt and mix together well, then stir in the mallow.

Pour the oil into a 9-inch (23-cm) skillet and place over medium heat. When the oil is very hot, add the contents of the bowl. Cover the skillet, reduce the heat to the very low, and cook for 10 minutes. Then remove the skillet from the heat, uncover, and, with a wooden spatula, check that the edges and the center of the frittata did not stick. Invert a plate slightly larger than the skillet on top of the pan and turn the skillet and plate together so the frittata falls onto the plate. Slide the frittata, browned side up, back into the skillet and cook, uncovered, over very low heat for 15 minutes. Turn off the heat and slide the frittata onto a plate. The frittata may be eaten hot or cold.

––––––––––––

POTATO AND MALLOW FRITTATA

Serves 4

Scant ½ pound (200 g) mallow leaves
1½ pounds (700 g) potatoes, peeled, cut into pieces, and rinsed
4 teaspoons (25 g) coarse salt
2 tablespoons (30 ml) extra-virgin olive oil
4 eggs
¼ teaspoon (2 g) fine salt
1 teaspoon (2 g) ground black pepper

Eliminate any mallow leaves that have turned yellow, then washing the remaining leaves well. Pour 2 quarts (2 l) water into a 4-quart (4-l) pot, toss in the potatoes, cover, and place over medium heat. When the water begins to boil, let 10 minutes pass, then add the coarse salt and the mallow leaves. Cook the mallow and potatoes together for about 10 minutes, timing from when the water starts to boil again. Remove the potatoes and mallow from the water with a wire skimmer and place on a large plate. Smash them with a fork while they are still hot, mixing them together.

Pour the oil into a 10-inch (25-cm) nonstick skillet and give the skillet a swirling motion so that the oil covers the sides as well. Place over medium heat for a full 3 minutes until the oil is very hot. Now pour in the potato and mallow mixture, flattening it uniformly with a fork, and let it cook for 10 minutes. Toss it in the pan once in a while so that it does not stick.

Meanwhile, in a bowl, beat the eggs with a fork for 1 minute, then add the fine salt and the pepper. When the potato and mallow mixture is ready, pour the contents of the bowl into the skillet. With a spoon, distribute the eggs uniformly so that no area remains uncovered. Cover the pan, reduce the heat to low, and cook for about 7 minutes. After 3 to 4 minutes, check the frittata and shake the pan if needed to keep it from sticking, using a wooden spatula if needed to loosen it from the pan edges. Turn off the heat and slide the frittata onto a serving plate (this frittata is not turned). The frittata may be eaten hot or cold.

MALLOW WITH OIL AND LEMON

Serves 4

1½ pounds (700 g) tender mallow shoots and leaves
2   tablespoons (40 g) coarse salt
    Lemon juice, to taste
    Extra-virgin olive oil, to taste

Eliminate any mallow leaves that have turned yellow, then wash the remaining leaves and the shoots carefully. Pour 4 quarts (4 l) water into an 8-quart (8-l) pot, cover, and place over high heat. When the water begins to boil, add the salt. When the water starts to boil again, add the mallow, cover the pan, and let the mallow cook for 2 minutes. Turn off the heat and remove the mallow from the water with a wire skimmer, draining well. Dry the mallow thoroughly so that not even a drop of water remains. Season at the table with the lemon juice and oil.

Milk Thistle

SILYBUM MARIANUM; ITALIAN: *CARDO;*
SALENTINE DIALECT: *GRATTALURO*

MILK THISTLES ARE JUST ONE of many types of thistle. There is the blessed thistle (also called holy thistle), which has long, thorny leaves and yellow flowers and whose infusion, added to bathwater, produces a toning effect.[1] "I suppose," Culpeper writes wittily "that the name was put upon it by some that had little holiness themselves" (*Complete Herbal,* 41). There's burdock, which has heart-shaped leaves and is useful for both cleaning the skin and eliminating excess uric acid. There's the carlina, whose scientific name is *Carlina acaulis* because it lacks a stem (*caulis*). It is also popularly known as the mountain or wind rose because of where it grows. It closes from view during bad weather and reopens when the weather is about to turn nice again, a quality that it retains (though not forever) even after it has been cut and brought home by vacationers who fail to heed the warnings of the alpine communities that urge respect for nature. The word *carlina* derives from Carolus and, ultimately, from Charlemagne, according to Enea Silvio Piccolomini of Pienza, the Humanist pope better known as Pius II, persecutor to the bitter end of the gentleman from Rimini, Sigismondo Malatesta. Being unable to burn him alive, Pius had to content himself with burning him in effigy. In his *Commentarii,* cited by De Gubernatis, he writes: "There is an herb called Carlina because it was miraculously revealed to Charlemagne" (*Mythologie,* vol. II, 60).[2]

There is also the woolworker's thistle, so-called because its thorny bracts were employed to eliminate the loose threads from fabrics, and the melancholy thistle, whose "virtues are but few," once again taking Culpeper at his word, "but those [are] not to be despised; for the decoction of the thistle in wine, being dr[u]nk, expels superfluous melancholy out of the body and makes a man as merry as a cricket; superfluous melancholy causes care, fear, sadness, despair, envy, and many evils more besides; but religion teaches to wait upon God's providence, and cast our care upon him who cares for us. What a fine thing were it if men and women could live so? And yet seven years' care and fear make a man never the wiser, nor a farthing richer" (*Complete Herbal,* 180).

And finally, there is the Marian thistle or Marythistle or milk thistle, which is what interests us here. We are dealing with an annual or biennial plant that, in all probability, is the ancestor of the artichoke. From the basal rosette, a hardy stem rises that easily reaches a height of three to five feet, at the top of which emerges a beautiful red-violet flower. It is very easy to recognize, thanks to the thorny green leaves streaked with white. It gets its common name from this characteristic, that is, the striations that would have been left (once and for always) by drops of milk fallen from the breast of Mary, *virgo et lactans,* who was searching among the thistles for a refuge in which to hide the newborn Jesus from the soldiers of Herod, who wanted him dead.

It is a sturdy legend that has prevailed even in the scientific name of the plant, *Silybum marianum.* And under the name of Mary, or Our Lady, or Her milk, this thistle has made the rounds of Europe. In England it is called St. Mary's thistle, Our Lady's thistle, milk thistle, or Mary's milkworts; in France, *chardon Marie, chardon de Notre-Dame, silybo de Marie;* in Spain, *cardo de Maria, cardo mariano, cardo lechal.*[3] A wider range, but still with a devotional flavor, can be found in Germany: *Mariendistel, Magendistel, Christi Krone, Heilandsdistel,* and *Gottesgnadechrut* (to which must also be added the lay term, *Silberdistel*). In Italy, it's the same: *cardo di Santa Maria, cardo di Maria,* or *cardo della Madonna,* but also, it may be said without offense, *cardo asinino,* "donkey's thistle."[4]

In his discussion of "our Ladies-Thistle" (Book II of *The Herball*), John

Gerard suggests that it would be good to simplify everything by calling the plant *Leucographus*, "of the white spots and lines that are on the leaves," but then he recalls that Pliny had already introduced the term *Leucographis* and states that he doubts very much if the Roman naturalist really had in mind our beloved thistle.

Pliny certainly does speak of thistles when he asserts, with poorly concealed enthusiasm (they "must be mentioned not without a feeling of shame"), that "at Carthage and particularly at Córdoba, crops of thistles yield a return of six thousand sesterces from small plots—since we turn even the monstrosities of the earth to purposes of gluttony and actually grow vegetables that all four-footed beasts without exception shrink from touching" (except, obviously, the Hellenic-Italic donkeys!). As for the gluttony-feeding delicacies, he gives us the recipe, feigning disinterest but nonetheless revealing how dear thistles are to him: "They are also preserved in honey diluted with vinegar, with the addition of laserwort root and cumin, so that *there may be no day without thistles for dinner*" (*Naturalis historia,* XIX, 43, 152–53, emphasis added.)

As to the medicinal virtues of the thistle "that puts forth in the middle of its points a purple flower, that quickly turns white and is gone with the wind," Pliny informs us that "pounded and compressed before it flowers, an application of the juice restores skin and hair lost by mange." Moreover, "it strengthens the stomach, and, if we may believe the report, it also affects the womb in such a way that male children are engendered. Glaucias,[5] at any rate, who seems to have been a most careful student of thistles, put this statement on record" (*Naturalis historia,* XX, 99, 262–63). Thank goodness!

According to Columella, it was used (in the absence of anything else) to make milk curdle: "it may also be brought into a consistency, both with the flower of the wild thistle and with the seeds of bastard-saffron, or the blessed [milk] thistle; and also with fig-tree-milk, which the tree emitteth if you wound its green bark" (*Of Husbandry,* VII, VIII, 324).

Hildegard von Bingen looks on the Marian thistle with suspicion. A plant that is born from the sweat of the earth cannot have great worth or power, asserts the Teutonic abbess. Hildegard clearly distinguishes the sweat of the earth from moisture (which produces plants that are edible or that have some benevolent function) and in particular from juices, which stand at the top of the scale and are produced by grapes and tree fruit. Despite this, she does not feel like ostracizing the thistle completely. She describes it as very harmful if eaten raw (it would weaken the blood, let a contaminating substance enter the body, and dilute someone's humors like water dilutes wine . . . to the point that the unfortunate person could lose his or her mind). If cooked and eaten by someone who is well, however, it won't do him much harm. Moreover, the "lady's-thistle has a coolness in it and is very useful. Anyone who has a stitch in his heart, or pain in any other part of his body, should take lady's-thistle and a little less sage and reduce them to a juice in a little water. When he is tormented by the stitch, he should immediately drink this and he will feel better" (*Physica*, XCIX).

As old as the world, the medicinal virtues of the milk thistle have been confirmed by more recent studies and analyses. In fact, silibinin, isolated for the first time toward the end of the 1960s by a group of researchers at the University of Monaco led by H. Wagner, L. Hörhammer, and R. Muster, is extracted from the achenes of this plant. This substance, which is really a mixture of substances with irresistible names (silibina, silidianina, isosilibina, and, last but not least, silicristina) is very effective in treating diseases of the liver. The roots have diuretic and fever-reducing properties, and the leaves have laxative properties. A milk thistle decoction[6] is good against motion sickness.

In the culinary world, this thistle, whose stems are noted in *The Oxford Companion to Food* as having a taste not dissimilar to asparagus,[7] was worthy of the elegies of John Evelyn, who talks about it in his *Acetaria*. He tells us: "Our Lady's milky or dappl'd Thistle, disarm'd of its Prickles[8] is worth esteem: The young Stalk about May, being peel'd and soak'd in Water, to extract the bitterness, boil'd or raw, is a very wholsome Sallet, eaten with Oyl, Salt, and Peper: some eat them sodden in proper Broath, or bak'd in Pies, like the Artichoke, but the tender Stalk boil'd or fry'd, some preferr; both Nourishing and Restorative" (*Acetaria*, 69).

Despite its Mediterranean origin, the thistle acquired a particular historic value in Scotland, becoming its symbol par excellence. No one knows exactly how that happened. Not even the official site of Scotland's national tourism organization departs from what has been repeated more or less everywhere, that is, that the thistle was chosen as a memento of an event that is plausibly historical, but certainly legendary. Some Scottish warriors were about to be attacked in their sleep by a band of Vikings (at some unknown time) and managed to save themselves only because one of the attackers trod on a thistle with his bare feet. The Vikings' imprecations and howls awakened the defenders, who put the Danes to flight. Thus, the thistle is for the Scots what the geese of the Capitoline Hill were for the ancient Romans besieged by the Gauls of Brennus. Its presence among the symbols of Scotland dates back at least to 1470, when James III had silver coins minted with the image of a thistle on them. In 1687, The Most Ancient and Most Noble Order of the Thistle was founded (as prestigious as the Order of the Garter in England). Its members sport a necklace of gold with rings that reproduce the figure of the thistle, obviously, and a nice medal in the form of a star, on which, in addition to a thistle, is the motto *Nemo me impune lacessit,* which translates as "No one provokes me with impunity."[9]

In 1503, on the occasion of the marriage of James IV of Scotland and Margaret of England, the poet William Dunbar (1460–1520?), called the Chaucer of Scotland, composed "The Thrissil and the Rois" (The Thistle and the Rose), a short poem to celebrate the climate of friendship that began between the two realms as a result of this marriage. The fearsome thistle, we read, is protected by many lances. The rose is like a fleur-de-lis, albeit red and white.

We cannot leave the world of thistles without reflecting for at least a moment on the relationship between the thistle and one of its amiable "exploiters," the goldfinch, which, when not imprisoned in some absurd cage but free to search for its food, seeks out the thistledown in the ripe flower head in which the plant "hides" the achenes that the bird craves. No one has spoken about this better that Henry David Thoreau, to whom we yield without another word: "I begin to see thistledown in the air about the second of August and thenceforward till winter. We notice it chiefly in August and September. What is called the Canada thistle is the earliest, and the goldfinch or thistle-bird (*Carduelis tristis*), for he gets his name from his food (*carduus* being the Latin for 'a thistle'), knows when it is ripe sooner than I. So as soon as the heads begin to be dry, I see him pulling them to pieces and scattering the down, for he sets it a-flying regularly every year all over the country, just as I do once in a long while. The Romans had their *Carduelis* or thistle-bird also, which Pliny speaks of as the smallest of their birds, for eating thistle seeds is no modern or transient habit with this genus. The thistle seed would oftener remain attached to its receptacle till it decayed with moisture or fell directly to the ground beneath if this bird did not come like a midwife to release it. . . . " (*Wild Fruits,* 100).

In conclusion, we remind all lovers that in order to know whether their love is returned, they must wait until the Feast of Saint John (June 24) and proceed according to what Alfredo Cattabiani, among others, recommends: Collect a thistle "in full flower and, after having scorched it, expose it during the night of the vigil in a glass of water. If it revives, the still-secret love is returned" (*Florario,* 232).

Milk thistle grows close to ruins and stone walls, at the sides of roads, and in pastures, often in large numbers, up to about thirty-five hundred feet in altitude. The foraging period runs from the beginning of October to the beginning of April.

BAKED MILK THISTLES

Serves 4

2¼ pounds (1 kg) milk thistles
 5 teaspoons (30 g) coarse salt
6½ tablespoons (100 ml) extra-virgin olive oil
 ¾ cup (80 g) dried bread crumbs
 4 teaspoons (5 g) chopped fresh parsley
 1 clove garlic, minced
5¼ teaspoons (15 g) capers in brine, rinsed
 ¾ teaspoon (2 g) ground red pepper
 ½ teaspoon (1 g) ground black pepper
 ¼ cup (30 g) pitted black olives

Don a pair of rubber kitchen gloves and peel the stems of the milk thistles to remove the thorns. You will use only the peeled stems. Repeatedly rinse the stems, making sure no bits of dirt remain. Pour 2 quarts (2 l) water into a 4-quart (4-l) pot, cover, and place over medium-high heat. When the water begins to boil, add the salt and milk thistles, re-cover, and boil for 10 minutes, timing from when the water begins to boil again. Remove the milk thistles from the water with a wire skimmer, draining well. Pat them dry and cut them in half.

Preheat the oven to 350°F (180°C). Grease a shallow 11-by-7-inch (28-by-18-cm) baking dish with half of the oil. Lay half of the thistles on the bottom of the dish, then sprinkle them with half each of the bread crumbs, parsley, and garlic; all of the capers; and half of each of the red pepper and black pepper. Scatter the olives over the top. Make a second layer with the remaining milk thistles and sprinkle them with most of the rest of the bread crumbs (set aside some to sprinkle on top) and all of the rest of the parsley, garlic, red pepper, and black pepper. Pour the remaining oil evenly over the surface and then scatter the reserved bread crumbs over the top. Then pour a generous ¾ cup (200 ml) water all around the edge of the dish and let it "lap" for a few moments to ensure that the layered ingredients do not move.

Bake until bubbling hot, about 20 minutes. Let rest for a few moments before serving.

STEWED MILK THISTLES

Serves 6

4½	pounds (2 kg) milk thistles
2	tablespoons (40 g) coarse salt
⅔	cup (60 g) grated pecorino cheese
3	to 4 tomatoes, peeled, seeded, and chopped
1	onion, finely chopped
	Scant 3 tablespoons (10 g) chopped fresh parsley
⅔	cup (150 ml) extra-virgin olive oil
1¼	teaspoons (3 g) ground red pepper, or 1 teaspoon (2 g) ground black pepper

Don a pair of rubber kitchen gloves and peel the stems of the milk thistles to remove the thorns. You will use only the peeled stems. Repeatedly rinse the stems, making sure no bits of dirt remain. Pour 4 quarts (4 l) water into an 8-quart (8-l) pot, cover, and place over high heat. When the water begins to boil, add the salt and milk thistles, cover, and cook for 10 minutes, timing from when the water returns to a boil.

When the milk thistles are ready, remove them from the water with a wire skimmer and place them in a 4-quart (4-l) saucepan. Pour about 2 cups (500 ml) of the cooking water into the pan and then cover the thistles with one-third each of the pecorino, tomatoes, onion, parsley, and oil. Now add a dusting of one-third of the red pepper or black pepper (these may also be used in combination, reducing each amount by half). Repeat the layering twice with the remaining ingredients. Cover the saucepan, place over very low heat, and cook for 20 minutes, stirring a couple of times. Let rest, uncovered, for about 15 minutes before serving. Serve hot or cold.

MILK THISTLES WITH OIL AND LEMON

Serves 4

2¼ pounds (1 kg) milk thistles
5 teaspoons (30 g) coarse salt
Lemon juice, to taste
Extra-virgin olive oil, to taste

Don a pair of rubber kitchen gloves and peel the stems of the milk thistles to remove the thorns. You will use only the peeled stems. Cut the stems in half lengthwise. Repeatedly rinse the stems, making sure no bits of dirt remain. Pour 4 quarts (4 l) water into an 8-quart (8-l) pot, cover, and place over high heat. When the water begins to boil, add the salt and milk thistles, re-cover, and cook for 15 minutes, timing from when the water begins to boil again. Turn off the heat and remove the milk thistles from the water with a wire skimmer, draining well. Dry the milk thistles thoroughly so that not even a drop of water remains. Season at the table with the lemon juice and oil.

BATTER-FRIED MILK THISTLES

Serves 6

FOR THE BATTER

3 whole eggs
2 cups (250 g) all-purpose flour
1 egg yolk
¾ teaspoon (4 g) fine salt
¾ cup plus 2 tablespoons (200 ml) sparkling mineral water, ice-cold
1 egg white
2¼ pounds (1 kg) milk thistles
5 teaspoons (30 g) coarse salt
All-purpose flour for dusting

2   cups (480 ml) extra-virgin olive oil
¾   teaspoon (4 g) fine salt

To prepare the batter: Break the whole eggs into a bowl and beat them well with a whisk. Whisk in the flour, egg yolk, and fine salt until thoroughly combined. Very slowly pour in the ice water while whisking constantly. Be sure to add it slowly, or no matter how much you whisk, the batter will be too liquid. Let the batter rest in the refrigerator for 2 to 3 hours. Then, just before using, whip the egg white with a clean whisk until stiff peaks form and fold it into the batter.

To prepare the milk thistles: Don a pair of rubber kitchen gloves and peel the stems of the milk thistles to remove the thorns. You will use only the peeled stems. Repeatedly rinse the stems, making sure no bits of dirt remain. Cut the stems into pieces about 1½ inches (4 cm) long. Pour 4 quarts (4 l) water into an 8-quart (8-l) pot, cover, and place over high heat. When the water begins to boil, add the coarse salt and milk thistles, re-cover, and cook for 15 minutes, timing from when the water begins to boil again. Remove the milk thistles from the water with a wire skimmer or slotted spoon, draining well. Pat the pieces dry with paper towels, then dust them lightly with a little of the flour and set them aside for the moment.

To fry the milk thistles: Line a large plate with paper towels. Pour the oil into a 9-inch (23-cm) skillet with 2½-inch (6-cm) sides and place over medium heat. When the oil is hot enough—small bubbles will be visible on the surface—dip the thistles, one at a time, into the batter and immerse in the oil. Do not put more than 10 pieces in the pan at a time. Let them fry, turning once, until golden, about 1½ minutes on each side. Remove from the skillet with a slotted spoon and drain on the towel-lined plate. Repeat until all the milk thistles are fried. Serve warm.

MILK THISTLE PIE

Serves 6

FOR THE DOUGH

2 cups plus 2 tablespoons (350 g) semolina flour, or 2¾ cups (350 g) all-purpose flour, plus more for sprinkling

6½ tablespoons (100 ml) extra-virgin olive oil

1¼ teaspoons (8 g) fine salt

¾ c up plus 2 tablespoons (200 ml) warm water

FOR THE FILLING

3⅓ pounds (1.5 kg) milk thistles

5 teaspoons (30 g) coarse salt

1 cup (240 ml) extra-virgin olive oil

1 to 2 onions, finely chopped

3 or 4 cherry tomatoes, halved

5 teaspoons (15 g) capers in brine, rinsed

2 teaspoons (12 g) fine salt

1 teaspoon (2 g) ground black pepper

¾ teaspoon (2 g) ground red pepper

⅓ cup (50 g) pitted black olives

Extra-virgin olive oil for preparing the pan and brushing the crust

To prepare the dough: Place the flour in a bowl. In a small pan, warm the oil over low heat for about 1 minute. Pour the oil into the flour, add the fine salt, and stir with a wooden spoon until well mixed. Gradually pour in the warm water while continuing to stir until everything comes together in a rough mass. Work the dough with your hands until it becomes soft and compact. Cover with a bowl or kitchen towel and let rest for about 1 hour.

To prepare the filling: Don a pair of rubber kitchen gloves and peel the stems of the milk thistles to remove the thorns. You will use only the peeled stems. Repeatedly rinse the stems, making sure no bits of dirt remain. Pour 4 quarts (4 l) water into an 8-quart (8-l) pot, cover, and place over high heat. When the water begins to boil, add the milk thistles and the coarse salt, re-cover, and cook for 10 minutes, timing from when the water returns to a boil. Remove the milk thistles with a wire skimmer, draining well. Pat dry with paper towels and cut into 1-inch (2.5-cm) pieces.

Pour the oil into a deep 12-inch (30-cm) skillet and place over low heat. Add the onion and cook until golden, about 10 minutes. Add the milk thistles, tomatoes, capers, fine salt, black pepper, and red pepper, raise the heat to medium, and cook until the milk thistles are tender and the flavors are blended, about 10 minutes. Stir occasionally with a wooden spoon to ensure that nothing sticks. Let cool.

To assemble: Sprinkle a little flour on a marble or wood work surface. Divide the dough in half and shape each half into a ball. Place a ball on the work surface and flatten with your palm. With a rolling pin, roll out the dough into a circle about 13 inches (32 cm) in diameter. Repeat with the second ball of dough.

Preheat the oven 350° to 400°F (180° to 200°C). Grease the bottom and sides of a 12-inch (30-cm) round baking pan with 1½-inch (4-cm) sides with the oil. Line the pan with a dough circle, pressing it against the bottom and sides and allowing it to extend slightly beyond the rim of the pan. Spoon the filling into the pan, spreading it evenly over the crust. Sprinkle the olives evenly over the top. Top the filling with the second dough circle and press along the edge of the pan with a fork to join the top and bottom crusts together well. Brush the top surface and the edges of the crust with the oil. With the fork, make some deep holes in the surface (say, as deep as the tines of a table fork) to vent the steam as the pie bakes.

Bake until the crust is golden, about 45 minutes. The pie may be served hot or cold.

Mint

MENTHA SPP.; ITALIAN: *MENTA*

MINT TAKES ITS NAME from a nymph. The myth regarding it is polymorphous, as always, but not exceptional. The few lines that Robert Graves dedicates to it in *The Greek Myths* seem more than sufficient to capture its spirit. "Hades, who is fierce and jealous of his rights, seldom visits the upper air, except on business or when he is overcome by sudden lust. Once he dazzled the Nymph Minthe with the splendour of his golden chariot and its four black horses, and would have seduced her without difficulty had not Queen Persephone made a timely appearance."[1] Victim of jealousy, instead of closing an eye (or opening it secretly and enjoying the scene), she flies off the handle and transforms the poor girl into the very fragrant plant we fierce consumers of alcoholic beverages slip into a mint julep.

The latter is a magnificent thirst quencher prepared with bourbon (from Kentucky, mind you, not the sour mash from Tennessee), sugar, crushed ice (lots of it), dried mint leaves (optional), and a nice sprig of mint (obligatory). The word *julep* comes from the Arabic *ğulēb*, which in turn comes from the Persian *gulāb*, which means, literally, "rose water." The Italian *giulebbe*, which should mean the same thing, instead overdoes it in current usage and carries the notion of excessive sweetness.

Mint juleps are traditionally associated with that great horse race, the Kentucky Derby, during which they are distributed free in large plastic cups. In 2007, some 120,000 were served. In 2006, a good number were placed on sale at a thousand dollars apiece: the bourbon was Woodford Reserve, the mint brought in from Ireland, the ice from the Bavarian Alps, and the sugar from Australia. The proceeds were donated to charities for retired racehorses.

There exist about thirty different types of mint, some more widespread than others, like *Mentha piperita, M. spicata, M. aquatica,* and *M. viridis,* all of which, on close examination, have similar medicinal qualities. Then there are what in Italy are called *mentastro* and *mentuccia,* which, as shown by their endings (*-astro* pejorative and *-uccia* diminutive), are treated a bit like poor or odd relatives. In reality, *mentuccia,* which originated in the mountain ranges surrounding the Mediterranean basin, now grows everywhere and should be given greater respect in its own right. It is also known as *puleggio* (*M. pulegium,* or pennyroyal in English) and *nepitella* (*Calamintha nepeta,* or lesser calamint).

Mint was one of the ingredients of the so-called *kykeon,* an ancient herbal soup or beverage whose composition is not completely confirmed but that, according to some, also included barley, honey, wine, cheese, and ergot. Some make it with many fewer ingredients, however: crushed barley, water, and mint leaves. The mint, however, is a must. It should not be surprising that the recipe has remained wrapped in mystery, given that it was served during the semiannual celebration, in spring and fall, of the Eleusinian mysteries in the sanctuary of Demeter at Eleusis, not far from Athens, which celebrated the respective reawakening and sleep of the life of the fields. The *Homeric Hymn to Demeter* speaks of it, saying that the goddess taught the rites to everyone so that, "reverently perform[ing] them" thereafter, they would win her heart's favor.[2]

The presence of ergot (assuming that it really was part of that swill) and the lysergic acid it contains has naturally raised suspicions that *kykeon* was a hallucinogenic beverage. But deductions of this sort pave the road that leads to hell, which is where, among others, all those who reject purification rights (like those proposed by Demeter) end up.[3]

In describing the movement—actually, the eviction—of various miserable and stinking odds and ends dragged around by the family of Vacerra, protagonist of the epigram, Martial mentions "a four-year-old chaplet of black pennyroyal" (*Epigrams,* XII, XXXII, 19).[4]

A crown of mint, also called *corona Veneris,* was traditionally placed on the head of young newlyweds to wish them much happiness and, given the plant's presumed (but not by everyone) aphrodisiac properties, "male children."

Both Columella and Pliny declare themselves convinced that cultivated mint is obtained, or can be, from the wild variety. "If the plants of it should happen to fail," writes Columella, "you may gather wild mint from off fallow lands and plant it with its tops inverted; which thing takes away its wildness, and makes it tame" (*Of Husbandry,* XI, III, 492). Pliny elaborates: "There is a wild kind of mint called *mentastrum;* this is propagated by layering, like a vine, or by planting stalks end downward." And he adds wonderful things (whether true or nice stories) like, for example, the "name of mint has been altered in Greece because of its sweet scent; it used to be called *mintha,* from which our ancestors derived the Latin name, but now it has begun to be called by a Greek word meaning 'sweet scented' [*hedýosmon,* from *hedýs* = soft, and *osmé* = odor, scent]" (*Naturalis historia,* XIX, 47, 159–160).

Yet according to a common belief of the Stoics, mint (like pennyroyal and lesser calamint, which Pliny distinguishes—thereby causing no little difficulty in identifying the specific plants in question) will "[flower] when it is in a larder" (Ibid.). A little like the blood miracle of the Neapolitan patron saint, San Gennaro, on September 19.

Further, Pliny does not rest until he has listed scores of diseases, illnesses, tribulations, and ailments that mint manages either to defeat or at least mitigate—either by itself ("prevents . . . chafing, even if only held in the hand") or in combination with honey, saltpeter, or vinegar, or with barley flour, cold water, salt, wine, and many other things. As usual, we will excerpt the observations which, from the distance of centuries, seem a bit . . . futuristic: "if these leaves are chewed and applied, elephantiasis is cured, as was discovered in the time of Pompeius Magnus by the chance experiment of someone who for shame smeared his face with them." Or, "taken in drink it brings on menstruation, but it kills the fetus." And this: "nor do those who carry, when in the sun, two sprays of pennyroyal behind their ears suffer from the heat." And to top it off, there is an associational touching of pathological realities that were perhaps once more plausible than they seem today: "Taken with salt it is beneficial for splenic trouble, bladder, asthma and flatulence; a decoction of it, quite as well as the juice, replaces a displaced uterus and is an antidote for the wound inflicted by scolopendra [centipede], whether the land or the sea variety; by scorpions; and especially the bite of man" (*Nauralis historia,* XX, 52–55, 144–157).

For Hildegard von Bingen (*Physica,* LXXV–LXXVIII), aquatic mint is not so good as food, although it's not bad either. It is effective against obstructions, however, whether they are due to an excess of food in the stomach or an excess of mucous in the lungs (in both cases, the patient has difficulty breathing and mint, eaten raw, helps rid him of it). Tied tightly together, the leaves of pennyroyal kill the worms and parasites that infect sores. Perhaps it's best just to take her word for that.

For Michele Savonarola, it "inhibits vomit, particularly of the phlegmatic sort, it is very good for digestion, cures hiccups, and induces the appetite just like other good foods, and if it is eaten with milk, it prevents its curdling in the stomach. And for women, whose good we must not forget [how kind of him], we will say regarding its utility that if cooked in water and placed as a plaster on their breasts swollen with milk, it removes that swelling or inflammation." Not satisfied, he adds, with a malicious smile on his lips, "And here, I would not shy away from such a thing, because I am certain that it will delight your Lordship. As Aristotle says in the twentieth of his problems, in ancient times, mint was banned in the army because it very much incites coitus, and they did that so that men would not be weakened. Now it is no longer banned, not even for women, etcetera" (*Libreto,* 544–552).[5]

Castore Durante insists on the benefits that mint provides to the digestive system (that it aids digestion and is useful against diarrhea is held as a hard fact, even today): "It is most agreeable to the stomach, to which it gives relief, particularly if the stomach tends toward coldness. It stimulates the appetite and prevents milk from depositing in the stomach or in the breasts, such that those who love milk should feed upon it often."[6]

Finally, Antonio Costantini and Marosa Marcucci, in *Grandma's Remedies,* assert that in the past, people put a few leaves of pennyroyal into their shoes, together with a fistful of bran, to prevent respiratory illnesses. But they say nothing about which herb should be employed to cure the blisters caused by the bran.[7]

And to conclude *sub specie gastronomiae: M. piperita* (a.k.a. peppermint) is good for liquors. To season salads and roast pig, however, it is better to use pennyroyal.

The harvest period for mint runs from October to May.

FRIED ANCHOVIES WITH MINT

Serves 4

21 medium-size anchovies
2 tablespoons plus 1 teaspoon (35 ml) white wine vinegar
2 or 3 fresh mint leaves, torn into pieces
1 clove garlic, chopped
   Pinch of coarse salt
¾ cup (100 g) all-purpose flour
1 egg
½ teaspoon (3 g) fine salt
2 cups (500 ml) extra-virgin olive oil

Remove the head from each anchovy, then rinse the anchovies. With a sharp knife, slit each anchovy along its belly and carefully remove the backbone without separating the fillets. Rinse the anchovies again, being careful to keep the fillets attached, and pat dry. Arrange the anchovies on a wide, deep plate. In a small bowl, mix together the vinegar, mint, garlic, and coarse salt, then pour the mixture evenly over the anchovies. Let marinate for 30 minutes.

Line a large plate with paper towels. Put the flour in a shallow bowl. In a second shallow bowl, beat the egg with a fork for about 1 minute, then beat in the fine salt. Remove the anchovies from the vinegar and pass both sides of each anchovy through the flour, shaking off the excess. Then pass the floured anchovies through the beaten egg. Pour the oil into an 8-inch (20-cm) skillet about 2 inches (5 cm) deep and place over medium heat. When the oil is hot, immerse about 7 of the anchovies in the oil and fry until golden, about 4 minutes. Remove the anchovies from the oil with a slotted spoon and place on the towel-lined plate to drain. Repeat with the remaining anchovies in two batches. Serve hot.

SAUTÉED ANCHOVIES WITH MINT

Serves 4

25 medium-size anchovies
⅓ cup (75 ml) extra-virgin olive oil

1   onion, thinly sliced
½   teaspoon (3g) fine salt
4   teaspoons (20 ml) white wine vinegar
¾   teaspoon (2 g) ground red pepper
3   or 4 fresh mint leaves, chopped

Remove the head from each anchovy, then rinse the anchovies. With a sharp knife, slit each anchovy along its belly and carefully remove the backbone without separating the fillets. Rinse the anchovies again, being careful to keep the fillets attached, and pat dry.

Pour the oil into a deep 12-inch (30-cm) skillet and place over very low heat. Add the onion and cook until golden, about 10 minutes. Add the anchovies and cook for 3 minutes. Season the anchovies with the salt and then pour the vinegar over them. Leave the anchovies on the heat for about 5 minutes, then sprinkle with the red pepper. Remove from the heat, transfer to a platter, and sprinkle with the mint.

CITRUS SALAD WITH MINT

Serves 4

6   blood oranges
⅔   teaspoon (4 g) fine salt
    Ground black pepper, to taste
4   teaspoons (20 ml) extra-virgin olive oil
14 to 15 fresh mint leaves, torn into pieces

Peel the oranges with a knife, removing both the peel and all of the white pith and membrane. Cut each orange crosswise into 3 slices, and then cut each slice in half. If there are seeds, remove them. Put the oranges in a bowl, add the salt, a few grinds of pepper, and the oil, and stir with spoon. Decorate with the mint and serve.

Myrtle Berries

MYRTUS COMMUNIS; ITALIAN: *MIRTO*

FOR THE FUTURE PRINCE of Montenevoso,[1] aka Gabriele d'Annunzio, who walked in the pine forest in the rain accompanied by Hermione, the tamerisks were "brackish and parched," the pines "scaly and bristly," while the myrtle, which could have been (who knows) "bushy and strong" or even "wide open and twisted," is described instead, simply and generically, as "divine." The reader will neither regret this *diminutio capitis* (from two epithets to one), nor the abandonment of the physical-environmental qualifiers that illuminated the first two shrubs (albeit expressed in learned language), because under that use of "divine" lies hidden a world of impulses and pleasures that will lead us directly (as anyone with even minimal knowledge of d'Annunzio's poetry knows) to ancient Hellas and its environs, a land of unfulfilled and metamorphic wonders.

Myrtó and similar names (Myríne, Myrsíne, Myrtílo, and so on), still common in Greek, all have beautiful stories behind them of one type or another, some with a transformative ending (for example, from woman to plant), as in the case of the athlete (who some call warrior) Myrsíne. Killed out of jealousy, or by accident, by a defeated male adversary, she elicits the compassion of Athena, who consoles her by allowing her to produce, seasonally, some lovely white flowers and berries of great enogastronomic value. There are other stories that lack the final mutation (but the name is there and you can't get away from it), like the very complicated one of Myrtilus, who, though not the best sort of character, managed to get a tomb behind the temple of Hermes (whose son he also was) at Feneos, in Arcadia. It is necessary to know that this young man was a "charioteer to Oenomaus [king of Pheneus]. When anyone came to court Hippodamia, Oenomaus's daughter, Myrtilus would skillfully race him with the king's chariot, and when he drew near the wooer, kill him with a javelin. Myrtilus himself was in love with Hippodamia, but not daring to attempt the contest, he submitted and acted as charioteer to Oenomaus. But they say that at last he turned traitor to Oenomaus, seduced by a promise made to him on oath by Pelops [a suitor of Hippodamia, to whom we owe the toponym Peloponnesus, or the island of Pelops] that he would allow Myrtilus to enjoy Hippodamia's company for one night. But when he reminded Pelops of his oath, Pelops pitched him overboard." That's how Pausanias puts it in his *Description of Greece* (VIII, 14, 10–12).[2]

In Greece, above and beyond all the names, myrtle is a plant particularly sacred to Aphrodite, who, as soon as she emerged from the sea spray from which she was born (and which, as Ovid recalls, was the basis of her name— *aphrós* = spray),[3] used a myrtle branch to conceal, from the lustful gaze of a satyr, her own nudity (something she would subsequently not worry much about). Also sacred to Aphrodite was the myrtle that (as Károly Kerény summarizes from different sources) grew near the temple of "poor Aphrodite" at Troezen: "They said that from [precisely] that point, Phaedra, who had fallen in love [with her stepson Hippolytus] could look down into the stadium . . . where the naked young man was exercising. Here there also grew myrtle, whose leaves she pricked with the pins in her hair, in her excitement."[4]

Permanent traces of the frenetic pricking of the myrtle leaves remain. If you hold the leaves up to the light, you will see small white dots on their surface. Nothing can convince us (as some crazy botanists would have it) that these are really just saturated glands of myrtle oil. The lugubrious events that follow this scene were captured by Euripides in two tragedies, *Hippolytus Veiled* (now lost) and *Hippolytus Crowned,* in which he takes up the theme of the young man who was shy, honest, and completely dedicated to venatic amusements, and who was tempted and ruined by a dissolute woman (though it must be said that at the beginning Phaedra does everything to keep her passion to herself). The conclusion could not have been more ill-fated: Phaedra kills herself and, by means of an inscription on a tablet, accuses Hippolytus of having violated her. Hippolytus's father, Theseus, curses his son and asks Poseidon (who "owes" him three wishes) to kill him. The god of the sea carries out the deed without hesitation: he frightens the horses with an apparition of an immense angry bull emerging from the waters, causing the young man to fall headlong from the chariot. Theseus then learns from Artemis (deus ex machina) how things really happened and is very upset about it.

According to other related myths, for which we will once again make use of Kerényi's syntheses, Artemis "pulled her beloved from death. Out of love for her, Asclepius, who lived very close by, in Epidaurus, brought him back to life with his medicinal herbs.... However, the inhabitants of the Alban Hills ... believed that the god Virbius, who kept himself hidden in a grove sacred to Diana (at Ariccia, in the thick forests around Lake Nemi) was none other than Hippolytus, who had been transported there by Artemis. Because of this, horses—animals that recalled the death of the resurrected god—could never be brought into the sacred enclosure."[5]

But not all myrtle ends up harmful. There is something to enjoy about it, too. The association with Aphrodite allows garlands of myrtle to compete doggedly with those of laurel in the symbolic representation of poetry, particularly (but not only) love poetry. Centuries later, Dante was able to write: "So sweet was my vocal spirit, that Rome drew / me from Toulouse, and in Rome I became worthy / to adorn my temples with myrtle" (*Purgatorio*, XXI, 88–90).[6] Thus spake Statius who, after his own introduction, starts weaving exaggerated praises of Virgil, eliciting a moment of cheerful embarrassment between Virgil and Dante. Statius, however, was not from Toulouse, but Naples.[7]

In the *Deipnosophistae*, Athenaeus asserts that even the so-called crown of Naucratis is made from myrtle fronds, and alleges, as proof, what Polycharmus (who was originally from Naucratis) said. Having escaped from a shipwreck, thanks to prayers addressed to a small statue of Venus he had with him on board the ship (a statuette that "rests" benevolently, filling "all the space near her with branches of green myrtle, and diffuse[s] a most delicious odour over the whole ship"), Herostratus (also from Naucratis and not otherwise known),[8] "having sacrificed to the goddess, ... invited all his relations and most intimate friends to a banquet in the temple and gave each of them a garland of myrtle branches which he called crown of Naucratis."[9]

Even among victorious generals there were those who preferred myrtle to laurel. With some diegetic angularity that is unusual for him, Pliny records the case of "Publius Postumius Tubertus, the first of all men who ever entered the city with an ovation [in 505 B.C.], . . . made his entry wearing a wreath made of the myrtle of Venus Victrix, and so made that tree a coveted object even for our enemies" (*Naturalis historia*, XV, 38, 125).

It is also thanks to Pliny that we know about the very special meaning myrtle had assumed in Rome across the centuries: "At the time of the foundation of Rome," he writes, "myrtles grew on the present site of the city, as tradition says that the Romans and Sabines, after having fought a battle over the carrying off of the maidens, laid down their arms and purified themselves with sprigs of myrtle at the place now occupied by the statues of Venus Cluacina" (XV, 36, 120). In fact, among the ancients, *cluere*, which now brings up associations with *cloaca* (sewer), simply meant "to purge, to clean, to purify."

Pliny also echoes a passage from Theophrastus describing the village of the Latins (it was a well-watered land on which grew "bay, myrtle, and wonderful beech: they cut timbers of it of such a size that they will run the whole length of the keel of a Tyrrhenian vessel") and the "district called by Circe's name" (a "lofty promontory but very thickly wooded, producing oak, bay in abundance, and myrtle" [*Enquiry into Plants*, V, VIII, 3]). Pliny states that the myrtle was "seen for the first time on the hither side of Europe . . . on the grave of Elpenor at Circello [Circaeus]." Homer, however, who reserves a few verses for Elpenor's death (by falling from the roof of Circe's palace after a bender) and burial to inform us that he was "none too brave in battle, none too sound in mind," does not mention any myrtle (*Odyssey*, X, v. 609).[10]

After stating his uncertainty regarding the possibility that the myrtle was truly "the first of all trees to be planted in public places at Rome," Pliny mentions that "the shrine of Quirinus, that is of Romulus himself, is held to be one of the most ancient temples. In it there were two sacred myrtles, which for a long time grew in front of the actual temple, and one of them was called the patricians' myrtle and the other the common people's. For many years the patricians' tree was the more flourishing of the two, and was full of vigour and vitality; as long as the senate flourished this was a great tree, while the common people's myrtle was shrivelled and withered. But after the latter had grown strong while the patrician myrtle began to turn yellow, from the Marsian war [91–88 B.C.] onward, the authority of the Fathers became weak, and by slow degrees [the tree's] grandeur withered away into barrenness. Moreover, there was also an old altar belonging to Venus Myrtea, whose modern name is Murcia" (*Naturalis historia*, XV, 36, 119–121).

Sometimes Pliny tells you more than you ever wanted to know: "In former times another use was . . . made of the myrtle-berry [in addition to extracting oil], which held the place of pepper before pepper was discovered; in fact, in the case of one kind of savoury dish the name is derived from this, it being to this day called myrtle sausage" (XV, 35, 118). It's entirely possible to recognize in this the ancestor of the large pork salami stippled with fat known as mortadella (from *mortella,* a popular name for myrtle).[11]

Whether *mortaio* or *mortella,* there is no doubt that the very aromatic berry of the myrtle aroused great curiosity on the part of the author of the *Problemata,* attributed to Aristotle. He asks himself: "Why is it that myrtle-berries which have been compressed in the hand seem to us sweeter than those which have not been so compressed? Is it for the same reason [that] dried grapes [are] sweeter than fresh clusters and undried grapes?" To which he responds, "dried grapes are, it appears, flavoured by the juice, which is naturally sweet, . . . but the grapes [that] are still in the cluster are not so flavoured. So too myrtle-berries, which are naturally sweet and have their sweetness within, like grapes when they are compressed, become saturated by the sweetness [that] is within them and are clearly sweeter externally." Not satisfied with such considered observations, our author also asks himself, "Why is it that the smaller myrtle-berries are, the more they tend to have no stones . . . ? Is it because, being less perfect, they have less distinctly formed stones? For the purpose of the stone is to contain the seed. Now the berries are smaller because they are mere offshoots and imperfect, and they are less sweet than those which have proper stones; for they are less concocted [that is, mature], and concoction is a process [that] produces perfection" (XX, 23–24, 925b). We have gone on at length about what is said in the *Problemata* to highlight this connection between maturity and perfection. This dual concept was also well known to Shakespeare ("Men must endure their going hence, even as their coming hither: ripeness is all" [*King Lear,* V, 11]), but very few devotees of consumerism know about it, enraptured as they are by the juvenile, compulsive myth of youth and of keeping themselves unripe.

But whether perfect or imperfect, myrtle berries remain divine, like the beautiful white flowers that precede them and shine in the underbrush and the Mediterranean scrub amid other very beautiful evergreen plants such as the mastic, the juniper, and the strawberry tree. They have a resinous, slightly peppery taste, with hints of rosemary, and they are used in all kinds of sauces for seasoning quail, partridges, wild boar, and even fish soup. In Europe, they are difficult to find north of the Alps. In Carinthia, however, it should not be a problem. At least that's what the poet Eugenio Montale assures, in a thought addressed to Dora Markus: "Now in your Carinthia / of myrtles and ponds, bend at the edge and observe / the timid carp bite"—a passage that proves that whether excellent or mediocre as a poet, he certainly was not a great fisherman.

The period for gathering myrtle runs from November to January. It must be done by "stripping" (that is, without breaking the branches), perhaps by using combs equipped with little receptacles or baskets.

MYRTLE BERRY LIQUEUR AND APERITIF

Makes about 1 pint (500 ml) liqueur and 1½ pints (700 ml) aperitif

Scant ¼ pound (100 g) myrtle berries
¼ cup (50 g) sugar
1⅔ cups (400 ml) pure alcohol (95 percent)
1¼ cups (300 ml) water
1 bottle (750 ml) red wine

Wash the myrtle berries well, let them drain in a tight-weave strainer, and then place them on paper towels to dry. Put the berries in a 2-quart (2-l) glass container with an airtight cap. Pour in 1¼ cups (300 ml) water, add the sugar, and mix with a spoon until it has dissolved. Pour in the alcohol and continue to mix for a few minutes. Cap and place in a cool, dark place for 40 days. Filter through a tight-weave strainer, reserving the berries, and store the liqueur in a capped bottle. It is an excellent digestif.

Put the berries back into the container in which the liqueur matured and pour in the bottle of wine. Cap and place in a cool, dark place for about 40 days, then filter through a tight-weave strainer and store in a capped bottle. Serve as an aperitif.

MYRTLE BERRY GRAPPA

Makes about 1 pint (500 ml)

Scant ¼ pound (100 g) myrtle berries

1⅔ cups (400 ml) unflavored grappa

¼ cup (50 g) sugar

Wash the myrtle berries well, let them drain in a tight-weave strainer, and then place them on paper towels to dry. Put the berries in a 2-quart (2-l) glass container with an airtight cap. Pour in the grappa, add the sugar, and mix well with a spoon until the sugar dissolves. Cap and leave in the open for 8 days (and nights). Filter through a tight-weave strainer and store in a capped bottle. This type of grappa is an excellent digestif.

Nettles

THE REPUTATION OF THE NETTLE as an invasive plant that is annoying to the epidermis (covered as it is with hairs containing formic acid) is solidly documented from antiquity to our times. The Latin name itself says that it is best to keep your distance from it, coming from the Latin *urere,* which means "to burn" and "to cause burning." Among others, Odo de Meung (a.k.a. Macer Floridus), a tenth-century herbalist, affirms this in his *De viri-bus herbarum* (On the virtue of herbs):[1] "a name that seems perfectly fitting given that it burns the fingers of those who hold it in their hands." Nicholas Culpeper wittily believes it unnecessary to describe them, since "they may be found by feeling in the darkest night" (*Complete Herbal,* 127).

But it is not just a matter of dermatology. If someone says of a piece of land that nettles grow there, that means that no one has passed through for some time. To reinforce this notion, there is a saying that when an Italian priest gets fed up with his profession, he chooses a place with nettles to cast off his cassock (*ha gettato le toniche alle ortiche*). Such space includes uncultivated land, particularly beside dilapidated dwellings, sheepfolds, and pens.

On the other hand, there is no lack of entries affirming that nettles are capable of every sort of benefit. According to more than a few ancient, protomodern, and modern physicians, they have hemostatic, antirheumatic, healing, anti-inflammatory, and antianemic properties, and they reinvigorate the scalp.

As usual, Pliny is full of encouraging news as well as radiant and authoritative advice: "What can be more hateful than the nettle?[2] Yet this plant, to say nothing of the oil that . . . is made from it in Egypt, simply abounds in remedies. Nicander assures us that its seed counteracts hemlock and also the poison of fungi and of mercury. Appollodorus says that [combined] with the broth of boiled tortoise it is good for salamander bites and as an antidote for henbane, snakebites, and scorpion stings. Moreover, its pungent bitterness itself, by the mere touch, forces to subside swollen uvulas, restoring prolapsus of the uterus, and of the anus of babies. . . . The same plant, with the addition of salt, heals dog bites" (*Naturalis historia,* XXII, 15, 31).

The naturalist Phanias (an author quoted among the sources for Pliny's books XXI–XXVI) praised the nettle highly, declaring that, eaten cooked or as a preserve, it is good "for the trachea, cough, bowel catarrh, stomach, superficial abscesses, parotid swellings and chilblains, that with oil it is sudorific, boiled with shellfish a laxative, with barley water it clears the chest and promotes menstruation, and mixed with salt it arrests creeping sores. A use is also found for the juice. An extract applied to the forehead checks bleeding at the nose." And like a perfect apothecary, he adds that the seed of nettles from Alexandria is prized above all others. "For all these purposes, though the milder and tender nettles are efficacious, the well-known wild variety [*Urtica urens*] is particularly so. . . . Certain of our countrymen have distinguished nettles by their season, stating that the disease is cured if the root of the autumn nettle is used as an amulet for tertian ague, provided that when [it] is dug up the names of the patients be uttered, and it be said for what man it is taken up and who his parents are; the same method is effective in quartan agues" (Ibid., XXII, 15, 35 and 16, 38).

Much less fantastical and certainly more of a party pooper is Hildegard von Bingen, who, in chapter 100 of her *Physica,* holds that eating raw nettles is harmful (but who would ever get the idea of putting it in their mouth without having cooked it first?). If, however, it is gathered as soon as it emerges from the earth and then cooked, it is an excellent food. What's more, it frees the stomach of mucous and the intestines of worms. To obtain this latter result, you must proceed as follows: In a pan, boil equal parts of nettle juice and mullein [another flowering herb common in the Mediterranean] and walnut leaves or bark. Add a little vinegar and lot of honey, skim it, and then bring it back to a boil. After it has boiled a little more, the brew is ready. Drink the potion for fifteen days in a row, a little after fasting and in abundance after meals. Those who have lost their memory can also avail themselves of the nettle's properties to get it back. You must make a paste out of it, which you add to olive oil. Then, on going to bed, you spread the mixture on your temples and on your chest. If you remember to do this often, the lack of memory decreases.

Of the hundreds of treatments based on nettles that Culpeper discusses, among the most attractive is the one in which "seed or leaves bruised and put into the nostrils stays the bleeding of them, and takes away the flesh growing in them called polypus" (*Complete Herbal*, 127). It is also a reliable remedy for dog bites, gangrene, cancerous ulcers, nosebleeds, and numerous illnesses of the respiratory system (particularly effective in the case of the latter is an infusion of nettles with the addition of honey).

In *Herbs in Cooking* by Maria and Nikos Psilakis,[3] we read that in Crete, in past (but not remote) times, an antidandruff soap was made with nettles. Beyond curing nearly everything (and facilitating coitus, both human and animal), some rumors, still popular just a few decades ago, held that it was extraordinarily effective against meteorological dangers. "In Tyrol, when a thunderstorm would break," writes Alfredo Cattabiani in his *Florario*, "locals would throw some nettles into the fire to keep away every danger, but particularly lighting, because according to one belief popular throughout central Europe, a thunderbolt never strikes nettle plants. They did the same thing in the town of Lugnacco, in the region of Canavese, convinced that it would keep away the witches that were believed to cause 'storm vapor.'"[4]

With macerated nettles, you can make particularly strong fabrics, table-cloths, sheets, and a paper of no mean quality. This was done in Scotland until relatively recently.

Nettles are also popular in cooking, formerly in the cuisine of the poor[5] and today in that of the rich. The shoots and the tips, before flowering, are used in the dough for green tagliatelle and lasagna noodles (both, preferably, with egg) and as an ingredient in soups, risottos, spaghetti, and vegetable pies. They are also good tossed in a skillet and can be used in place of basil in pesto. Apicius, who dedicates only one recipe to nettles (for a type of frittata; *De re coquinaria*, IV, 11, 36, *Patina de urtica*), talks about it in the previous book (Ibid., III, XVII) with a detachment that, if not arrogant, is certainly chauvinist: "*Urticam feminam sole in ariete posito adversus aegritudinem sume si voles*" (The female nettle, when the sun is in the position of the Aries, is supposed to render valuable services against ailments of various kinds). Taking a cue from that *feminam,* someone truculently translated it into English as "stinging." In reality, the species commonly known as the stinging nettle is *U. dioica,* a dioecious variety (that is, with either masculine or feminine flowers).[6] On the other hand, *U. urens* is monoecious and has both masculine and feminine flowers on the same plant. This is the one that burns the most. The trichomes (hairs), which break on touch, release a liquid containing irritating substances that include histamine and, as we have said, formic acid.

The gathering period for nettles runs from December to May, though in moist soils it runs all year.

SPAGHETTI WITH NETTLES

Serves 4

14	ounces (400 g) nettle tops and leaves
6½	tablespoons (100 ml) extra-virgin olive oil
1	clove garlic
¾	teaspoon (2 g) ground red pepper
2	tablespoons (40 g) coarse salt
1	pound (450 g) spaghetti
⅓	cup (30 g) grated pecorino cheese

Don rubber kitchen gloves (raw nettles sting and trigger a lot of itching) and carefully wash the nettle tops and leaves, discarding the stems. Pour the oil into a 12-inch skillet. Cut the garlic clove in half lengthwise and, if necessary, remove the shoot. Finely crush the garlic, add to the oil, and place over low heat for 3 minutes. Turn off the heat, let cool, and add the red pepper.

Pour 4 quarts (4 l) water into an 8-quart (8-l) pot, cover, and place over high heat. When the water begins to boil, add the salt. When the water begins to boil again, toss in the spaghetti, cook for 6 minutes, and then toss in the nettles and cook for 1 minute longer. Scoop out 5 tablespoons (75 ml) of the cooking water and immediately drain the spaghetti and nettles in a colander.

Add the spaghetti and nettles, the reserved cooking water, and the cheese to the skillet, place over medium heat, and cook for about 3 minutes, stirring everything with a spoon and fork until well mixed. Serve hot.

RICE SFORMATO WITH NETTLES
Serves 6

FOR THE NETTLES

1½ pounds (700 g) nettle tops and leaves

¼ cup (60 ml) extra-virgin olive oil

½ cup (50 g) finely chopped sliced spring onions (white part only) or white onion

1½ teaspoons (9 g) fine salt

FOR THE RICE

5 cups (1.2 l) vegetable broth

   Coarse salt

6½ tablespoons (100 ml) extra-virgin olive oil

¼ cup (30 g) finely chopped spring onions (white part only) or white onion

1¾ cups (350 g) Arborio or Vialone Nano rice

2 tablespoons (30 g) butter

⅓ cup (40 g) grated Parmesan cheese

FOR THE BÉCHAMEL

3½ tablespoons (100 g) butter

⅓ cup (50 g) all-purpose flour

2 cups (500 ml) whole milk, heated

¾ teaspoon fine salt

   Freshly grated nutmeg, to taste

TO ASSEMBLE

4 teaspoons (20 g) butter

3 tablespoons (20 g) dried bread crumbs

⅔ cup (80 g) plus 2½ tablespoons (15 g) grated Parmesan cheese

1 cup (100 g) coarsely shredded Emmentaler cheese

1 to 2 ladlefuls vegetable broth

To prepare the nettles: Don rubber kitchen gloves (raw nettles sting and trigger a lot of itching) and carefully wash the nettle tops and leaves, discarding the stems. Squeeze the nettles well with your hands (without taking off the gloves!) to remove as much water as possible. Pour the oil into a 12-inch skillet and place over low heat for 3 minutes. Add the onions and cook until golden, 7 to 8 minutes. Divide the nettles into thirds and lay one-third in the skillet. Raise the heat to high, leave the nettles for 1 minute, then, using a spoon and a fork, stir and turn the nettles for 1 minute, adding about one-third of the fine salt. Repeat with the remaining nettles and fine salt in two additions. All of this takes place with the skillet uncovered, naturally, which allows the water to evaporate completely. Remove from the heat and let cool.

To prepare the rice: Pour the vegetable broth into a 3-quart (3-l) pot filled with 1½ quarts (1.5 l) water, place it over medium-high heat and bring to a boil. When the mixture begins to boil, add coarse salt to taste. The rice will be cooked in this broth, which must be kept at a simmer. Meanwhile, pour the oil into a 4-quart (4-l) pot and place over very low heat. Add the onions and cook for about 3 minutes. Take care that they do not burn. Raise the heat to medium, add the rice, and stir with a wooden spoon for another 5 minutes to toast it.

Now begin to add the broth, a little at a time, stirring after each addition and allowing it to evaporate before adding more. After 15 to 20 minutes of cooking, turn off the heat. At this point the rice should be tender but still slightly firm at the center of each grain and *all'onda*—in other words, firm but not dry. Add the butter and Parmesan and stir so everything is well mixed. Remove from the heat.

To prepare the béchamel: Melt the butter in a 2-quart (2-l) saucepan over medium heat. It shouldn't take any longer than 1 minute. Remove from the heat, add the flour, and stir vigorously with a whisk so that no lumps form. Return the pan to medium heat and stir constantly for another 2 minutes. Pour in the milk while whisking vigorously. Add the fine salt and a few gratings of nutmeg, then abandon the whisk and stir with a wooden spoon for another 10 minutes. The mixture should have the consistency of thick cream. Turn off the heat and let cool, stirring often to prevent a skin from forming on the surface.

To assemble the *sformato*: Preheat the oven to 400°F (200°C). Generously grease the bottom and sides of an 11-by-7-inch (28-by-18-cm) baking dish with 2-inch (5-cm) sides with 2 teaspoons (20 g) of the butter. Add half of the bread crumbs, swirling the dish to distribute them evenly on the bottom and sides. Layer half of the rice on the bottom of the dish, then top with the nettles. Sprinkle evenly with ⅔ cup (80 g) of the Parmesan cheese and then with the Emmentaler. Pour the béchamel evenly over the surface and then the broth. Stir the remaining rice once or twice and spoon it on top, flattening it well. Combine the remaining bread crumbs and the remaining 2½ tablespoons (15 g) Parmesan and sprinkle evenly over the surface. Dot the top with the remaining 2 teaspoons (10 g) butter.

Bake until piping hot and the top is golden, 40 to 45 minutes. Let rest for a few minutes before serving.

NETTLE FRITTATA

Serves 4

- 5 ounces (150 g) nettle leaves
- 2½ teaspoons (15 g) coarse salt
- 4 eggs
- 5 teaspoons (10 g) grated pecorino or Parmesan cheese
- ½ teaspoon (1 g) ground black pepper
- ¼ teaspoon (2 g) fine salt
- 2 tablespoons (30 ml) plus 4 teaspoons (20 ml) extra-virgin olive oil

Don rubber kitchen gloves (raw nettles sting and trigger a lot of itching) and carefully wash the nettle leaves. Pour 2½ quarts (2.5 l) water into a 5-quart (5-l) pot, place over high heat, cover, and bring to a boil. When the water begins to boil, add the coarse salt and nettles and cook for no more than 1 minute. Remove the nettles from the water with a wire skimmer, draining well. Chop the nettles roughly.

In a bowl, beat the eggs with a fork for about 1 minute. Add the cheese, pepper, and fine salt and mix together well.

Pour 4 teaspoons (20 ml) of the oil into a 9-inch (23-cm) nonstick skillet over medium heat. Add the nettles and cook, stirring occasionally, for about 3 minutes. Add the contents of the bowl to the skillet, reduce the heat to low, and cook for about 3 minutes. Uncover and slowly pour in the remaining 2 tablespoons (30 ml) oil, adding it in a swirling motion. Lift the edges of the frittata with a wooden spatula to making sure it is not sticking, then cook, uncovered, for another 5 minutes. Turn off the heat and slide the frittata onto a plate (this frittata is not turned). The frittata may be eaten either hot or cold.

POTATO PIE WITH NETTLES

Serves 6

FOR THE DOUGH

3⅓ pounds (1.5 kg) potatoes, of uniform size

1 egg

1½ teaspoons (10 g) fine salt

1 teaspoon (2 g) ground black pepper

FOR THE FILLING

14 ounces (400 g) nettle tops and leaves

4 teaspoons (25 g) coarse salt

1¼ cups (300 ml) extra-virgin olive oil

⅓ cup (35 g) thinly sliced spring onions (white part only)

¾ teaspoon (2 g) ground red pepper

3½ teaspoons (10 g) capers in brine, rinsed

⅓ cup (40 g) pitted black olives

2 tablespoons (20 g) dried bread crumbs

To prepare the dough: Put the potatoes into a 4-quart (4-l) pot, add water to cover by 1 inch (2.5 cm), cover, and place over medium heat. When the water begins to boil, cook the potatoes until tender, about 50 minutes. To test if the potatoes are ready, pierce a potato with a fork. If the fork slides easily into the potato, they are ready. Do not overcook them or they will absorb too much water. Drain the potatoes and let them cool just until they can be handled, then peel them and let them cool. Work the potatoes with your hands until a uniform, compact dough forms. Add the egg, salt, and pepper and work the dough for a few more minutes until it is smooth and uniform. Cover with a kitchen towel.

To prepare the filling: Don rubber kitchen gloves (raw nettles sting and trigger a lot of itching) and carefully wash the nettle tops and leaves, discarding the stems. Pour 2 quarts (2 l) water into a 4-quart (4-l) pot, cover, and place over high heat. When the water begins to boil, add the salt. When the water starts to boil again, add the nettles tops and leaves, re-cover, and cook for 1 minute. Turn off the heat and remove the nettles from the water with a wire skimmer, draining well.

Pour ⅔ cup (150 ml) of the oil into a 9-inch (23-cm) skillet and place over low heat. Add the spring onions and cook until golden, about 10 minutes.

Add the red pepper and the nettle tops and leaves and cook, stirring vigorously with a wooden spoon, for 5 minutes. Finally, stir in the capers, turn off the heat, and stir in the olives.

To assemble: Preheat the oven to 400°F (200°C). Grease the bottom and sides of a baking dish 11 inches (28 cm) in diameter and 2 inches (5 cm) deep with ⅓ cup (75 ml) of the oil. Divide the dough in half and shape each half into a ball. Pour ⅓ cup (75 ml) of the remaining oil into a bowl, and use the oil to grease your palm. Working with half of the dough, pinch off small quantities of the dough, press each portion in your greased palm, and then put them in the prepared baking dish, placing them side by side and leveling the surface with your greased hand. Sprinkle the dough evenly with half of the bread crumbs, then press gently in place. Lay the nettles mixture evenly over this crumb-topped base. Cover the nettles with the remaining potato dough in the same manner, again leveling it well with your greased hand. Sprinkle the top potato layer with the remaining bread crumbs.

Bake until the top is lightly golden, about 50 minutes. If the surface is still pale after 50 minutes, turn the oven to broil and continue to cook for about 10 minutes. Remove from the oven and let cool (so that it sets better) for about 15 minutes before serving.

NETTLES WITH OIL AND LEMON

Serves 4

3⅓ pounds (1.5 kg) tender nettle tops and leaves
2 tablespoons (40 g) coarse salt
Extra-virgin olive oil, to taste
Lemon juice, to taste

Don rubber kitchen gloves (raw nettles sting and trigger a lot of itching) and carefully wash the nettle tops and leaves, discarding the stems. Pour 4 quarts (4 l) water into an 8-quart (4-l) pot, cover, and place over high heat. When the water begins to boil, add the salt. When the water starts to boil again, add the nettles tops and leaves, re-cover, and cook for 1 minute. Turn off the heat and remove the nettles from the water with a wire skimmer, draining well. Dry the nettles thoroughly so that not even a drop of water remains. Season at the table with the oil and lemon juice.

NETTLE RISOTTO

Serves 4

½ pound (250 g) nettle tops and leaves
6½ cups (1.5 l) vegetable broth
    Coarse salt
¼ cup (60 ml) extra-virgin olive oil
1 small onion, finely chopped
1¾ cups (350 g) Vialone Nano or Arborio rice
¼ cup (60 ml) dry white wine
4 tablespoons (60 g) butter
⅓ cup (40 g) grated Parmesan cheese

Don rubber kitchen gloves (raw nettles sting and trigger a lot of itching) and carefully wash the nettle tops and leaves, discarding the stems. Pour the broth into a 3-quart (3-l) pot, place over medium-high heat, and bring to a boil. Season to taste with salt. The rice will be cooked in this broth, which must be kept at a simmer. Meanwhile, pour the oil into a 4-quart (4-l) pot and place over very low heat. Add the onion and cook for about 3 minutes. Take care that the onion does not burn. Raise the heat to medium, add the nettles, and continue to cook, stirring often, for 5 minutes. Add the rice and stir with a wooden spoon for another 5 minutes to toast it. Pour in the wine and continue to stir until it has evaporated.

Now begin to add the broth, a little at a time, stirring after each addition and allowing it to evaporate before adding more. After 15 to 20 minutes of cooking, turn off the heat. At this point the rice should be tender but still slightly firm at the center of each grain. Add the butter and Parmesan and stir so everything is well mixed. Let rest for 5 minutes before serving.

POLENTA WITH NETTLES

Serves 4

1½ pounds (700 g) nettle tops and leaves

6½ tablespoons (100 ml) extra-virgin olive oil

½ cup (50 g) finely chopped spring onions (white part only) or white onion

1 tablespoon (15 g) coarse salt

1½ teaspoons (3 g) ground black pepper

2 cups (300 g) polenta (cornmeal)

⅓ cup (40 g) grated Parmesan cheese

Don rubber kitchen gloves (raw nettles sting and trigger a lot of itching) and carefully wash the nettle tops and leaves, discarding the stems.

Pour the oil into an 8-quart (8-l) pot and place over very low heat for 1 minute. Add the onions and cook, stirring occasionally, until golden, about 15 minutes. Make sure that they don't burn. Add the nettles and stir well with a spoon and a fork until the nettles and onions are well mixed and the flavors blended. Raise the heat to medium, add one-third of the salt, and stir again. Repeat with the remaining salt in two additions, stirring after each addition. When the nettles seem properly "bruised," add the pepper and stir well once again. Cover the pan and cook for 2 to 3 minutes. Uncover, stir, add 6½ cups (1.5 l) water, cover again, and bring to a boil. When the water begins to boil, uncover the pan and pour in the polenta, letting it rain down very slowly while whisking vigorously to make sure that no lumps form. Everything must be mixed together perfectly. Reduce the heat to medium-low and cook for about 50 minutes, never forgetting to stir. The polenta is ready when it pulls away from the sides of the pan and no longer tastes grainy. Turn off the heat, sprinkle the polenta with the Parmesan, stir in the cheese, and serve.

NETTLE RAVIOLI

Serves 4

FOR THE DOUGH

1⅔ cups (200 g) all-purpose flour, plus more for rolling

2 eggs

FOR THE FILLING AND SAUCE

1½ pounds (700 g) nettle tops and leaves

4 tablespoons (60 g) coarse salt

1 cup (100 g) grated Parmesan cheese

1 cup (100 g) coarsely shredded Emmentaler cheese

1 egg

Freshly grated nutmeg

5 or 6 fresh sage leaves

4 tablespoons (60 g) butter

To make the dough: Mound the flour on a marble or wood work surface and hollow out a crater in the center. Crack the eggs into the crater and beat them with a fork until blended. Then, using the fork, draw the flour from the walls of the crater little by little into the eggs. Once the mixture becomes pasty, work it with your hands until a soft, compact dough forms. Divide the dough in half, shape each half into a ball, and then flatten each ball into a thick disk. Place the disks under a bowl or wrap in plastic and let rest for about 1 hour.

To make the filling: Don rubber kitchen gloves (raw nettles sting and trigger a lot of itching) and carefully wash the nettle tops and leaves, discarding the stems. Pour 3 quarts (3 l) water into an 8-quart (8-l) pot, cover, and place over high heat. When the water begins to boil, add 2 tablespoons (30 g) of the salt. When the water starts to boil again, add the nettle tops and leaves, re-cover, and cook for 1 minute. Turn off the heat and remove the nettles from the water with a wire skimmer, draining well. Let the nettles cool, then, with your hands, form them into a tight ball and squeeze firmly so that no water remains. Using kitchen shears or a knife, finely cut the nettles.

In a bowl, combine the nettles, ⅔ cup (65 g) of the Parmesan, all of the Emmentaler, the egg, and a few gratings of nutmeg and mix well.

To make the ravioli: Lightly dust a work surface with 1 to 1½ teaspoons (3 to 4 g) flour and place half of the dough on it. With a rolling pin, roll out the dough into a paper-thin sheet. (Or, roll out the dough on a pasta machine.) Fold the pasta sheet in half, creasing lightly, then unfold the sheet flat again. Starting from the line of the fold, spoon small mounds of the filling onto half of the dough, arranging them in rows and spacing the mounds about 1 inch (2.5 cm) apart. When you have finished, cover the mound-topped dough with the other half of the dough and, with your fingers, press down firmly around the mounds to remove any air pockets. Now, with a pastry wheel, cut between the rows crosswise and then lengthwise to create square ravioli. Sprinkle a large tray with 1 to 1½ teaspoons (3 or 4 g) flour, and transfer the ravioli to the tray. Repeat with the remaining dough and filling and add the ravioli to the tray.

To cook the ravioli and make the sauce: Pour 3 quarts (3 l) water into the same 8-qt (8-l) pot, cover, and place over high heat. When the water beings to boil, add the remaining 2 tablespoons (30 g) salt. When the water begins to boil again, drop in the ravioli and cook until their rise to the surface, about 5 minutes.

Meanwhile, incise the sage leaves with a fingernail so they will release their essence. In a small saucepan, melt the butter over high heat. When it begins to foam, add the sage leaves and heat for 1 minute, then remove from the heat.

Drain the ravioli carefully in a colander and place them onto a serving platter. Pour the melted butter with the sage leaves over the ravioli, then sprinkle with the remaining ⅓ (35 g) Parmesan. Stir gently and serve.

Pine Nuts

PINUS SPP.; ITALIAN: *PINOLO*

"'WHAT NAME SHOULD I GIVE HIM?' said [Geppetto] to himself. 'I want to call him Pinocchio. This name will bring him luck. I knew an entire family of Pinocchios: Pinocchio the father, Pinocchia the mother and Pinocchi the kids. The richest among them begged for charity, yet they all did alright'" (chap. III). There is no one in the world (the book has been translated into every language, including Chinese, Swahili, and even Latin)[1] who does not recognize the bitter irony with which Carlo Collodi baptized his creation, even before the pile of wood was carved and transformed into a puppet—one of the few "Made in Italy" products to have firmly inserted itself into the universal imagination, along with Dante Alighieri, Machiavelli, Casanova, Sophia Loren, and Ferrari sports cars.

The last lecture of the noted linguist Gianfranco Folena in the athenaeum of Padua concerned this anthroponym. From the text of his lecture,[2] we learn that "The *Tommaseo-Bellini Dictionary* defines *pinocchio* as 'seed of the pine closed in a shell or pod, which is also called Pinocchio (capitalized), and which holds the pinocchio within it.' ... The *Tommaseo-Bellini*, the vocabulary of Italian unification, was completed in 1879 ... that is, shortly before the birth of *Pinocchio,* whose adventures date from 1881." The real surprise in Folena's lecture, however, is not that a common noun was adopted and transformed into a proper noun, but the fact that "the immediate success of *Pinocchio* also had repercussions in the vocabulary of the language, ... almost causing the traditional and more widespread term that indicated the seed of the pine, *pinocchio*, to disappear—to the benefit of the more popular and lower register term *pinolo*." After reviewing a whole series of variants (*pinoccolo, pignolo, pignuolo, pinottolo*), Folena concludes by noting that "fifty years later, everyone said *pinolo*, and *Pinocchio* had become an almost mysterious name." But we would do the scholar a great injustice if we did not add the illuminating consideration he offers as the underlying reason for that adoption: "Of course, the wood that was so-baptized was not pine, but a piece of firewood. For me, Tommaseo's definition highlights a wonderful metaphor ... that [the] 'very hard wooden shell [the *pigna*] containing the tender seed' represents Pinocchio's wooden body and his boy's soul."

The fact that *pinocchio* had previously been the widespread term, rather than *pinolo*, is also shown by the dictionary entry *pignoccata*, which was used to designate a dessert made with sugary dough and pine nuts that was de rigueur among the credenza dishes served in banquets of the late Middle Ages and the Renaissance. Here is the version, with the Anglo-Norman name *pynnonade*, from the English recipe book *The Forme of Cury:* "Take blanched almonds and boil them until [they are] somewhat thick with good broth or with water and set on the fire and simmer it; add yolk of boiled egg. Take some pine nuts fried in oil or in fat, add to the rest with mixed powdered spices, sugar and salt, color it with alkenet [*Alcanna tinctoria*] a little."[3] Curiously, in the sweets known today in Sicily and Calabria as *pignoccata* (or more commonly, *pignolata*), there is traditionally no trace of pine nuts.

Since we find ourselves talking about recipes, permit me to relay a very sweet and easy one, pine nut bruschetta, which Alain Denis champions in *Erbe spezie condimenti* [Herbs, Spices, Seasonings]: "Whip 3½ tablespoons toasted pine nuts (the sublime flavor of the pine nuts is best expressed after light roasting), 3½ teaspoons capers, and 2 drops of balsamic vinegar. Spread this cream on some pieces of toast lightly scented with oil. Lay some raw fillets of mullet on top, sprinkled with more crushed pine nuts and broil everything until the fish is cooked and the pine nuts lightly toasted."[4]

The goodness of pine nuts needs no publicity, and as everyone knows, they definitely make a contribution in the preparation of fillings, vegetables, sauces, and seasonings. Their presence shines in Genoese pesto and, along with wild fennel, in Sicily's pasta with sardines. Italians are probably their most devoted consumers, continuing gastronomic traditions that have been widespread since the time of ancient Rome and that were well documented by Apicius under the heading *Dulcia domestica et melcae* of his *De re coqui-naria* (Book VII, XIII), where pine nuts are called *nuclei*: "In a chafing-dish put honey, pure wine, raisin wine, rue, pine nuts, ... [and ground] pepper."[5]

Pliny speaks of pine nuts with the same care with which a mother in times past might have spoken of her baby's pink bottom powdered with talcum: "The largest fruit and the one that hangs highest is that of pine-cones, which encloses inside it small kernels lying in fretted beds and clothed in another coat of rusty colour, showing the marvelous care that Nature takes to provide seeds with a soft place to lie in" (*Naturalis historia*, XV, 9, 35). Other authors from bygone ages, however, have shown a less enthusiastic attitude and have advised taking some precautions. The meticulous Michele Savonarola, for example, having found female pine nuts preferable to the male ones, does not neglect to note that "both are difficult to digest, irritate the stomach, and have sharp and oily parts, which make them harmful to those who are cough-ing.... They give great nourishment if they are not prepared [that is, cooked], but if they are first placed in an infusion of hot water, they will release the sharpness and oiliness that make them inflammatory [and] they will lose their heat. If their temperament is reduced beforehand [that is, with the hot water infusion], they are good for those who must be treated. And prepared thusly, they provide nourishment and induce coughing because they are cold and draw the pus from one's chest. And if eaten with melon seeds, they are useful against burning urine. They can also be given to consumptives and to the exhausted. They give strength and enrich the blood" (*Libreto, 98–99*).

In his *Herbario novo* (under "pignoli"), Castore Durante confirms that the best pine nuts are those extracted from feminine pinecones. But whether masculine or feminine, he proceeds with a paroxysmal list of virtues and benefits: "Eaten fresh with other foods, they are very nutritious ... .They are helpful for the paralytic, the stupid, and those with tremors. They purify the lungs and its ulcers, drawing out rot..... Pine nuts eaten with sugar or with honey, softened first in warm water and then washed with cool water, are good for coitus. They are beneficial in destroying ulcers of the kidneys and the bladder.... They fatten the thin and cure the gnawing of the stomach." And if a tenth of all that (plus what we have omitted for reasons of brevity) were true, it would be sufficient to increase the consumption of pine nuts across the globe.

In Europe, the pine that produces the best pinecones (and therefore, the best pine nuts) is the domestic variety, commonly called the pine nut pine

(*Pinus pinea*). Two pine nuts are set under each layer. It is best to heat the pinecone before taking a hammer to it to remove the seeds from their natural home. Or, you can do as they do in the park of Migliarino-San Rossore (near Pisa), where apparently the pinecones are laid in the open air for about six or seven months, after which time the nuts fall out of their own accord.

The gathering period for pinecones runs from November to April. People used to climb the trees or wait for the pinecones to fall by themselves. Now shaking machines are used.

CREAM PIE WITH PINE NUTS
Serves 6

FOR THE CRUST

2 cups plus 2 tablespoons (265 g) all-purpose flour
½ cup (100 g) sugar
⅛ teaspoon (1 g) fine salt
⅔ cup (135 g) cold butter, cut into cubes
1 egg
4 teaspoons (20 ml) sparkling mineral water, ice-cold
  Butter and all-purpose flour for preparing the pan
¾ cup (150 g) dried cannellini beans

FOR THE CREAM

3 egg yolks
½ cup (100 g) sugar
2 cups (500 ml) whole milk
½ cup (70 g) all-purpose flour
  Zest of 1 untreated (unwaxed) lemon, in strips

FOR THE TOPPING

2 to 4 pinecones, to yield ¾ cup (110 g) nuts

To prepare the crust: In a bowl, combine 2 cups (250 g) of the flour, the sugar, the salt, the butter, and the egg. Mix everything while gradually adding the sparkling water, mixing just until the ingredients come together in a rough mass. Shape the dough into a ball, flatten it into a disk, put it in a covered bowl, and then in the refrigerator for 2 hours.

Preheat the oven to 350°F (180°C). Remove the dough from the refrigerator.

Sprinkle some of the remaining 2 tablespoons (15 g) flour on a marble or wood work surface and set the dough on the surface. Sprinkle the remaining flour on top of the dough. With a rolling pin, roll out the dough into a circle 11 inches (28 cm) in diameter. If the dough begins to tear, press it together with your hands. Butter a 9-inch (23-cm) round pan with 1¼-inch (3-cm) sides. Then, with a swirling motion, add a little flour to the pan so that it sticks well everywhere, tapping out the excess. Line the pan with the dough circle, pressing it against the bottom and sides of the pan. Cut a sheet of parchment paper into a 9-inch (23-cm) circle, place the circle on top of the dough, and spill the beans onto the paper. This will keep the dough from swelling in the oven.

Bake the crust until you see that it has a nice golden color, about 30 minutes. Remove from the oven, scoop out the beans and lift out the parchment, and let the crust cool on a wire rack. Now invert a flat 10-inch (25-cm) plate on top of the pan and turn the pan and plate together so the crust falls onto the plate. Turn the crust over again onto a second plate of the same size.

To prepare the cream: Place the egg yolks and the sugar in a bowl and stir with a wooden spoon to combine. Add the flour little by little while stirring with the wooden spoon constantly to prevent lumps from forming. Add the milk, always pouring it slowly and without ever ceasing to stir. Pass everything through a tight-weave strainer into a 3-quart (3-l) saucepan and add the lemon zest. Place the pan over medium heat and continue to stir, always in the same direction, for 30 minutes (be careful not to let the mixture start to boil). Then reduce the heat to very low and cook for another 5 minutes, never forgetting to stir (otherwise the cream will stick to the bottom). Remove from the heat, remove and discard the lemon zest, and continue to stir the cream often as it cools.

To extract the nuts from pinecones: Heat 2 to 4 pinecones until they open. Let them cool and then shake out the pine nuts. You will need ¾ cup (110 g) nuts.

Pour the cooled cream into the crust and arrange the pine nuts on top.

BAKED QUINCE WITH PINE NUTS

Serves 4

4 quinces (about 2¼ pounds/1 kg)
1 tablespoon (15 g) butter

5½ teaspoons (15 g) pine nuts

5 teaspoons (20 g) sugar

Preheat the oven to 350°F (180°C). Wash the quinces very carefully and dry them with paper towels. With a sharp knife, and working from the stem end, extract the core from each fruit, leaving a hole 1½ inches (4 cm) in diameter and about 1 inch (2.5 m) deep. Divide the butter evenly among the holes, then the pine nuts, and finally the sugar. Place the quinces in a baking dish about 9 inches (23 cm) in diameter (or just large enough to accommodate them) and about 2½ inches (6 cm) deep.

Bake the quinces until tender when tested with a knife, about 1 hour. Let cool and serve.

BAKED APPLES WITH PINE NUTS

Serves 4

4 apples (see note)

1 tablespoon (15 g) butter

5½ teaspoons (15 g) pine nuts

5 teaspoons (20 g) sugar

½ cup (120 ml) extra-virgin olive oil

Preheat the oven to 350°F (180°C). Wash the apples very carefully and dry them with paper towels. With a sharp knife, and working from the stem end, extract the core from each fruit, leaving a hole about 1½ inches (4 cm) in diameter and about 1 inch (2.5 cm) deep. Divide the butter evenly among the holes, then the pine nuts, and finally the sugar. Place the apples in a baking dish about 9 inches (23 cm) in diameter (or just large enough to accommodate them) and about 2½ inches (6 cm) deep.

Bake the apples until tender when tested with a knife, about 40 minutes. Let cool and serve.

Note: The Italian recipe calls for rennet apples (*mele renette*), which are not grown in North America. Rennets are small, sweet, golden apples tinged with red, similar to Fuji or Gala apples. —Trans.

Pomegranate

PUNICA GRANATUM; ITALIAN: MELOGRANO

WITH THE POMEGRANATE, we don't know whether it's better to begin by following the thread of the biblical tradition or that of Greek mythology. Heads or tails? The Bible wins—and so it is. This small tree, by now more often found cultivated than wild, is one of the candidates to interpret the role of the Tree of Life (in addition to the tree of knowledge of good and evil) that God planted at the center of the terrestrial Paradise and that has given so much trouble to that part of humanity said to be of the Judeo-Christian persuasion.

It's good to recall that there were two trees, and that eating from the first would have rendered man "one of us" (as far as God's knowledge goes).[1] It is extraordinarily significant that God Himself pronounced this judgment, very worried that "the man [but woman, why was she left out?] . . . might reach out his hand and take also from the tree of life, and eat, and live forever." In order not to have too many immortals around, YHWH saw himself forced to drive Adam out, and "at the east of the garden of Eden he placed the cherubim, and a sword flaming and turning to guard the way to the tree of life" (Genesis 3:22–24).

Fortunately, the pomegranate, in the Hebrew Bible, the so-called Old Testament, also appears in much more joyful circumstances (and less "pregnant" with consequences). The Song of Solomon, for example, is a text that, if annoying commentators had not interfered with it,[2] would seem to present itself "to whomever reads it, like a love poem . . . expressed by two protagonists in alternating songs with a tone that is strongly erotic and set predominantly in a mannerist, pastoral frame."[3]

To give an idea of these pastoral-erotic suggestions, here is a brief list of quotes in the book in which the word *rimmôn* appears, which in Hebrew indicates both the pomegranate tree and its fruit, the latter the symbol of love and fertility (as it is, after all, throughout the Mediterranean and Middle East). The groom says of the bride (4:3, repeated in 6:7): "Your lips are like a crimson thread, / and your mouth is lovely. / Your cheeks are like halves of a *pomegranate* / behind your veil." And again (4:13): "Your channel is an orchard of *pomegranates* / with all choicest fruits, / henna with nard, / nard and saffron, calamus and cinnamon. . . . " And again (6:11): "I went down to the nut orchard . . . / to see . . . / whether the *pomegranates* were in bloom," where a malicious allusion to Genesis 3 might also be made but where what really counts is understanding the impatience of someone awaiting the maturity of his beloved so he might exhaust his own sexual and (why not?) procreative desire. The same thing emerges even more explicitly in 7:12: "Let us go out early to the vineyards / and see whether the vines have budded, / whether the grape blossoms have opened / and the *pomegranates* are in bloom. / There I will give you my love." As for the beloved, it would seem that not only is she mature and available—as much as or more than the man himself—but also (notwithstanding the fact that Origen, in his commentary to the Song of Solomon, carefully avoids mentioning the pomegranate) a little impudent (8:1–2): "O that you were like a brother to me / who nursed at my mother's breast! / If I met you outside, I would kiss you / and no one would despise me. . . . / I would give you spiced wine to drink, / the juice of my *pomegranates*." Indeed!

The pomegranate is also at the center of the very complicated myth of Persephone, who would like to return to her mother Demeter but cannot abandon the kingdom of the dead because she ate the "sweet pomegranate seed" her husband (who not only knew what was what but was also a smooth talker) had given her "secretly" (*Homeric Hymn to Demeter,* v. 372). Why secretly? is the question that springs to mind. To hide it from Hermes, who gave to Hades Zeus's order to return Persephone to her mother. But the circumstances are not clear. Face to face, Persephone will tell Demeter that having been forced to eat the pomegranate, she will have to spend a few months in hell. "When the luck-bringing Hermes came, swift messenger from my father the Son of Cronos [Zeus] and the other Sons of Heaven, bidding me come back from Erebus that you might see me with your eyes and so cease your anger and fearful wrath against the gods, I sprang up at once for joy; but he secretly put in my mouth sweet food, a pomegranate seed, and forced me to taste against my will" (vv. 407–413).[4] I'm sorry to say that some doubts persist concerning whether she was forced. Persephone's description of the pomegranate seed as "sweet" raises suspicions as to whether she really wanted to leave. Not to mention the fact that there would always have been the possibility of not swallowing, like Bill Clinton, who admitted to having smoked marijuana but not to having inhaled it. Today, of course, anyone might inhale it publicly, provided he gets a medical certificate that says that cannabis, other than making adolescents giggle, lowers the blood pressure in adults.

But whether Persephone was coerced or consenting, the question remains: Who planted the pomegranate in Tartarus? Who had made it the tree of the dead? A surreptitious response comes from a thread of the (exceedingly complex) myth regarding Orion, whose first wife, Side, had dared to compete in beauty with Hera and, because of this, had not merely fallen *ad inferos,* but had also been transformed into a pomegranate. But right now, this is a path down which we can go no further without losing our way.

Aside from some Greek myths and some juicy poems with a paleotestamentarian stamp that foreshadow amorous ecstasies, the pomegranate is present in scores of representations as a symbol of the fertility and prosperity granted by God as a sign of His benevolence: "You shall make the rope of the ephod [a sacred garment] all of blue. It shall have an opening for the head in the middle of it. . . . On its lower hem you shall make pomegranates of blue, purple, and crimson yarns . . . with bells of gold between them . . . a golden bell and a pomegranate alternating all around the lower hem of the robe. Aaron shall wear it when he ministers, and its sound shall be heard when he goes into the holy place before the Lord, and when he comes out, so that he may not die."[5] So states the book of Exodus (28:31–35).

Sandro Botticelli painted wonderful pomegranates, held in the hands of both the Madonna and the baby Jesus in a painting completed in 1487 and known, in fact, by the name *Madonna of the Pomegranate.* It can be seen at the Uffizi and is, in itself, worth a trip to Florence. At the sides of the painting are lilies of purity, which traditionally accompany the Madonna, but it is the pomegranate that fixes and shocks the gaze at the center of the canvas: carnal, exuberant, contradictory. It is to the artist's credit that the flesh is not overcome by chastity and a bit of honest Epicureanism is brought back to life.

After all, the pomegranate is also a fruit that is good for your health (although there are some contraindications). It can be both eaten and drunk.[6] Pliny, who nimbly summarizes the medical-scientific wisdom of the ancient world, calls the pomegranate *Malum punicum* (because of Carthage, where he believed it originated) and he subtly compares its structure to "the cells in a honeycomb" (*Naturalis historia,* XIII, 34, 113). Elsewhere, he praises its virtues against various illnesses of the mouth, nostrils, ears, eyes, anus, male genitals, and red splotches on the hands. He asserts (but he does this regarding who knows how many other plants and herbs) that it also fights the venom of scorpions and sea slugs.[7] The most surprising assertion, however, is the following: "The first bud of this fruit when it is beginning to blossom is called *cytinus* by the Greeks; it has a wonderful feature, which has come under the notice of many investigators. If a person, after freeing himself from every kind of [binding]—girdle, shoes, even his ring—plucks one of these buds with . . . the thumb and the fourth finger of his left hand, brushes his eyes with it, lightly touching them, and then swallows it without its touching any tooth, he will suffer, it is said, no eye-trouble during the same year." To top it all off, Pliny offers some final praise for the pomegranate: the smoke of its burning skin drives away gnats (*Naturalis historia,* XXIII, 58, 108–10, 115).

The pomegranate is an essential ingredient of many Middle Eastern cuisines, such as those of Syria, Iran, and Lebanon. Within Italy, it is particularly popular in Sicily, but its reputation is also rising sharply among devotees of *nouvelle cuisine* (along with those chocolate scribbles with which the most fashionable chefs ensnare their infinitesimal dishes). Finally, with pomegranates you can (or should) make grenadine. The traditional, very simple method consists of boiling the juice recovered from crushing the seeds and adding an almost equal dose of sugar or honey. In commercial grenadines today, however, there is nearly no pomegranate juice. It is made with currants, raspberries, and God knows what else. Grenadine—the real kind—is indispensible for the preparation of a tequila sunrise: three parts tequila, six parts orange juice, and one part pomegranate syrup. Since the sight of this cocktail must remind us of the rising sun and its different gradations of red and orange, you must succeed in depositing the grenadine at the bottom of the glass (pouring it very slowly along the edge) in which you have already mixed (no shaking, please!) the tequila and orange juice.

Originally from a vast zone of the globe ranging from Iran to the slopes of the Himalayas, the pomegranate is widespread in the entire Mediterranean basin and in the Caucasus region, but it really grows everywhere. The harvest period runs from August to October.

POMEGRANATE RISOTTO

Serves 4

1 pomegranate
6½ cups (1.5 l) vegetable broth
Coarse salt
¼ cup (60 ml) extra-virgin olive oil
1 onion, thinly sliced
1¾ cups (350 g) Arborio or Vialone Nano rice
¼ cup (60 ml) dry white wine
1½ tablespoons (20 g) butter
¼ cup (40 g) grated Parmesan cheese

With a sharp knife, divide the pomegranate into 4 or more pieces. Remove the seeds and place them in a bowl. Pour the broth into a 3-quart (3-l) pot, place over medium-high-heat, and bring to a boil. Season to taste with the salt. The rice will be cooked in this broth, which must be kept at a simmer. Meanwhile, pour the oil into a 4-quart (4-l) pot and place over very low heat. Add the onion and cook for about 3 minutes. Take care that the onion does not burn. Raise the heat to medium, add the rice, and stir with a wooden spoon for 5 minutes to toast it. Pour in the wine and continue to stir until it has evaporated.

Now begin to add the broth, a little at a time, stirring after each addition and allowing it to evaporate before adding more. After 15 minutes of cooking, add the pomegranate seeds and stir for another 5 minutes. At this point the rice should be tender but still slightly firm at the center of each grain. Turn off the heat, add the Parmesan and butter, and stir so everything is well mixed. Let rest for 5 minutes before serving.

SPAGHETTI WITH POMEGRANATE

Serves 4

1 pomegranate
2 tablespoons (40 g) coarse salt
1 pound (450 g) spaghetti
1⅔ cups (400 g) plain yogurt
⅓ cup (40 g) Parmesan cheese

With a sharp knife, divide the pomegranate into 4 or more pieces. Remove the seeds and place them in a bowl. Pour 4 quarts (4 l) water into an 8-quart (8-l) pot, cover, and place over high heat. When the water begins to boil, add the salt. When the water begins to boil again, toss in the spaghetti and cook for 7 minutes, timing from when the water begins to boil again.

Drain the spaghetti and place in a serving bowl. Add the yogurt and Parmesan and stir until well mixed. Finally, add the pomegranate seeds, stir again until everything is perfectly mixed, and serve.

Prickly Pear

OPUNTIA FICUS-INDICA; ITALIAN: FICODINDIA

THE ITALIAN NAME FOR PRICKLY PEAR is *ficodindia,* or Indian fig, but it is neither. Rather, it comes from what is known as the West Indies and is actually the Greater and Lesser Antilles—the *nuevo mundo* that Christopher Columbus came across, intent on "finding the East by way of the West." Facing the Indies is Tierra Firme, or New Spain, a land of dreams and mirages—unless, of course, you were at the wrong end of the harquebuses of Hernán Cortés and other gentlemen sent by Providence to ensure the Indians' entrance into the Christian paradise. It appears certain that the first exemplars of prickly pear were brought to Spain by Captain (later Admiral) Columbus of the *Santa María.*

For a detailed (if not very precise) description of the plant, however, we need to wait a few years. We find one—two, in fact—in the book *Historia general y natural de las Indias y Tierra Firme del mar Océano* of the Spanish historian and naturalist Gonzalo Fernandéz de Oviedo y Valdés (1476–1557). In Chapter XXVII, of the first part of the ninth book, he speaks of "*los cardos de la tunas e su fructa* [the prickly pear thistle and its fruit]" but warns that in Chapter I of the following book he will describe "*l'arbol de las sol-daduras* [the soldering tree]" with which "a man can weld fragile or broken things together." With regard to this second plant, Fernández de Oviedo asserts that "the Indians make a type of paste and cut it into square pieces," which can also be done with the blades of the first plant, with which it "has much similarity." Some taxonomic caution, then, is not only desirable but necessary.

The plant that interests us is, however, the one that produces "some very painful figs" that are "full of small seeds like true figs, and the skin of this fruit is also like them (or a little thicker)."[1] This excerpt clearly demonstrates that even among the most cunning explorers, this plant tends to dampen curiosity and tone down the differences that, if left free to express themselves, would give to life less predictable and boring colors and flavors.

A native of central Mexico according to many, it passed from there to other Mesoamerican regions, that is, to Cuba and Hispaniola, where Europeans first saw it. But the prickly pear has since spread to all temperate zones of the globe, and anyone can identify it without having to touch it (since, covered as it is with needles, it stings like the dickens).

It seems to have existed forever in places like Sicily, whose landscape would be unimaginable without the *Opuntia ficus-indica*, as it came to be called through the initiative of the Scottish botanist Philip Miller (1691–1771). In the Nahuatl language it was known as *nōpalli* or *nohpalli*, from which the Spanish *nopales* is derived. Specifically, this term refers to the blades (or the cladodes, for those who want to amaze their friends or impress women) and, therefore, to the plant, while the fruit were called *nōchtli*.

The presence of this signifier in Tenochtitlán, the original name of what we know today as Mexico City, is certainly not accidental. The matter is etymologically complicated but not irresolvable: you need only succeed in harmonizing the name of a fourteenth-century mythical founder, *Ténoch*, with *tetl*, meaning "stone" or "rock" and *nōchtli*, with which we are already familiar, and insert it all into the foundation myth of the city. It seems that the nomadic population of the Aztecs (or, more correctly, the Mexica) had received from their god, Huitzilopochtli, the order to settle in the place where an eagle with a snake in its beak could be found, perched on a rock in the middle of the waters. After about two hundred years of wandering, the divine sign appeared on a small island in the middle of Lake Texcoco. At that point, their leaders effectively said *hic manebimus optime* (here we'll be fine), so they set to work building what was, according to Bernal Díaz del Castillo (1492–1584),[2] who saw it in 1519 (nearly two hundred years after construction began in 1325), a city so splendid that "we [that is, he and the other invaders there with him] hardly knew what to say, not even being certain that what we had before our eyes was a real city."

This etiological fable is confirmed by the first folio of the Mendoza Code, named for Antonio de Mendoza, viceroy of New Spain, who, about twenty years after the conquest, had it drawn up with the intention of sending it to Charles V. His *dominus et imperator* (of the Holy Roman Empire) never received it, however, because it was seized by French pirates who attacked the ship on which the precious manuscript was traveling.[3] It contains the pictographic history of the Aztecs, their leaders, their conquest, and even the tributes paid by the populations they subjugated. Explanations and comments are written in Spanish. In the center of the first folio stands, lo and behold, an eagle supported by a prickly pear growing from a stone—only the snake is missing. The motif is repeated, *talis et qualis,* on the Mexican flag (serpent restored).

The prickly pear reproduces with frightening speed, such that it quickly transforms itself into a weed. The only natural agents capable of combating its invasiveness effectively are phytophagous insects, among which another scourge of the fields excels, the cochineal (*Dactylopius opuntae*). The cochineal invites itself to dinner, turning the entire prickly pear plant into a feast. However, this insect is very useful—essential, in fact—in the preparation of a natural colorant, carmine, which is obtained by grinding the desiccated bodies of thousands of cochineals. Because of this, in some places, rather than being considered infamous beasties that destroy the balance between the prickly pear that is visually beautiful and the prickly pear that tastes good, the wickedness of their massacre is turned to profit. Well known as a shade of dark red, carmine has been used to color fabrics and other goods (including Easter eggs) for centuries.

Today, all of this has lost its importance. The colorants extracted from the cochineals have been replaced by synthetic dyes. This is also true of *alchermes*—from *al-qirmiz,* an Arabic term meaning, precisely, "cochineal"—an Italian liquor much respected by bakers (at least once upon a time). Nowadays, those of us who love insects (especially Hemiptera) and cakes with *alchermes* and/or colored with carmine no longer must wrinkle our noses at the idea of putting an extract of sessile parasites into our bellies. No, at most, we nervously try to determine the collateral effects of the chemical compound that we stick in our mouths in place of cochineal carmine, knowing that it will pass through our defenseless bodies very slowly, organ by organ.

There are prickly pears of different types and with different qualities. The color of the fruit varies (for example, from the orange-yellow of the Sulfurine variety to the red-purple of the Sanguine to the greenish white of the Muscareda). The shape also varies (much rounder at the beginning of the season, oblong toward the end). The medicinal virtues—still relentlessly debated—differ from species to species as well. Ever stronger, if not yet prevailing, is the opinion that they are effective in curing diabetes. This hope is not a good excuse to throw yourself into Bajtra, a prickly pear–based liquor produced in Malta, where the plant has reigned supreme across the landscape for centuries: for a brief while (1975–88) it acted as its national symbol.

There is one place where coming across the prickly pear is even more amazing: the travertine Fountain of the Four Rivers, erected in 1651 by Gian Lorenzo Bernini in the center of Piazza Navona in Rome. The rivers, which include the Nile, the Ganges, the Danube, and La Plata, representing the four continents known to the geographers of the Late Renaissance, each have their dowry of fauna and flora. For example, everyone knows the lion is there, and the palm can also be easily seen. For the prickly pear, you have to look to the right of the Río de la Plata and not let yourself be distracted by the raised hand with which the personification of this river tries to protect itself from the feared collapse of the façade of the church that faces it, Sant'Agnese in Agone. . . . This is a good story of which tourist guides in Rome are very fond, but it is a joke: the church was constructed many years later (by Borromini).

Wherever prickly pears are found, the problem is harvesting and peeling them without filling one's hands with—in addition to the needles we have already mentioned (which, being quite visible, can be avoided)—the thin and very insidious prickly hairs that the well-spoken call glochids. The clever proceed in this manner: they equip themselves with a *coppo*, a rod with a basket at the end with a serrated upper edge, with which they detach the pears from the blades. With rubber kitchen gloves, they transfer the pears to a basin filled with water or rinse them under a faucet so the glochids wilt. Then, with a knife, they remove both ends and cut the surface of the fruit lengthwise, which by now has become a slightly bent cylinder. They separate the halves and scoop out the edible part, which is rich in magnesium and potassium. Native Americans, who had little water and no kitchen gloves, would gather the prickly pears in the early morning when the fruits were covered with dew. Then they would rub them in the sand, getting more or less the same result one gets in the sink.

That they knew how to open them skillfully is evident from what was written by Fernández de Oviedo, who not only defines prickly pear fruit as "good tasting and good to digest" (despite the fact that they gave him a great fright when, having eaten too many, he began to urinate red and thought he was having an internal hemorrhage) but also notes that his involuntary hosts sold them "in the plaza of this city, at all times, as good fruit." One wonders what this Spanish polygraph would have said had he been able to read Matilde Serao's nineteenth-century description of a street in Naples: "It is picturesque for a lover of color, wandering in via Roma in the evening, to see a cart laid out as a table on which, on many small plates, you can see little stacks of peeled prickly pears."[4]

In addition to eating the fruit raw, the Indians would also boil the prickly pears to reduce them to a mush similar to puréed apples. The conquistadores, boiling them a little longer and adding some of their own devilry, converted them into a syrupy paste to which they gave the name *queso de tuna,* or "prickly pear cheese." The blades are also edible. They must be peeled, cut into strips, and boiled. Then they must be washed aggressively to remove the rubbery substance that they emit during boiling. At this point, they can be mixed with greens in salads, or they can be added to omelets. They can also be pickled. "The blades, freed from the needles and skin, baked or heated on the fire, were applied to the backs of those sick with pleurisy," according to Antonio Costantini and Marosa Marcucci.[5]

The harvest period for the fruits runs from August through September.

RIGATONI (DITALONI RIGATI) WITH PRICKLY PEAR AND RICOTTA

Serves 4

5 ounces (150 g) prickly pears
1¼ cups (300 g) sheep's milk ricotta cheese
5 teaspoons (30 g) coarse salt
¾ pound (350 g) rigatoni

Wearing rubber kitchen gloves, cut each prickly pear lengthwise with a sharp knife, making one cut on the right, a second one on the left, and a third, more delicate one at the center of the fruit. Remove the 2 strips of skin. Then, using your hands, remove the flesh from the remaining skin. Cut the flesh into small pieces and place in a bowl. Put the ricotta in a second bowl large enough to hold the pasta once it is cooked.

Pour 3 quarts (3 l) water into a 6-quart (6-l) pot, cover, and place over high heat. When the water begins to boil, add the salt. When the water begins to boil again, add the rigatoni and cook for 10 minutes. Scoop out 5 tablespoons (75 ml) of the cooking water and immediately drain the pasta.

Add the reserved cooking water to the ricotta and mix well, then add the pasta and mix well. Finally, add the prickly pear and carefully stir everything together again before serving.

SPAGHETTI WITH PRICKLY PEAR AND YOGURT

Serves 4

2 to 3 prickly pears
1⅔ cups (400 g) plain yogurt
⅓ cup (40 g) grated Parmesan cheese
6½ teaspoons (40 g) coarse salt
¾ pound (350 g) spaghetti

Wearing rubber kitchen gloves, cut each prickly pear lengthwise with a sharp knife, making one cut on the right, a second one on the left, and a third, more delicate one at the center of the fruit. Remove the 2 strips of skin. Then, using your hands, remove the flesh from the remaining skin. Cut the flesh into small pieces and place in a wide bowl large enough to accommodate the pasta. In a small bowl, combine the yogurt and Parmesan and mix well.

Pour 3 quarts (3 l) water into a 6-quart (6-l) pot, cover, and place over high heat. When the water begins to boil, add the salt. When the water begins to boil again, toss in the spaghetti and cook for 7 minutes.

Drain the spaghetti and add to the bowl holding the prickly pear. Add the yogurt mixture to the pasta, stir and toss until everything is well mixed, and serve.

PRICKLY PEAR RISOTTO
Serves 4

2 or 3 prickly pears
6½ cups (1.5 l) vegetable broth
 Coarse salt
¼ cup (60 ml) extra-virgin olive oil
1 onion, finely chopped
1¾ cups (350 g) Arborio or Vialone Nano rice
¼ cup (60 ml) dry white wine
4 tablespoons (60 g) butter
⅓ cup (40 g) grated Parmesan cheese

Wearing rubber kitchen gloves, cut each prickly pear lengthwise with a sharp knife, making one cut on the right, a second one on the left, and a third, more delicate one at the center of the fruit. Remove the 2 strips of skin. Then, using your hands, remove the flesh from the remaining skin. Cut the flesh into small pieces and place in a bowl.

Pour the broth into a 3-quart (3-l) pot, place over medium-high-heat, and bring to a boil. Season to taste with the salt. The rice will be cooked in this broth, which must be kept at a simmer. Meanwhile, pour the oil into a 4-quart (4-l) pot and place over very low heat. Add the onion and cook for about 3 minutes. Take care that the onion does not burn. Raise the heat to medium, add the rice, and stir with a wooden spoon for a good 5 minutes to toast it. Pour in the wine and continue to stir until it has evaporated.

Now begin to add the broth, a little at a time, stirring after each addition and allowing it to evaporate before adding more. After 15 to 20 minutes of cooking, turn off the heat. At this point the rice should be tender but still slightly firm at the center of each grain. Add the butter and Parmesan and stir until well mixed. The time has finally arrived for the prickly pear, which must be mixed with everything else. Don't forget to keep stirring until the last moment. Let rest for 5 minutes before serving.

Purslane

PORTULACA OLERACEA; ITALIAN: *PORTULACA;*
SALENTINE DIALECT: *PRUCACCHIA*

THE PLANT THAT IN THE SALENTO is called *prucacchia* or *brucacchia* (depending on which labial consonant you favor) commonly goes by the name of *portulaca* (and more rarely, *porcellana*) elsewhere in Italy. The lineage of this appellation is not at all obvious. In lexicography, as in the best families, while the *mater est semper certa,* the *pater* is, if not quite *semper incertus,* at least more difficult to identify. For example, those who hold that *portulaca* descends directly from the Latin of Pliny (*Naturalis historia,* XX, 81, 210) usually forget that the most accredited textual tradition assigns to the Roman naturalist the term *porcillaca* (and not *portillaca*). Pliny's term, however, would justify the rarer Italian *porcellana* and would connect the plant nicely to the avidity with which pigs (Italian and Latin, *porci*) feed on them, rather than to the idea of a door (*porta*) or an opening (*apertura*), inspired by the dehiscence of the small pod that contains the seeds.[1]

Native to India and Persia, it now grows everywhere, even in places like Union Square in San Francisco, which can get so saturated with exhaust fumes that the purslane must have a constitution of iron (in addition to the courage of a lion) not to die from asphyxiation. Stubborn but not rebellious, the small reddish stem of wild purslane remains prostrate, whereas it tends to stand upright if cultivated. It is naturally found in fields and vegetable gardens, at the edges of roads, on the plains and in the mountains, and even close to the sea, in both fertile and arid soils.

Many consider it an invasive plant that is nearly impossible to get rid of. Every plant produces around fifty thousand seeds, each of which can remain buried thirty or forty years without losing the power to resuscitate itself, provided it is not too deep in the soil. A plow need only cut some furrows in a field, bringing the seeds back to the surface, to give purslane another chance. Furthermore, a purslane plant that is pulled up, if left in situ, will take root again. Sometimes even a piece of the plant is enough.

But as Sandra Mason says, slightly modifying the American proverb "If you can't beat 'em, join 'em," "If you can't free yourself from purslane, eat it,"[2] because this very tenacious plant is also an excellent and healthful food. It contains more omega-3 fatty acids (the same type found in fish[3] and in certain algae) than almost any other green, not to mention vitamins A, B, and C and beta carotene. In short, it's a health bomb. Appropriately, Massimo Vaglio reports that "those who eat purslane and the meat of animals that graze where purslane is abundant develop a more efficient metabolic life . . . which leads to the formation of eicosapentaenoic and docosahexaenoic acids which, in turn, contribute to . . . stimulating the contraction of muscles and the functioning of the circulatory system, and in essence reduce the incidence of coronary diseases."[4]

Although practically forgotten today, archeological evidence from the excavations undertaken around the sanctuary of Hera, on the island of Samos, dates the consumption of purslane to the mists of time—that is, to the era in which, in the swamps formed by the Imbrasos River, the locals began to practice the cult of this goddess who would subsequently be unhappily married to the supreme head of the Olympic gods and end up being called (in Homeric style) white-armed Hera. It is worth remembering that in Roman times, her sanctuary, having become famous and rich, was the object of severe plundering by Gaius Verres, eloquently denounced during the trial against him by no less than Marcus Tullius Cicero.[5]

In the Canadian province of Ontario, at the bottom of Crawford Lake, microfossils have been found of plants and herbs that were cultivated by the Iroquois, who once lived in the area. In addition to those of corn, sunflowers, and various types of squashes, the presence of purslane was noted. Dating the findings to sometime between 1268 and 1468, we can now confidently state that purslane may not be indigenous to North America like certain beans, the tomato, and, of course, corn, but it is certainly pre-Columbian.

Fortunately, it was not forgotten everywhere. It is very much sought after in Turkey, where young purslane is eaten raw in salads, together with tomatoes and cucumbers. The entire sprig or, preferably, the leaves are used. If the plant is mature, however, it is best to cook it and use it for seasoning the stuffing for lamb or for a nice plate of lentils (it tastes vaguely like lemon but can also recall spinach or watercress).

In the Balkans, in Egypt, in Greece, and particularly in Crete, we find purslane leaves (often accompanied by cucumbers and slices of green pepper) seasoned with yogurt—treated, in turn, *ad libitum* with olive oil, garlic (often in excessive quantities), coriander, mint, chervil, and other herbs . . . and salt. Another country where purslane has never ceased to satisfy people's appetites and tastes is Mexico, where it is called *verdolaga*. Very popular (at least as much as nopales, or the paddles of the prickly pear), handfuls of purslane are used in omelets, tortillas, soups, and stuffings. The famous Mexican *verdolaga* stuffing is easy to make and requires (in addition to the purslane) oil, garlic, onion, tomato, beaten egg, salt, and, to add some spice, finely chopped jalapeño.

Purslane was also a rather common salad ingredient even in Europe through the Renaissance. This is what Castelvetro writes about it: "Purslane is eaten a lot as salad on its own, or with other herbs; we always add pepper and finely chopped onion to counteract its coldness" (*The Fruit, Herbs & Vegetables of Italy*, 77). John Evelyn is also not opposed to purslane, but he recommends it be pickled or at least mixed with hotter greens. But if you insist on eating it by itself, seasoned with oil and vinegar, you should do it "with Moderation, as it has been sometimes found to corrupt in the Stomach" (*Acetaria*, 162).

Both Castelvetro and Evelyn reverse or strongly soften the negative judgment of purslane expressed by Hildegard von Bingen, who really could not stand it and dismisses it with prejudice in a line and a half: "Purslane (*burtel*) is cold and, when eaten, produces mucus in a person. It is not profitable for a person to eat" (*Physica*, LXXIV). Nor is Michele Savonarola kind to purslane, *sub specie gastronomiae*, although he recognizes some worth in its curative properties: "Taken as food it gives little nourishment and is no good, because it is cold, moist and viscous and, hard to digest, it weakens the appetite, but it nonetheless confers warmth to the stomach and represses cholera and vomit, and takes away the appetite for coitus. Finally, it removes pain from teeth when it is chewed" (*Libreto*, 78).

Also cautious is Castore Durante, for whom "eating too much of it, and too often, causes no little harm, because it is difficult to digest, it weakens the stomach [but if the stomach is overheated, then it is a good remedy], it offends vision, nourishes little and poorly, and then, being cold, it takes away appetite and diminishes reproductive and sensual desire" (*Herbario novo,* LVIII). But note that here, as in Savonarola, those who are too often aroused can take some to cool off!

Long before modern science could confirm how effective purslane was for lowering blood pressure, cholesterol, arthritis, or other things, Pliny (in antiquity) and Culpeper (in the protomodern era) praised its therapeutic qualities, each in his own way. The list of benefits is immoderately extensive in the first and not miserly in the second. We can excerpt only a few of their peculiarities: "[Wild purslane] counteracts the impurities of water, and if pounded and applied in wine it cures headache and sores on the head; other sores it heals if chewed and applied with honey.... For eye-fluxes in persons of all ages [it is applied] with pearl barley, to the forehead and temples, but to the eyes themselves in milk and honey; also, if the eyes should fall forwards, pounded leaves are applied with bean husks.... Whether eaten or drunk it is good for epilepsy.... It checks lust and amorous dreams. A Spanish prince, father of a man of praetorian rank, because of unbearable disease of the uvula, to my knowledge carries except in the bath a root of peplis [wild purslane] hung round his neck by a thread, being in this way relieved of all inconvenience" (all this—and more—in *Naturalis historia,* XX, 81, 210).

As for Culpeper, he thinks that the seeds are more effective than the leaves, and they are particularly effective in treating cystitis. Like many, he is also convinced that purslane calms sexual excitement. Not only does it eliminate sensual dreams, but if used too much, it often extinguishes all ardor and even the capacity to procreate (*Complete Herbal,* 146). It is unclear whether "extinguishes the heat and vi[r]tue of natural procreation" should be interpreted as "renders sterile" or as "renders impotent," but we lean toward the former. For both reasons, limiting its use seems advisable. Full speed ahead, however, for the juice, which, mixed with rose oil, cures grazes from lightning, gunpowder burns, and even pains of the breasts caused, presumably, by too much milk production.

Purslane (*Portulaca oleracea* to the experts), which has what it takes to become a cultivated green in the future (some gardeners have already begun), is gathered when young in June and July.

SPAGHETTI WITH PURSLANE

Serves 4

2¼ pounds (1 kg) purslane
½ cup (120 ml) extra-virgin olive oil
1 onion, finely chopped
4 tomatoes, diced
1 clove garlic, minced
¾ teaspoon (2 g) ground red pepper
⅛ teaspoon (1 g) fine salt
1 pound (450 g) spaghetti
2 tablespoons (40 g) coarse salt
Ground black pepper

Use only the tips of the sprigs and the most tender leaves of the purslane. Wash them repeatedly until no bits of soil remain. Pour the oil into a 12-inch (30-cm) skillet and place over very low heat. Add the onion and cook, stirring occasionally, until golden, about 10 minutes. Add the tomatoes, garlic, red pepper, and fine salt and mix well. Set aside off the heat.

Pour 3½ quarts water into a 5½-quart (5-l) pot, cover, and place over high heat. When the water begins to boil, add the coarse salt. When the water begins to boil again, toss in the purslane and cook, uncovered, for about 5 minutes. Remove the purslane from the water with a wire skimmer, draining well, and set aside. Now add the spaghetti to the same boiling water and cook for about 6 minutes, timing from when the water begins to boil again.

When the pasta is ready, scoop out 5 tablespoons (75 ml) of the cooking water and add to the skillet with the tomatoes. Then drain the spaghetti and add to the skillet along with the drained purslane. Cook everything over medium heat for 3 to 4 minutes, stirring constantly with a spoon and fork. Grind in some pepper, stir once again, and serve.

PURSLANE FRITTATA
Serves 4

1 pound (500 g) purslane
4 teaspoons (25 g) coarse salt
6 eggs
½ teaspoon (3 g) fine salt
Ground black pepper
2 tablespoons (15 g) grated pecorino or Parmesan cheese
2 slices (50 g) stale bread, soaked in water and
    wrung out lightly
4 teaspoons (20 ml) extra-virgin olive oil

Use only the tips of the sprigs and the most tender leaves of the purslane. Wash them repeatedly until no bits of soil remain. Pour 2½ quarts (2.5 l) water into a 5-quart (5-l) pot, cover, and place over high heat. When the water begins to boil, add the coarse salt. When the water begins to boil again, toss in the purslane and cook for 5 minutes, timing from when the water returns to a boil. Remove the purslane from the water with a wire skimmer, draining well. Mince with kitchen shears or a sharp knife.

In a bowl, beat the eggs with a fork for about 1 minute. Add the fine salt, a few grinds of pepper, the pecorino, and the bread and beat again, this time with a whisk or a spoon, making sure everything is perfectly mixed. Add the purslane and stir vigorously with a spoon.

Line the bottom and sides of a 9-inch (23-cm) nonstick skillet with parchment paper (which prevents the frittata from sticking to the bottom, and makes turning it easier). Pour in the oil and place the pan over medium-low heat for 3 minutes, swirling the pan once or twice to help distribute the oil evenly. After 3 minutes, add the contents of the bowl to the pan, taking care to spread it evenly. Cover and cook for 10 minutes. Uncover about every 3 minutes and, with a wooden spatula, check that the edges of the frittata are not sticking. After 10 minutes, uncover, invert a plate slightly larger than the skillet on top of the pan, and turn the skillet and plate together so the frittata falls onto the plate. Slide the frittata, browned side up, back into the skillet and cook, uncovered, over low heat for 10 minutes. Turn off the heat and slide the frittata onto a plate. The frittata may be eaten cold or hot.

PURSLANE SALAD

Serves 4

2¼ pounds (1 kg) purslane
Juice of 2 lemons
⅛ teaspoon (1 g) fine salt
Ground black pepper
Extra-virgin olive oil, to taste

Use only the tips of the sprigs and the most tender leaves of the purslane. Wash them repeatedly until no bits of soil remain, then place in a colander to drain thoroughly. Dry any remaining moisture with paper towels and put the purslane in a salad bowl.

In a small bowl, whisk together the lemon juice, salt, and a few grinds of pepper, then whisk in the oil. Pour the dressing over the purslane, toss well, and serve right away.

PURSLANE WITH OIL AND LEMON

Serves 4

4½ pounds (2 kg) purslane
2 tablespoons (40 g) coarse salt
Lemon juice, to taste
Extra-virgin olive oil, to taste

Use only the tips of the sprigs and the most tender leaves of the purslane. Wash them repeatedly until no bits of soil remain.

Pour 3½ quarts (3.5 l) water into a 6-quart (6-l) pot, cover, and place over high heat. When the water begins to boil, add the salt. When the water begins to boil again, toss in the purslane and cook, uncovered, for 10 minutes. Remove the purslane from the water with a wire skimmer, draining well. Dry the purslane thoroughly so that not even a drop of water remains. Season the purslane at the table with the lemon juice and oil.

POTATOES AND PURSLANE

Serves 4

2¼ pounds (1 kg) purslane
6½ tablespoons (100 ml) extra-virgin olive oil
   1 clove garlic, halved lengthwise and green sprout removed
      if necessary
2¼ pounds (1 kg) yellow-fleshed potatoes, peeled, cut into
      chunks, and rinsed
   2 teaspoons (12 g) coarse salt
      Ground black pepper, or 1 small dried chile, halved

Use only the tips of the sprigs and the most tender leaves of the purslane. Wash them repeatedly until no bits of soil remain. Pour the oil into a pot about 10 inches (25 cm) in diameter and 4 inches (10 cm) deep and add the garlic and then the potatoes. Pour in 1¼ cups (300 ml) water, add the salt and a few grinds of pepper (or the chile, if you prefer), and stir to mix. Now add the purslane, cover, place over medium heat, and cook for about 15 minutes, checking occasionally to make sure the contents are not sticking to the bottom.

Uncover and stir the contents carefully with a wooden spoon, or grasp the pot by its handles (but don't burn yourself!) and give it a swirling motion, so that what is on the bottom moves to the top and vice versa without breaking. Re-cover and cook for about 15 minutes longer. Check that the potatoes are cooked before turning off the heat and serving.

PICKLED PURSLANE SPRIGS

Makes 1 small jar

3½ ounces (100 g) purslane sprigs (2⅓ cups)
   1 cup (240 ml) white wine vinegar

Gather only the tenderest sprigs of the purslane plant and wash and dry them well. Then let them "bruise" for 4 days—that is, let them dry on a tray (even better if it is perforated) placed in an airy and cool place.

Break up the purslane sprigs and place them in a glass jar about 3¾ inches

(8 cm) in diameter and 4 inches (10 cm) deep with an airtight cap. Pour in the vinegar, then press on the purslane with a wooden spoon until it is completely submerged in the vinegar. Cap tightly, place in a cool, dark place, and let 40 days pass before eating. The purslane is good in salads or in savory pies.

PURSLANE RISOTTO

Serves 4

- 1 pound (500 g) purslane
- 5 teaspoons (30 g) coarse salt
- 6½ tablespoons (100 ml) extra-virgin olive oil
- 1¾ cups (350 g) Arborio or Vialone Nano rice
- ⅓ cup (40 g) grated Parmesan cheese
- Ground black pepper

Use only the tips of the sprigs and the most tender leaves of the purslane. Wash them repeatedly until no bits of soil remain. Pour 2½ quarts (2.5 l) water into a 5-quart (5-l) pot, cover, and place over high heat. When the water begins to boil, add 2½ teaspoons (15 g) of the salt. When the water begins to boil again, toss in the purslane, cover with the lid slightly ajar, and cook for 10 minutes. Remove the purslane with a wire skimmer, draining well. Using kitchen shears or a sharp knife, cut into ¾- to 1-inch (2- to 3-cm) pieces.

Pour 6½ cups (1.5 l) water into a 3-quart (3-l) pot, place over medium-high heat, bring to a boil, and add the remaining 2½ teaspoons (15 g) salt. The rice will be cooked in this water, which must be kept at a simmer. Meanwhile, pour the oil into a 4-quart (4-l) pot and place over very low heat for about 3 minutes. Add the purslane and cook, stirring, for 4 to 5 minutes. Raise the heat to medium, add the rice, and stir with a wooden spoon for another 5 minutes to toast it.

Now begin to add the water, a little at a time, stirring after each addition and allowing it to evaporate before adding more. After 15 to 20 minutes of cooking, turn off the heat. At this point the rice should be tender but still slightly firm at the center of each grain. Add the Parmesan and pepper to taste and stir so everything is well mixed. Let rest for 5 minutes before serving.

PURSLANE WITH PARMESAN

Serves 4

4½ pounds (2 kg) purslane
2 tablespoons (40 g) coarse salt
½ cup (120 ml) extra-virgin olive oil
1 onion, finely chopped
¾ teaspoon (2 g) ground red pepper
1 cup (100 g) grated pecorino or Parmesan cheese

Use only the tips of the sprigs and the most tender leaves of the purslane. Wash them repeatedly until no bits of soil remain. Pour 3½ quarts (3.5 l) water into a wide 6-quart (6-l) pot, cover, and place over high heat. When the water begins to boil, add the salt. When the water begins to boil again, toss in the purslane, cover with the lid slightly ajar, and cook for 10 minutes. Remove the purslane with a wire skimmer and drain well. Scoop out ⅔ cup (150 ml) of the cooking water and set aside.

Discard the remaining cooking water and wash and dry the pot. Pour the oil into the pot and place over very low heat. Add the onion and cook, stirring occasionally, until golden, about 10 minutes. Remove the pot from the heat and let the oil cool.

Add the red pepper to the cooled oil, then add half of the purslane and sprinkle it evenly with half of the pecorino. Top with the remaining purslane and sprinkle evenly with the remaining cheese. Add the reserved cooking water, place over very low heat, and cook, uncovered, for about 15 minutes. Serve warm.

SAUTÉED PURSLANE

Serves 4

4½   pounds (2 kg) purslane
2   tablespoons (40 g) coarse salt
⅔   cup (150 ml) extra-virgin olive oil
1   onion, finely chopped
     Ground red pepper, or 1 small dried chile, halved

Use only the tips of the sprigs and the most tender leaves of the purslane. Wash them repeatedly until no bits of soil remain. Pour 3½ quarts water into a 6-quart (6-l) pot, cover, and place over high heat. When the water begins to boil, add the salt. When the water begins to boil again, toss in the purslane and cook, uncovered, for 10 minutes. Remove the purslane from the water with a wire skimmer, draining well, then dry thoroughly with paper towels.

Pour the oil into a pot about 10 inches (25 cm) in diameter and 5 inches (13 cm) deep and place over very low heat. Add the onion and cook, stirring occasionally, until golden, about 10 minutes. Take care that the onion does not burn. Add a little red pepper (or the chile, if you prefer), stir well, and then add the purslane. Cover and cook over very low heat for 3 to 4 minutes. Uncover and, using a slotted spoon, turn the purslane so that what was on the bottom of the pot is now on the top. Or, better yet, grasp the pot by its handles (but don't burn yourself!) and give it a swirling motion. This is how you avoid the danger of the purslane becoming a mush. Let cook, uncovered, over low heat for about 5 minutes longer, then serve.

Red Poppy

PAPAVER RHOEAS; ITALIAN: *PAPARINA*

EVERY ITALIAN WHOSE MEMORY extends back to 1952 knows that poppies are tall, tall, tall and goslings very small—consequently blocking that "most natural" impulse that goslings have in their hearts to gobble up poppies. In that year, the song "Papaveri e papere" (Poppies and goslings)—lyrics by Mario Panzeri, music by Vittorio Mascheroni—achieved "unequaled" success at Italy's Sanremo Music Festival and then spread throughout the Italian peninsula and even beyond the country's borders.[1]

To those who, driven by irresistible desire, would like to discover how that highly inconvenient love story between a representative of the floral world and one from the fauna world ends up, we offer here the (translated) lyrics in their disconcerting entirety:

> Through a wheat field (I can't tell you which)
> A gosling passed with her father
> And saw some tall poppies shining in the sun . . .
> And she was spellbound.

> The gosling said to her father: "Papa,
> How do you eat the poppies?"
> "*You* can't eat the poppies," said Papa.

And then he added, picking at his salad:
"What do you expect, that's life . . .

You know that poppies are tall, tall, tall,
And you are very small . . . and you are very small
You know that poppies are tall, tall, tall,
You were born a gosling, what can you do about it?"

Near a stream (which one I couldn't say),
One day a poppy looked into the water
And saw a small blonde gosling . . .
And he was spellbound.

Poppy said to his Mama, "Mama,
How do you gobble a gosling?"
"*You* can't gobble a gosling," said Mama.
"If you let yourself fall for her,
The whole world will no longer be able to say . . .

You know that poppies are tall, tall, tall,
And you are very small . . . and you are very small.
You know that poppies are tall, tall, tall,
You were born a gosling, what can you do about it?"

And one day in May (which one I couldn't say),
What everyone thought would happen did.
Poppy waited for his Gosling in the light of the moon,
and then he married her.

But this romance didn't last very long . . .
Soon came the sickle that cut down the grain . . .
And a gust of wind carried the poppies away.
And so Little Poppy was gone
leaving his Gosling in the lurch.

You know that poppies are tall, tall, tall,
And you are very small . . . and you are very small.
You know that poppies are tall, tall, tall,
You were born a gosling, what can you do about it?

Opinion is widespread that this song testifies not only to the cultural back-
wardness in which Italy found itself in the 1950s, but also to the embarrassing
fatuousness "inscribed in the genetic code of Italians." While America was
giving birth to cool jazz and then to rock and roll, and George Brassens and
Juliette Gréco were starting out in France, the national taste in Italy, placed
on display annually at Sanremo, persisted for songs that were sentimental

and melodramatic or pseudorustic and surrealistic. While Italian cinema was experiencing its superlative season of neorealism, Italian song plummeted into the saddest insipidness.

Alternatively, those who won't surrender when faced with the evidence and who prefer to suspect a less rash and almost revolutionary subtext, will welcome what the author of the words had to say: "The lyrics of 'Papaveri e papere' were suggested to me by the presumptuousness of certain political figures. I believe that even a simple popular song may be a satire of customs." Panzeri's intention seems to find confirmation in Gigi Vesigna, who wrote, "The words came to be read as referring to the political class and, in particular, to Amintore Fanfani—small in stature but a very powerful representative of the Christian Democrats." Another antigovernment reading is seen by Dario Salvatori: "That same year, the electoral campaign of the PCI [the Italian Communist Party] was based on a manifesto in which the tall Christian Democratic poppies were mowed down by the revolutionary wind of communism. The goslings left in the lurch were the oppressed people with no choices; the tall poppies [were] the Christian Democrats."[2]

According to Gianni Borgna, however, the subliminal message hidden in the fable's impossible zooifloral love was, instead, of an ultraconservative stamp. "Papaveri e papere" has a "decidedly remissive moral that preaches resignation to the end and supine acceptance of one's own state of social inferiority. That the 'gosling' may be identified with women confirms such a reading."[3]

We might not give credit to the cryptopolitical values for which Panzeri would like to be the spokesman, but in order to show the historical and linguistic materials to which he could or might have turned, we must not neglect what is explained under the heading *papavero* in the dictionary of Salvatore Battaglia. "*Figurative.* An important person who occupies a position at the highest level in a city, in a community, in a political or cultural organization, or the like; authority (particularly in the expressions *Alto, grosso papavero* [tall, fat poppy]) and, with this meaning, derived from an anecdote according to which Lucius Tarquinius Superbus (the last king of Rome, from 535 to 509 B.C.) knocked down the poppies in his garden with a cane to symbolize to his son that the easiest way to take possession of the city of Gabi was to eliminate its most important and influential citizens. In modern usage, the term has a strongly ironic meaning."[4]

Behind this is a long and very beautiful story presented with extreme precision and intelligence by the great classical scholar, Gabriella Giglioni of the University of Pisa, in her essay, "Cutting the Tallest Ears: Individual Ambition and Collective Interest in the Polis."[5] The anecdote of the cutting down of the poppies actually begins with the ears of wheat in Herodotus, an author of whom Giglioni is undoubtedly our best reader. Thrasybulus, tyrant of Miletus, sent a "silent message" to Periander, tyrant of Corinth, who, through a messenger of his own, had asked for advice regarding the best way "to govern the city, after having introduced the most secure of constitutions." Thrasybulus then led Periander's envoy outside the city into a cultivated field where, as they walked, he asked him again and again why he had been sent from Corinth. At the same time, whenever Thrasybulus saw an ear of wheat that stood out, he would cut it and throw it away, destroying the most beautiful and tallest of the crop in the process. Once back in Corinth, the messenger maintained that he had never received any advice, but in describing what had happened, he made it clear to Periander that cutting the heads of the nobility is the only sure way to keep oneself in power.

In his *Politics* (XIII), Aristotle uses the same example to justify states that are built on supporting democracy ostracizing their most powerful citizens in the interest of "aspiring to equality above all things." It is only with Titus Livy that the ears of wheat become poppies, a substitution that has the particular merit of silencing critics who would accuse tyrants of squandering resources.

But the marriage of poppies and goslings, and the desire of the latter to fall for the former, remains a sticking point. There is a document that might render the match less mysterious, but it is improbable that Panzeri and Mascheroni (the Italian Gilbert and Sullivan, so to speak) were aware of it. This would be the phonological observation set within *Hortulus,*[6] a poem in Latin composed in Charlemagne's time by Walafrid Strabo (ca. 808–849). In it, we read some amazing things. Not only would the poppy be most effective in repressing those "*ructus . . . amaros . . . adusque*" (disgusting and acrid belches) that an ulcer "*ab imo pectore*" sends to the mouth, but it would derive its very "*nomen formidabile*" from the sound produced by the chewer (*sono mandentis*), or from the Latin verb *papare* (the Italian *pappare*—"to eat greedily"—is not far from it). Walafrid's influence is somewhat problematic. I repeat, however, that it is improbable that the protagonists of the Sanremo Music Festival, both then and now, were aware of this text, which is not exactly popular.

Perhaps the explanation is closer at hand than it seems. In the pages of any dictionary of the Italian language, the entry *papavero* (poppy) is immediately followed by the entry *papera* (gosling), and although you sometimes find, placed between them, the entry *pape* (an interjection expressing wonder or admiration), this does not prevent the eye from connecting the two originally unrelated nouns. And there's more. In most dialects of southern Italy, the poppy is called *paparina,* not *papavero*

With regard to the name *Papaver rhoeas* (which distinguishes the red poppy from others that do not interest us here), Pliny assures us that its origin is the Greek *rhoiás,* in turn connected to the verb *rhéo,* which means "pass by, flow rapidly" and therefore, "wilt quickly," which, in fact, the poppy does (*Naturalis historia,* XIX, 53, 169).

Rivers of ink have been spilled regarding the poppy's medicinal qualities. It would be difficult to channel them here into a few lines. Everyone knows that the poppy is an excellent sleep inducer, but it is not enough simply to smell its scent, as do those who must cross the field of poppies surrounding the city of Oz. You must chew them, drink a decoction, or smoke them. But even here, be careful. The omniscient Pliny informs us that "it acts as a purge; five heads boiled in three heminae of wine also induce sleep" (*Naturalis historia,* XX, 77, 204).

On the culinary side, we eat the small, electric blue seeds that are often found in sandwiches, sweets, and pastry rings in many European countries and in America (like the *pasteli* made in Greece and the bagels of New York). We also eat the leaves, which must be gathered, preferably between February and the end of April—long before the stem lengthens and the flowers emerge. But this depends on many factors and thus it cannot be excluded that the lowest and most tender leaves may be gathered as early as November or December.

An odorless oil (*oglietta*) that is excellent for salads is extracted from the white poppy, but it is now used almost exclusively by painters.

BAKED RED POPPY LEAVES

Serves 6

4½ pounds (2 kg) red poppy leaves
5 teaspoons (30 g) coarse salt
¾ cup (200 ml) extra-virgin olive oil
1 cup (100 g) grated Parmesan cheese
½ teaspoon (1 g) ground black pepper

Wash the poppy leaves several times (don't use any leaves that are dry or too close to the root) to make sure no trace of soil remains. Pour 2 quarts (2 l) water into a 6-quart (6-l) pot, cover, and place over high heat. When the water begins to boil, add the salt and then drop in the leaves, cover, and when the water begins to boil again, cook for 2 minutes. Remove the leaves with a wire skimmer, draining well, then dry thoroughly with paper towels.

Preheat the oven to 350°F (180°C). Grease a shallow 13-by-9-inch (32-by-23-cm) baking dish with ⅔ cup (150 ml) of the oil. Lay half of the poppy leaves on the bottom of the dish and dust them evenly with half each of the Parmesan and pepper. Drizzle half of the remaining oil over the top. Repeat the layers, ending with the remaining oil.

Bake until piping hot and the top is golden, about 20 minutes.

SAUTÉED RED POPPY LEAVES

Serves 4

4½ pounds (2 kg) red poppy leaves
5 teaspoons (30 g) coarse salt
½ cup (100 ml) extra-virgin olive oil
1 onion, finely chopped
¾ teaspoon (2 g) ground red pepper

Wash the poppy leaves several times (don't use any leaves that are dry or too close to the root) to make sure no trace of soil remains. Pour 4 quarts (4 l) water into an 8-quart (8-l) pot, cover, and place over high heat. When the water begins to boil, add the salt. When the water begins to boil again, drop in the leaves, cover, and cook for 3 minutes. Remove the leaves from the water with a wire skimmer, draining well, then dry thoroughly with paper towels.

Pour the oil into a 9-inch (23-cm) skillet and place over very low heat. Add the onion and red pepper and cook, stirring occasionally with a wooden spoon, until the onion is golden, about 10 minutes. Take care that the onion does not burn. Add the poppy leaves and continue to cook, stirring constantly with a wooden spoon, for about 5 minutes, then serve.

RED POPPY LEAVES WITH OIL AND LEMON

Serves 6

4½ pounds (2 kg) red poppy leaves
5 teaspoons (30 g) coarse salt
Lemon juice, to taste
Extra-virgin olive oil, to taste

Wash the poppy leaves several times (don't use any leaves that are dry or too close to the root) to make sure no trace of soil remains. Pour 4 quarts (4 l) water into an 8-quart (8-l) pot, cover, and place over high heat. When the water begins to boil, add the salt and then drop in the leaves, cover, and when the water begins to boil again, cook for 10 minutes. Remove the leaves from the water with a wire skimmer, draining well. Dry the leaves thoroughly so that not a drop of water remains. Season at the table with the lemon juice and oil.

RED POPPY LEAF PIE

Serves 6

FOR THE DOUGH

2 cups plus 2 tablespoons (350 g) semolina, or 2¾ cups all-purpose flour, plus more for sprinkling
6½ tablespoons extra-virgin olive oil
1¼ teaspoons (8 g) fine salt
¾ cup plus 2 tablespoons (200 ml) warm water

FOR THE FILLING

2¼ pounds (1 kg) red poppy leaves
5 teaspoons (30 g) coarse salt
⅔ cup (150 ml) extra-virgin olive oil
2 to 3 onions, finely chopped
1¼ teaspoons (3 g) ground red pepper
8 grape or cherry tomatoes, finely chopped
1 teaspoon (2 g) ground black pepper
⅓ cup (50 g) pitted black olives
Extra-virgin olive oil for preparing the pan and brushing the crust

To prepare the dough: Place the flour in a bowl. In a small pan, heat the oil over low heat for about 1 minute. Pour the oil onto the flour, add the fine salt, and stir with a wooden spoon until well mixed. Gradually pour in the water while continuing to stir until everything comes together in a rough mass. Work the dough with your hands until it becomes soft and compact. Cover with a bowl or kitchen towel and let rest for about 1 hour.

To prepare the filling: Wash the poppy leaves several times (don't use any leaves that are dry or too close to the root) to make sure no trace of soil remains. Pour 4 quarts (4 l) water into an 8-quart (8-l) pot, cover, and place over high heat. When the water begins to boil, add half of the coarse salt. When the water begins to boil again, drop in the leaves, cover, and cook for 3 minutes. Remove the leaves from the water with a wire skimmer, draining well, then dry thoroughly with paper towels.

Pour the oil into a deep 12-inch (30-cm) skillet and place over low heat. Add the onions and red pepper and cook, stirring occasionally, until golden, 10 to 15 minutes. Add the poppy leaves, tomatoes, pepper, and the remaining coarse salt, raise the heat to medium, and cook until the poppy leaves are tender and the flavors are blended, for about 10 minutes. Stir occasionally with a wooden spoon to ensure that nothing sticks. There should be no water on the pan bottom; only a little oil should remain. If any water remains, raise the heat and stir to evaporate it. Turn off the heat and let the filling cool.

To assemble: Sprinkle a little flour on a marble or wood work surface. Divide the dough in half and shape each half into a ball. Place a ball on the work surface and flatten with your palm. With a rolling pin, roll out the dough into a circle about 13 inches (32 cm) in diameter. Repeat with the second ball of dough.

Preheat the oven to 350° to 400°F (180° to 200°C). Grease the bottom and sides of a 12-inch (30-cm) round baking pan with 1½-inch (4-cm) sides with the oil. Line the pan with a dough circle, pressing it against the bottom and sides and allowing it to extend slightly beyond the rim of the pan. Spoon the filling into the pan, spreading it evenly over the crust. Sprinkle the olives evenly over the top. Top the filling with the second dough circle and press along the edge of the pan with a fork to join the top and bottom crusts together well. Brush the top surface and the edges of the crust with the oil. With the fork, make some deep holes in the surface (say, as deep as the tines of a table fork) to vent the steam as it bakes.

Bake until the crust is golden, about 45 minutes. The pie may be served hot or cold.

RED POPPY LEAVES WITH ONION AND OLIVES

Serves 4

4½ pounds (2 kg) red poppy leaves
2 tablespoons (40 g) coarse salt
½ cup (120 ml) extra-virgin olive oil
½ onion, thinly sliced
¾ teaspoon (2 g) ground red pepper
½ teaspoon (1 g) ground black pepper
¼ cup (30 g) black olives

Wash the poppy leaves several times (don't use any leaves that are dry or too close to the root) to make sure no trace of soil remains. Pour 4 quarts (4 l) water into an 8-quart (8-l) pot, cover, and place over high heat. When the water begins to boil, add the salt. When the water begins to boil again, drop in the leaves, cover, and cook for 3 minutes. Remove the leaves from the water with a wire skimmer, draining well, then pat dry with paper towels.

Pour the oil into a 4-quart pot and place over very low heat. Add the onion and cook until golden, about 5 minutes. Add the red pepper, black pepper, and poppy leaves and stir well. Cover and cook for 5 minutes. Uncover, add the olives, stir again to mix well, and cook for another 5 minutes. Let rest for a few minutes before serving.

Samphire

CRITHMUM MARITIMUM;
ITALIAN: *FINOCCHIO DI MARE*

SAMPHIRE IS A SMOOTH, HAIRLESS PERENNIAL plant with a woody base, plump leaves that function as reservoirs for water (like all succulents), and yellow-green umbrella-shaped flowers. It grows in bushes on the cliffs of the Mediterranean and the Atlantic, up to the latitudes of Scotland. But it has also been recorded along the rocky coasts of the Black Sea, the Canary Islands, Asia, and North America.[1] It literally emerges from clefts in the rocks and is often inundated by saltwater. It protects itself from this (and from the wind and the sun) by lining its leaves with a thin, peelable outer layer.

Searching for samphire can be gratifying because it is often found in the middle of a breathtaking panorama, but reaching it is not always easy. At a minimum, the rocks sting and scratch, or the plants are very high up. Bothered by ravens and other birds of ill omen, you need to be very careful not to fall into the sea or, even worse, onto the beach, as the Shakespearean character Edgar insinuates when speaking with Gloucester: " . . . half way down [the face of the rock] / Hangs one that gathers samphire, dreadful trade!" (*King Lear,* V, VI).

At first glance, it's difficult to imagine what you are seeing is an edible plant, even if the desire to take a walk with a sprig of samphire in your mouth surpasses that of any other herb, except perhaps purslane (see page 150). But it is edible without a doubt, as those who consumed it almost daily as a way to combat hunger still remember, and as readers of Dioscorides know. He was among the first to compare it to purslane, with the stipulation, however, that it tasted like salt (*De materia medica*, II, 129).

Usually, it is the leaves of the plant that are eaten. Their taste vaguely recalls that of fennel, even if they are more bitter, and decidedly more salty. Raw, they are good for seasoning salads. Boiled, sprinkled with salt, and then pickled along with some spices, they make an excellent side dish for meat or fish. When prepared this way, the highest part of the stem, which is the most tender, is used. On the Isle of Wight, in England, local cooks prepare a sauce from chopped samphire and butter.

John Evelyn, the greatest expert on salads of the seventeenth century, recommends eating the tender shoots raw and says he prefers samphire to most salad greens—it cleans your pipes and stimulates the appetite. He asks himself why it is not cultivated in the vegetable gardens of his village, "as it is in France; from whence I have often receiv'd the Seeds, which have prosper'd better, and more kindly with me, than what comes from our own Coasts:" He adds that it is good pickled, and as an ingredient for salad, there is nothing better (*Acetaria*, 62). Besides these two predominant uses, the tops and the flowers can be fried or used to flavor frittatas.

As for medicinal uses, Culpeper, who defines it as "a safe herb, very pleasant both to taste and stomach," bemoans the fact that it is no longer used as much as it once was, asserting that indigestion and blockage, of which the fragile nature of man is so often victim, could be avoided or at least rendered more tolerable by frequent use of samphire (*Complete Herbal*, 164).

For Castore Durante, samphire produces effects of a totally different sort: "It enflames the blood. It is not good for the young nor in warm weather. But it is good for the old in winter, in small quantities" (*Il tesoro della sanità* [Treasure Trove of Health], 92).

The scientific name of samphire is *Crithmum maritimum*, from the Greek *krithé*, or "barley" (whose grains resemble fennel seeds), and *maritimum*, for the environmental reason explained above. But there is a second reason. Particularly rich in vitamin C, samphire leaves, treated with salt to dehydrate them and then pickled, were once used by sailors to prevent and cure scurvy.

The step from sailors to fishermen is relatively short. And since the patron saint of fishermen is Saint Peter, who fished for fish as much as for men, this green is dedicated to him and often carries his name. But as is well known, Peter is an added name. Before being christened such by the Master, he was called Simon. The reason for the rechristening is also known: needing to establish a church, it was better (if it was to last a long time) to construct it on a rock (*petra* in Latin, hence Petrus, hence Peter), rather than on the sand. The events of the last two thousand years seem to have proven him right.

All of this explains why what is known in Italy as *finocchio di mare* or *finocchio marino* (sea fennel), in France as *fenouil de mer,* and in Spain as *hinojo marino* is not only called Saint Peter's herb in England but also samphire or rock samphire, camphire, passper, roch semper, samper, shamsher—whatever suits the fancy of the *C. maritimum* gatherer hanging from the cliffs of Dover.

We must not forget, in *cauda sine veneno*, that samphire is also the green that timidly challenges sow thistle for the privilege of having nourished Theseus before his struggle against the bull at Marathon (see Pliny, *Naturalis historia,* XXVI, 509, and page 175 in this volume).

The flowers, which are hermaphroditic, are gathered from June to August, and the seeds from August to October. For culinary uses, it is best to gather the leaves when they are the most tender, that is, in spring.

PICKLED SAMPHIRE

Makes 1 small jar

1½ cups (50 g) flower clusters of samphire, pickleweed, or saltwort
1 cup (250 ml) white wine vinegar

Gather only the tenderest parts of the samphire—that is, the umbrellas with the flowers—and wash and dry them well. Then let them "bruise" for 2 days—that is, let them dry on a tray (even better if it is perforated) placed in an airy and cool place.

Place the flower clusters in a jar about 3¾ inches (8 cm) in diameter and 4 inches (10 cm) deep with an airtight cap. Pour in the vinegar, then press on the samphire with a wooden spoon until it is completely submerged in the vinegar. Cap tightly, place in a cool, dark place, and let 40 days pass before eating. The samphire is good in salads and savory pies.

BREAD WITH SAMPHIRE SEEDS

Makes 1 large loaf

3 cups (500 g) semolina flour

2 tablespoons (25 g) active dry yeast

1¼ cups (300 ml) warm water

1½ teaspoons (10 g) coarse salt

3½ teaspoons (10 g) samphire seeds, pickleweed, or saltwort

Pour 1½ cups (250 g) of the flour into a large bowl and make a small well in the center. Add the yeast to the well, then pour ½ cup (120 ml) of the warm water into the well. Using a wooden spoon, combine the yeast mixture with the flour (this will take at least 5 minutes). Cover the bowl with plastic wrap and then with a kitchen towel. Let the dough rise overnight in a draft-free spot.

The next day, mound the remaining 1½ cups (250 g) flour on a work surface and make a well in the center. Transfer the risen dough from the bowl to the well, and then pour ½ cup (120 ml) of the warm water into the well. Starting from the center of the mound and working toward the edge, mix everything well with your hands. In a small bowl, combine the salt with the remaining ¼ cup (60 ml) warm water, stirring until dissolved. Pour this water, a little at a time, into the dough while working the dough vigorously. Continue to knead the dough until it is smooth and elastic and small bubbles appear on the surface (this is a sign that the yeast is working), about 15 minutes. Form the dough into a ball, cover it with plastic wrap and then a kitchen towel, and place in a warm, draft-free spot. Let rise until doubled in volume, at least 1 hour.

Punch down the dough and shape it into a rectangle. Sprinkle with the samphire seeds, then knead the dough for about 5 minutes to distribute the seeds evenly throughout the dough.

Line a loaf pan 11½ inches (29 cm) long, 4½ inches (11 cm) wide, and 2¾ inches (6 cm) deep (or of similar size) with parchment paper. Transfer the dough to the pan, leveling it well with your hands. Cover with plastic wrap and let rise for about 20 minutes. Meanwhile, preheat the oven to 350°F (180°C).

Make a lengthwise slash or a cross in the surface of the loaf. Bake until browned, about 50 minutes. Remove from the oven and then remove from the pan. Let cool in a wicker bread basket.

POTATOES AND SAMPHIRE

Serves 4

3 cups (100 g) samphire, pickleweed, or saltwort
6½ tablespoons (100 ml) extra-virgin olive oil
1 clove garlic, halved lengthwise and green sprout removed if necessary
2¼ pounds (1 kg) yellow-fleshed potatoes, peeled, cut into chunks, and rinsed
1½ teaspoons (10 g) coarse salt
Ground black pepper

Use only the tips of the samphire sprigs, which must be tender and green. Wash them well, then place in a colander to drain. Pour the oil into a pot about 10 inches (25 cm) in diameter and 4 inches (10 cm) deep and add the garlic and then the potatoes. Pour in 1¼ cups (300 ml) water, add the salt and a few grinds of pepper, and stir to mix. Now add the samphire, cover, place over medium heat, and cook for about 15 minutes, checking occasionally to make sure the contents are not sticking to the bottom.

Uncover and stir the contents carefully with a wooden spoon, or grasp the pot by its handles (but don't burn yourself!) and give it a swirling motion, so that what is on the bottom moves to the top and vice versa. Re-cover and cook for about 15 minutes longer. Check that the potatoes are cooked before turning off the heat and serving.

RICE SFORMATO WITH SAMPHIRE

Serves 6

14 ounces (400 g) samphire, pickleweed, or saltwort
1½ teaspoons (10 g) coarse salt
 2 tablespoons (30 ml) extra-virgin olive oil
 2 teaspoons (10 g) butter
 2 tablespoons plus 1 teaspoon (15 g) dried bread crumbs
4¼ cups (1 l) whole milk
1½ (300 g) Arborio or Vialone Nano rice
 ½ cup (55 g) plus 2 teaspoons (5 g) grated Parmesan cheese
 1 whole egg
 2 egg yolks

Use only the tips of the samphire sprigs, which must be tender and green. Wash them well, then place in a colander to drain. Pour 2 quarts (2 l) water into a 4-quart (4-l) pot, cover, and place over high heat. When the water begins to a boil, add the salt. When the water begins to boil again, toss in the samphire and cook for 5 minutes. Remove the samphire from the water with a wire skimmer and drain well. Cut into small pieces with kitchen shears or a sharp knife. Discard the water in the pot and keep the pot handy.

Pour the oil into a 9-inch (23-cm) skillet and place over medium heat for about 1 minute. Add the samphire and stir with a wooden spoon for 2 minutes. Turn off the heat.

Preheat the oven to 400°F (200°C). Grease the bottom and sides of a 13-by-9-inch (32-by-23-cm) baking dish with 1 teaspoon (5 g) of the butter. Add the bread crumbs, swirling the dish to distribute them evenly on the bottom and sides. Pour the milk into the pot in which you parboiled the samphire, place over medium heat, and bring just to a boil. Add the rice and boil for 5 minutes. Remove from the heat and stir for about 3 minutes to cool slightly. Add the samphire and stir vigorously. Then add ½ cup (55 g) of the Parmesan and stir vigorously. Now add the whole egg and stir well, and finally the egg yolks. Make sure that everything is mixed perfectly. Pour the mixture into the prepared baking dish and level the surface. Dot the top with the remaining 1 teaspoon (5 g) butter, then sprinkle the remaining 2 teaspoons (5 g) Parmesan evenly over the surface.

Bake until the rice is tender and the top is golden, about 40 minutes. Let rest for a few minutes before serving.

SAMPHIRE SALAD

Serves 4

⅔ pound (300 g) samphire, pickleweed, or saltwort
   Juice of 2 lemons
⅛ teaspoon (1 g) fine salt
   Ground white or black pepper
   Extra-virgin olive oil, to taste

Use only the tips of the samphire sprigs, which must be tender and green. Wash them well, then place in a colander to drain. If any water remains, dry with paper towels. Put the samphire on a serving plate.

In a small bowl, whisk together the lemon juice, salt, and a few grinds of pepper, then whisk in the oil. Pour the dressing over the samphire and serve right away.

Sow Thistle

SONCHUS OLERACEUS; ITALIAN: *CRESPIGNO;*
SALENTINE DIALECT: *ZANGONE*

IN HIS *PIANTE MEDICINALI SPONTANEE DEL SALENTO*,[1] Salvatore
Presicce writes that sow thistles grow in various types of soil, which is somewhat comforting. Less reassuring, however, is his statement that they grow
particularly well in "disturbed" ground. Fortunately, the author immediately
clarifies the type of disturbance. Sow thistles are found in untilled fields, at
the base of stone walls and ruins, and along country roads and paths—basically, everywhere man has put his hand to subvert the natural order of things.

A favorite plant of those who love the rustic cuisine of the Salentine peninsula, the sow thistle, whose original habitat includes Eurasia and tropical
Africa, now grows throughout the world. It has been spotted in different
parts of California and Arizona (adjacent to urbanized areas, having sprung
up like mushrooms in the desert) and even in Hawaii—all places where it is
considered a foul weed, much like the dandelion (discussed in this volume
under wild chicory).

But not wanting to stray too far—and given that we find ourselves in the
former Magna Graecia (in an area of Salento called, in fact, Graecìa, where
they still speak a type of Greek even today)—how can we not be seized by the

desire to claim that *zangone*, the Salentine term for sow thistle, derives from the *sonchus*[2] that Theophrastus speaks of in *Enquiry into Plants* (VI, IV, 8), where he tells us that it grows in bunches and is good to eat. On the same day one plant is merely sprouting, one is in full bloom and has already formed the blowpipe that will allow it to scatter its seed everywhere at the first breeze.

The English (who do not use it much) call it sow thistle, a term that might seem vaguely derogatory or politically incorrect. John Evelyn gives it only a few lines, as swift as they are mysterious: "Sow-thistle, *Sonchus;* of the *Intybus*-kind. Galen was us'd to eat it as Lettuce; exceedingly welcome to the late Morocco Ambassador and his Retinue" (*Acetaria*, 66).

Much less cryptic is John Gerard, from whom we learn not only that the sow thistles flower all summer and have a flavor that tends toward the sweet and the bitter at the same time, but that "they are eaten as other potherbs are . . . . Sowthistle . . . increase[s] milke in the breasts of nurses, causing . . . children whom they nurse to have a good colour" (*The Herball*, II, 31, 232). The notion of the coloring comes from Pliny (see below). The predilection of Tuscans (indeed, of Italians in general) for salad was fostered by Giacomo Castelvetro, who wrote *The Fruit, Herbs & Vegetables of Italy* in London in 1614. Reflecting on the reasons why his countrymen ate more greens and fruit than meat, he observed the following: "Firstly, Italy, though beautiful, is not as plentifully endowed as France or this fertile island [Great Britain] with meat, so we make it our business to devise other ways of feeding our excessive population [not counting foreigners] found in such a small circuit of land. The other equally powerful reason is that the heat, which persists for almost nine months of the year, has the effect of making meat seem quite repellent, especially beef, which in such a temperature one can hardly bear to look at, let alone eat. . . . This is why we prefer our fruit and vegetables, for they are refreshing, they do not thicken the blood and above all they revive the flagging appetite" (p. 99).

Culpeper adds to the list of benefits of sow thistle, although some of them are over the top: "Three spoonfuls of the juice taken, warmed in white wine, and some wine [this time cold, presumably] put thereto, causes women in travail to have so easy and speedy a delivery that they may be able to walk presently thereafter." He also points out that bringing sow thistle juice to a boil or warming it in some bitter almond oil inside the skin of a pomegranate is a sure remedy for deafness and tinnitus (*Complete Herbal*, 173).

Pliny, in the indispensable (for us) Book XXII of his *Naturalis historia*, asserts that Theseus dined on sow thistle before confronting the monstrous and extremely dangerous bull that roved the plain of Marathon (thus, ground even more "disturbed" than that discussed in this volume's chapter on wild fennel). It was offered to him by an old woman in whose hut he took refuge (a bad thunderstorm drove him indoors) while en route to performing his feat.

To confirm that he was speaking of *sonchus* (and in particular, *Sonchus oleraceus*),[3] Pliny mentions *Hecale*, a poem by Callimachus (ca. 305–240 B.C.), which has reached us in such fragmentary condition that no trace remains of the green that interests us here. Therefore, we have one of two choices. Either we integrate Callimachus with Pliny, or we lament the lacunae in the text that has survived to our time, from which we can deduce only that "she [Hecale, presumably] took a sparkling hollow bowl . . . and poured from the basin, and mixed something else with it . . . , and she pulled breads from the basket and set them down, taking away / those that women set aside for the cowherds . . . normal, the remains of which the miller had not sifted . . . brought olives . . . and placed *ghergherina,* fine bran and that which was still white / in salt to soak, the autumnal . . . " A literal Italian translation of the section regarding this frugal meal sounds like something written by a Language poet.

Pliny must have read Callimachus very closely, given that he returns to this dinner a second time in *Naturalis historia* (XXVI, 50). Here, however, he changes the cards on the table a bit and asserts that *Crithmum maritimum*[4] "is also one of the wild plants that are eaten—at any rate, in Callimachus, the peasant Hecale puts it on the table." To give us an exact idea of the contents of the poem (but not necessarily the dinner) and of the meeting between the very young hero and the old woman,[5] we must go back to the first of Plutarch's *Parallel Lives* and perhaps into the sources of his story.[6]

To give us a sense of sow thistles, however, Pliny is enough (and perhaps more than enough). He writes that there are two types, one white and one black, and that they would look like lettuce "except that they are prickly, with a stem a cubit high . . . which on being broken streams with a milky juice." Then, drawing from the physician Erasistratus of Ceos, he adds that "it carries away stone in the urine, and that to chew it purifies foul breath." However, according to the great Roman naturalist, the most astonishing results can be obtained by drinking "three cyathi of the juice warmed in white wine [to] aid delivery [of infants], but the expectant mother must take a walk immediately after drinking it."[7] He also notes that "a decoction of the stem itself makes the milk abundant in nurses and improves the complexion of the babies." Would it be too much to report Pliny's news that sow thistles can be applied "externally for abscesses at the anus"? And that the juice, particularly of white sow thistles, is an excellent antidote to snakebite and scorpion stings? (*Naturalis historia,* XXII, 44, 88–90).

In the kitchen, the young plant, cooked or raw, is used in salads. You can also cook the young leaves of the basal rosette together with other natural plants like chicory and dandelion. (The sow thistle is easily distinguished from the dandelion because the tip of each caulis has several yellow heads, as opposed to the single head of the dandelion.) The leaves can be dried (in the shade) and served as an infusion (left to steep for about ten minutes). If a cup is taken before the first course of a meal, it favorably disposes the stomach—and perhaps the heart and spirit as well—for the repast to come.

The gathering season for the sow thistle is spring and summer.

SOW THISTLES WITH OIL AND LEMON

Serves 4

2¼ pounds (1 kg) sow thistles
5 teaspoons (30 g) coarse salt
Lemon juice, to taste
Extra-virgin olive oil, to taste

Wash the sow thistles well, taking care to remove any leaves that are not extremely green, such as those closest to the root. Pour 3½ quarts (3.5 l) water into a 6-quart (6-l) pot, cover, and place over high heat. When the water begins to boil, add the salt and then immediately drop in the sow thistles. Cover and cook for 10 minutes, timing from when the water begins to boil again. Remove the sow thistles from the water with a wire skimmer, draining well, then dry thoroughly with paper towels. Season at the table with the lemon juice and oil.

SMOTHERED SOW THISTLES

Serves 4

2¼ pounds (1 kg) sow thistles
6½ tablespoons (100 ml) extra-virgin olive oil

½ teaspoon (1 g) crushed black peppercorns
¾ teaspoon (2 g) ground red pepper
1⅛ teaspoons (7 g) coarse salt

Wash the sow thistles well, taking care to remove any leaves that are not extremely green, such as those closest to the root, then drain thoroughly. Pour the oil into a 5½-quart (5.5-l) pot and add the peppercorns and red pepper. Top with the sow thistles and sprinkle with the salt. Cover, place over medium heat, and cook for 5 minutes. Uncover and turn the sow thistles with a wooden spoon so that those that were on the bottom are now on the top. Re-cover and cook for 5 minutes longer, then uncover and turn the sow thistles again. Repeat the cooking and turning two more times. The sow thistles may be eaten hot or cold.

Strawberry Tree/Arbutus

ARBUTUS UNEDO; ITALIAN: CORBEZZOLO

THE STRAWBERRY TREE IS A BEAUTIFUL and, in Italy at least, an "exclamatory" plant. It is somewhat less exclamatory today than it was in the nineteenth and early twentieth centuries, when pronouncing the pluralized name of the plant (and its fruit)—*Corbezzoli!*—indicated that you were scandalized or surprised, or that you wanted to reinforce an observation.

In some lexicographic repertories, we read that the exclamation *Corbezzoli!* has little to do with the plant with which it continues to be associated, but rather with the (usually) pendulant parts of the male body of mammals (humans included). Indeed, you would be hard-pressed not to find some formal affinity between such parts and the spheroid configuration of the arbutus fruit.

There are, however, many other names with which to indicate this evergreen plant of variable dimensions (usually from nine to thirteen feet) that prefers[1] to grow among the mixed Mediterranean scrub or in coastal pine forests, where it can be found beside mastic and myrtle trees (which are also plants with poor trunks), and beside the holm oak, the downy oak, and, of course, pines. A scroll of its names in Italian would include *lellarone, ciliegia marina, frola marina, fragola marina, albastro, albatro, albatrello,* and *arbuto*. The idea of the strawberry (which its fruit distantly resembles) exists not only in English (strawberry tree) and in Italian (*fragola marina*), but also in French (*arbre à fraises*).

The strawberry tree's scientific name is *Arbutus unedo*. The etymology of *arbutus* is in dispute, and so we must content ourselves with stating that this was the name given to the plant by Latin writers. In the case of *unedo*, however, there is agreement today that it seems to be a witticism of Pliny's: "The fruit is held in no esteem, the reason for its name being that a person will eat only one! Nevertheless the Greeks call it by two names, *comaron* and *memaecylon*, which shows that there are two varieties of the plant; and with ourselves it has another name, the arbutus. Juba states that in Arabia the strawberry tree grows to a height of 75 feet" (*Naturalis historia*, XV, 28, 99).[2]

Gastronomic enthusiasm for the fruit of the strawberry tree appeared in later times. However, the first steps were taken by Lucretius, whose notion of mankind was pre-agricultural and crudely venatic. At first the poet writes, a bit disconsolately: "What the rain and sun / And earth supplied was gift enough for them. / Acorns were staple diet, or they fed / On arbute-berries, which we see today / Scarlet in wintertime—but long ago / There were more of them, much bigger, and the earth / Out of her blooming newness offered much—/ No fancy fare, but adequate" (*De rerum natura*, V, vv. 937–44).[3] But several verses later, from a perspective that seems to recall the animal world, he offers us something much more appetizing: "And Venus joined / The bodies of lovers, in the woods; a girl / Shared a man's appetite, or perhaps succumbed / To his insistent force, or took a bribe: / Acorns, or arbute-berries, or choice pears" (Ibid., vv. 962–65). Although tainted, perhaps, by suspicions of convenience on the woman's part and blackmail on the man's, it is a beautiful game of seduction nonetheless.

With Virgil, the tone of the narration brightens, but the strawberry tree clearly remains confined to the animal world. We read in his *Georgics,* with regard to how the flocks must be cared for during the winter months: "First I decree that all the sheep shall feed, while waiting for the leafy Spring's return, in comfortable folds. Let the hard ground be deeply strewn with straw and carpeted with bundles of fresh fern, lest icy frost harm the soft lambs, inducing foul disease in foot or fell. I also give command the goats shall have good store of arbute boughs, and running brooks to drink of. Let the stalls, screened from the wind, confront the winter sun and meet his beam at noon, what time Aquarius from cold declining star drops on the year's last days his dew and rain" (III, 294–304).[4]

Elsewhere, illustrating Aeneas's grief over the death of Pallas and his orders for the restitution of the body to Pallas's father, Virgil shadows the rough and innocent gaiety of the strawberry tree with funereal colors: "Mourning done, / he commands his troops to lift the stricken body high / and sends a thousand men, . . . / to escort the rites and join in the father's tears / Others lost no time, / braiding with wickerwork a soft, pliant bier, / weaving shoots of arbutus, sprigs of oak, / shrouding the piled couch with shady leaves. / Here on his raised rustic bed they place the boy / and there he lies like a flower cut by a young girl's hand (*Aeneid,* XI, 69–79).[5]

An entreaty of this sort could not elude Giovanni Pascoli, the exceptional Latinist and poet inclined to the funereal lament, who opens his ode, "Al corbezzolo" (To the strawberry tree),[6] with the following verses: "you who . . . / keep your fruit safe / from the snow and frost: // that which takes away from others gives you joy and gives you strength / to fly toward life; / you put forth flowers when every other / throws its leaves to the ground." Pascoli grafts onto this trunk of refined allusiveness an interior monologue filled with the buzzing of female prophets and cruel memories ("Wandering people arrived, and war / was with them; you could hear bellowing / the horns of fierce buffalo from the land, / conch shells from the sea.") Then he adds an evocation of a funereal rite still dripping with Virgilian dew: "The cows turned their heads toward the bier, / green, for on the dead one's forehead were / placed some white flowers and red / berries on his eyes."

And now, leaving the classics and their imitator behind, we find the strawberry tree at the center of one of the most famous paintings of all time and all places: *The Garden of Earthly Delights* by Hieronymus Bosch (1450–1516), now preserved in the Prado museum in Madrid. In the central panel, the painter depicts numerous, hyperbolic berries of the strawberry tree (and other wild berries) bitten or embraced by nude human figures. The mysterious presence of this fruit (and there is very little in this triptych that is not mysterious) explains why in the inventory of objects possessed by the Spanish crown drawn up in 1593, at the time of Philip II (a great admirer of Bosch), the painting appears with the title *The Picture of the Strawberry Trees.* There may or may not be a connection with the painting, but a bear with her front paws leaning against a strawberry tree is, even today, the symbol of the city of Madrid, like the wolf nursing the twins in Rome or the dragon eating a child in Milan.

The *A. unedo* flowers and bears fruit at the same time, such that our gaze brightens on seeing it, due to the green of its leaves, the white of its flowers, and the red of its mature berries. This is a tricolor plant, ladies and gentlemen, something that will make those who still believe in a united Italy very happy.

Arbutus berries are used, above all, to make jam, but in Portugal they also use them to make a brandy called *medronho*.

ARBUTUS BERRY RISOTTO

Serves 4

5 ounces (150 g) arbutus berries (about 12 berries)
6½ cups (1.5 l) vegetable broth
  Coarse salt
¼ cup (60 ml) extra-virgin olive oil
1 onion, thinly sliced
1¾ cup (350 g) Arborio or Vialone Nano
¼ cup (60 ml) dry white wine
⅓ cup (40 g) grated Parmesan cheese
3 tablespoons (45 g) butter

Wash the berries, drain well, and set them on paper towels to dry. Once they are dry, cut them in half and set aside. Pour the vegetable broth into a 3-quart (3-l) pot, place over medium-high heat, and bring to a boil. Season to taste with the salt. The rice will be cooked in this broth, which must be kept at a simmer. Meanwhile, pour the oil into a 4-quart (4-l) pot and place over very low heat. Add the onion and cook until golden, about 5 minutes. Take care that the onion does not burn. Raise the heat to medium, add the rice, and stir with a wooden spoon for another 5 minutes to toast it. Pour in the wine and continue to stir until it has evaporated.

Now begin to add the broth, a little at a time, stirring after each addition and allowing it to evaporate before adding more. After 15 minutes of cooking, add the arbutus berries and stir for 5 minutes. At this point the rice should be tender but still slightly firm at the center of each grain. Turn off the heat, add the Parmesan and butter, and stir so everything is well mixed. Let rest for 5 minutes before serving.

Thyme

THYMUS SPP.; ITALIAN: *TIMO*

FOR A CLASSICIST, OR ANY SELF-RESPECTING reborn aficionado of ancient literature (that is, someone beyond their fifties),[1] a tiger can only be Hyrcanian; a marble sculpture must be Parian; Monte Soratte must be snowy (and the Apennines forested); Sulmona will always be *"gelidis uberrima undis"*; the lover of a poet (Tibullus, for example) will always be a slut who, in the narrow alleyways of Imperial Rome, exhausts the loins of the grandsons of Romulus; and honey—ah yes, the only honey that matters—is from Hymettus. The latter is for the simple reason that on Hymettus, the Athenian mountain that was once very green but is now completely denuded by cyclical (and very suspicious) fires and which has at its peak a cluster of monstrous metal antennae crowning the devastation, grew a thyme so aromatic that the bees were more attracted to it than to any flower. A predictable result of this, of course (no less welcome because of its predictability), was a honey *sans pareil* whose goodness was undisputed throughout the world wherever there were men capable of expressing, in writing, their gratitude for nature's gifts and their enogastronomic preferences.

There are many varieties of thyme (confusing them is legitimate, as well as innocuous), of which at least two are useful in healthcare and cooking: *Thymus vulgaris* and *T. serpyllum*. Pliny speaks extensively of the latter, repeating what Theophrastus had written almost word for word (in *Enquiry into Plants,* VI, VII, 2, and elsewhere), informing us that "most mountains teem with thyme . . . for instance the mountains of Thrace, and so people pluck off sprays of them and bring them down into the valleys to plant them there; and they do the same at Sicyon [not far from Corinth] from mountains there and at Athens from [obviously] Mount Hymettus" (*Naturalis historia,* XIX, 55, 172). In the following book, in addition to speculating that this species of thyme is "thought to be so-named from its being a creeping plant,"[2] Pliny offers us, *more solito,* a list of remedies that are, to say the least, amazing (XX, 90, 245): It is "an especially potent antidote for the poison of marine creatures. For headache a decoction in vinegar is applied to the temples and forehead, rose oil being added; so also for phrenitis and lethargus. For griping and strangury, for quinsy and vomiting, four drachmae of it are taken in water" (Ibid., 246). *Dulcis in fundo*—practically at the end of Book XX, which deals with herbal remedies—Pliny finds thyme in a "very famous" prescription that "is used to counteract the poison of venomous animals. It is carved in verse upon a stone in the temple of Aesculapius at Cos. Take [the weight of] two denarii of wild thyme and the same of opopanax and of spignel, respectively; one denarius [in weight] of trefoil seed; of aniseed, fennel seed, ami and parsley, six denarii respectively, and twelve denarii of vetch meal. These are ground and passed through a sieve and then kneaded with the best wine obtainable into lozenges, each [with the weight] of one victoriatus. One of these is given at a time mixed with three cyathi of wine. King Antiochus the Great is said to have used this preparation as an antidote for the poison of all venomous creatures except the asp" (*Naturalis historia,* XX, 100, 264). Lucky Antioch, who knew how much a victoriatus weighed! Presuming that no reader would want to experiment with the effectiveness of this formula, we will refrain from further specifications.

Virgil proposes a much simpler preparation in his second eclogue (vv. 10–11), where Croydon recalls that Thestylis, whose love is unrequited by the cruel Alexis, grinds together flavorful herbs in a mortar (for harvesters consumed by the midsummer heat) that turn out to be thyme (and rue) and garlic. But who knows what flavor garlic had in antiquity? In any case, the consoling rural and woodsy atmosphere we breathe in Virgil allows us to overlook these practical details. The important thing is to stay far away from bricks and from the paved streets of the city. "Though Pallas blessed the towered citadels she herself did build, dearer than they to us [are] our woods and wilds." (vv. 61–62).[3]

Hildegard von Bingen teaches that if you can't tolerate garlic, thyme can be used in its place. If someone has leprosy, writes the musical and medicinal abbess, "season thyme with other herbs and spices [but which ones?]. Rub this on the leprosy. Its heat and strength will diminish the rotten matter in any kind of leprosy." It should never be used by itself, however, because "its strength would perforate ulcers"—and we wouldn't want that. Further, if a bit of soil remains attached to the roots and a fragrant bath is prepared, or if it is placed in a cauldron of water (again with other herbs and some surrounding soil), it can be used to make something resembling a sauna. But the important thing is never to remove the soil and to repeat the operation often, after which the *pravos humores* [nasty fluids] will certainly decrease (unless, of course, God has decided otherwise). No divine interference, however, is recorded for ocular diseases: "If old age or some other infirmity is causing blood and water in someone's eye, weakening him beyond measure, he should stare at green thyme until his eyes are damp, as if by crying. This makes them pure and clear, since the greenness of that herb carries away the eye disorder" (*Physica,* CCXXIII). Back in my day, to cure sties, you held your eye pressed against the neck of a bottle filled with olive oil.

Culpeper is a little like Pliny in that, for him, thyme cures almost everything, from whooping cough to worms, from gout to migraines—not to mention its excellent results in facilitating both the menstrual cycle and childbirth (since it's a plant subject to the influence of Venus). This is true for both cultivated thyme and, in particular, for the wild variety (also known as mother of thyme). The latter is "excellently good" in the treatment of frenzy and of lethargy "although they are two contrary diseases" (*Complete Herbal,* 183–84).

From Cattabiani comes the invitation to reread what Cesare Ripa,[4] the scholar and *trinciante,* or "carver" (that is, one skilled at the cutting of meats), wrote at the end of the sixteenth century in his verbal-visual *Iconologia, overo Descrittione Dell'imagini Universale cavate dall'Antichità et da altri Luoghi* (Iconology, or a Description of Universal images drawn from Antiquity and from other Places) regarding the most suitable icon for expressing the concept of diligence: "A woman with a lively aspect, she would hold in her right hand a sprig of Thyme [clearly not *serpyllum*], above which flies a bee. In her left hand she would hold the branch of an Almond tree and one of Mulberry. At her feet a rooster scrapes about. Some call it diligence *a diligendo,* which means 'to love,' because the things that we love delight us, and thus we use all diligence in pursuing them. Diligent industry, or rather industrious diligence, in selecting, choosing the best [he's not talking about politics] is depicted by the Bee that flies above the Thyme. Plutarch, in his treatise *De tranquilitate animi,* reports that although thyme is a very dry herb, bees take honey from it, just as men of sense "draw from the most unfavourable circumstances something which suits them and is useful."[5]

Ripa's book was supposed to be useful "to Poets, Painters, and Sculptors, to represent the human virtues, vices, affections, and passions." Whether it was effectively useful to the progress or perfection of the arts is a question that can gladly be avoided in order to continue our journey—a little bit forward, a little bit back, and a little to the side. Abandoning the georgic-medicinal virtues of thyme,[6] our path now leads to some gastronomic uses not readily available on our dinner tables. To do this, however, it is necessary to introduce a third type of thyme (after the two mentioned at the beginning): *T. creticus* or *capitatus* (so-called because of the conical shape of its flower heads).[7] There are also those who call it Persian hyssop, even if, in Arabic, its name is *za'atar farsi,* that is, "Persian thyme."[8] Under the name *za'atar,* in addition to thyme, we also find a mixture of three aromatic herbs, of which thyme is the principal component; the other two are sumac and sesame. In Lebanon, this mixture and olive oil are worked into bread dough before placing it in the oven. The bread is called *mana'eesh bil-za'tar* and it is eaten in the morning, for breakfast. In addition to bread, thyme or its mixture is used to season fried eggs and *labneh*—that is, the type of cheese that also goes by the name Greek yogurt. Finally, returning to local latitudes, thyme is an obligatory component of a bouquet garni (or aromatic bundle) together with mint, sage, and rosemary.[9] Thyme is further recommended because it maintains its fragrance the longest of all of the herbs.

The gathering period for thyme leaves and for the plant's flowering crowns lasts all spring and all summer.

LAMB STEW WITH THYME

Serves 4

½ cup (120 ml) plus 2 tablespoons (30 ml) dry white wine
1⅓ pounds (600 g) boneless lamb (shoulder, leg, loin), cut into about 12 pieces

⅓ cup (75 ml) extra-virgin olive oil
⅓ cup (40 g) finely chopped spring onions (white part only)
  or white onion
1 clove garlic, minced
5 thyme sprigs
1½ teaspoons (3 g) ground black pepper
¾ teaspoon (5 g) coarse salt

In a 2½-quart (2.5-l) bowl, combine ⅓ cup (80 ml) water and ½ cup (120 ml) of the wine. Immerse the lamb in the liquid and let it marinate for 5 minutes. Remove the pieces and dry well with paper towels.

Pour the oil into a wide 3-quart (3-l) pot, place over medium heat, and warm for about 2 minutes. Add the lamb and brown well, about 3 minutes on each side. Add the onions, garlic, thyme, and pepper and stir continuously for 5 minutes. Add the salt and continue to stir for another 5 minutes. Pour in the remaining 2 tablespoons (30 ml) wine and cook until the wine evaporates. At this point, pour in 1¼ cups (300 ml) water, then, when it starts to boil, reduce the heat to the lowest setting. Everything must simmer for 2½ hours. The lamb is ready when about 6½ tablespoons (100 ml) of sauce remains. Remove from the heat and leave covered for 10 minutes before serving.

PHEASANT WITH THYME AND MYRTLE BERRIES

Serves 4

1 pheasant with feathers, about 3⅓ pounds (1.5 kg), or
  plucked and gutted, about 2 pounds (900 g)
¼ cup (60 ml) extra-virgin olive oil
3½ ounces (100 g) pancetta, sliced
2 tablespoons (30 ml) brandy
1 white onion, thickly sliced
8 fresh or dried myrtle berries
2 thyme sprigs
1½ teaspoons (3 g) ground black pepper
¾ teaspoon (4 g) coarse salt

If the bird still has its feathers and viscera, pluck and gut it. Wash the pheasant carefully and dry well with paper towels. Pour the oil into a 5-quart (5-l) pot and warm over medium heat for about 1 minute. Add the pheasant and brown on both sides, about 5 minutes on each side. Add the pancetta and continue to brown for another 5 minutes. Pour in the brandy and cook until it evaporates. Add the onion, myrtle berries, thyme, pepper, and salt and cook until the onion wilts, about 10 minutes. Pour in 4¼ cups (1 l) water, cover, reduce the heat to medium-low, and cook the pheasant for 2 hours. Uncover, raise the heat to medium, and cook for 20 minutes longer.

Transfer the pheasant to a plate. Retrieve the myrtle berries and the thyme sprigs from the pot, pass them through a food mill, and then stir the purée into the sauce remaining in the pot. Using poultry shears, cut the pheasant into pieces and arrange on a platter. Pour the sauce over the pheasant and serve.

Wallrocket

DIPLOTAXIS ERUCOIDES;
SALENTINE DIALECT: *RAMASCIULO*

IT IS NO SMALL STEP from the name wallrocket (*ramasciulo* in the Salento, although some insist on *gramasciulo*) to *Diplotaxis erucoides,*[1] even if the terms refer to the same annual herbaceous plant (although some assert it's a perennial) that grows pretty much everywhere in Italy and the western Mediterranean basin (Spain, southern France, Algeria), preferring fields cultivated for grains and beets, vineyards, uncultivated fields, and the base of stone walls.

The world is divided into two camps on wallrocket: on one side are those who consider it a weed and on the other those who doggedly seek out its leaves because they are good to eat, either raw in salads (when they are very tender) or cooked: first boiled in a lot of water and then sautéed in a skillet with oil, garlic, and maybe a little bit of tomato, as is done with wartycabbage (see page 68). Called *cime di ciucce* (donkey tops) in some villages, the leaves are also excellent substitutes for turnip greens with classic pastas like *orecchiette, cavatelli,* or *strozzapreti.*

Even animals crave them: sheep, goats, and some cows called *modicane* (from Modica in the province of Ragusa) that produce the milk from which Ragusano cheese[2] is made and detest being confined in a stall to chew on hay and sainfoin. These cows give their best only if they are left free to choose a nice plate of *Anthemis arvensis, Medigago ispida, Scorpiurus subvillosus, Calendula arvensis*, and other aromatic plants, *D. erucoides* among them.[3]

The question as to the origin of the name *ramasciulo* yields either silence or hypotheses that need careful verification. Some of my informants support the notion that it comes from the Italian stem *ramo*, meaning "branch." Others claim it is an apheresis of *gramasciulo* and hold that *gramo*—"miserable, unhappy, poor"—was the name given to it by those who were forced to eat it morning and night when there was nothing else to eat. Finally, there are those like Gaetano Tenore, who invites his listeners to think of May (*maggio*), a month in which wallrocket expresses itself in its greatest (*maggiore*) abundance, tenderness, and tastiness.[4]

Better etymological waters flow, as we hoist the sails of scientific caution by recalling the Greek origin of the plant's name: from *diplóas*, or "double," and *taxis*, or "arrangement, order." The seeds are in fact arranged in two rows within the siliqua (the seedpod). On the other hand, the specific name *erucoides* refers to the fact that wallrocket resembles arugula, even if your naked eye and trained taste buds don't really agree.[5]

Various species exist, but they all have the same characteristics: the basal leaves are robust, a little hairy, up to six inches long, and lobed on both sides of the central rib. The upper ones usually lack a stalk. The flowers are showy, characterized by four white petals. They flower all year and are much loved by photographers, who cannot manage to pull their lenses away from the downiness of the plant in general or from the contrast between the white of the petals and the yellow of the pistils.

The *Journal of Allergy and Clinical Immunology* (November 6, 2000) notes two cases, one of rhinitis and the other of asthma, in which the victims were two workers in a vineyard during the period of pollination of *Diplotaxis* (insects take care of that). These are things that happen only in America.

Like all the members of the Brassicaceae (or Cruciferae) family (mustard, cabbage, broccoli, turnips, watercress, and so on), wallrocket needs clay soil and water. It can easily tolerate temperatures even below freezing, but during the coldest months, the leaves disappear. In the summer, they are too hard. They emerge again during the first autumn rains and in spring.

One gathering period is as good as another but the leaves should be tender.

WALLROCKET WITH OIL AND LEMON
Serves 4

3½ pounds (1.5 kg) wallrocket
    Scant 3 tablespoons (50 g) coarse salt
    Juice of 2 lemons
    Extra-virgin olive oil, to taste

Clean the wallrocket well, removing any yellowed leaves and the part close to the root. Wash repeatedly until no bits of soil remain. Pour 4 quarts (4 l) water into an 8-quart (8-l) pot, cover, and place over high heat. When the water begins to boil, add the salt and the wallrocket, cover, and cook for 10 minutes, timing from when the water begins to boil again. Remove the wallrocket from the water with a wire skimmer, draining well, then pat thoroughly dry with paper towels. Season the wallrocket at the table with the lemon juice and oil.

BAKED WALLROCKET WITH PARMESAN
Serves 4

2¼ pounds (1 kg) wallrocket
    Scant 3 tablespoons (50 g) coarse salt
⅓   cup (75 ml) extra-virgin olive oil
1¾ teaspoons (4 g) ground black pepper
1   cup (100 g) grated Parmesan cheese

Clean the wallrocket well, removing any yellowed leaves and the part close to the root. Wash repeatedly until no bits of soil remain. Pour 4 quarts (4 l) water into an 8-quart (8-l) pot, cover, and place over high heat. When the water begins to boil, add the salt and the wallrocket and cook for 5 minutes, timing from when the water begins to boil again. Remove the wallrocket from the water with a wire skimmer, draining well.

Preheat the oven to 350°F (180°C). Drizzle about half of the oil over the bottom of a shallow 12-by-8-inch (30-by-20-cm) baking dish. Fill with the wallrocket, arranging it in an even layer. Sprinkle with the pepper, drizzle the remaining oil evenly over the top, and then sprinkle with the Parmesan. Bake until piping hot and the top is golden, about 20 minutes.

BAKED WALLROCKET WITH
CAPERS AND OLIVES

Serves 4

4½ lb. (2 kg) wallrocket
Scant 3 tablespoons (50 g) coarse salt
⅔ cup (150 ml) extra-virgin olive oil
¾ cup (80 g) dried bread crumbs
2½ tablespoons (10 g) chopped fresh parsley
1¾ teaspoons (5 g) minced garlic
¼ cup (40 g) capers in brine, rinsed
2¾ teaspoons (6 g) ground black pepper
⅓ cup (40 g) pitted black olives

Clean the wallrocket well, removing any yellowed leaves and the part close to the root. Wash repeatedly until no bits of soil remain. Pour 4 quarts (4 l) water into an 8-quart (8-l) pot, cover, and place over high heat. When the water begins to boil, add the salt and the wallrocket and cook for 5 minutes, timing from when the water begins to boil again. Remove the wallrocket from the water with a wire skimmer, draining well.

Preheat the oven to 350°F (180°C). Pour about half of the oil into a shallow 12-by-8-inch (30-by-20-cm) baking dish. Fill with the wallrocket, arranging it in an even layer. Sprinkle the bread crumbs evenly over the wallrocket, then top evenly with the parsley, garlic, capers, pepper, and olives. Sprinkle a ladleful of water evenly over the surface, then drizzle the remaining oil over the top. Bake until piping hot, about 20 minutes.

WALLROCKET FRITTATA

Serves 4

1 pound (450 g) wallrocket
1 tablespoon (20 g) coarse salt
4 teaspoons (20 ml) extra-virgin olive oil
¾ teaspoon (5 g) fine salt
1 teaspoon (2 g) ground black pepper
4 eggs
½ cup (50 g) grated Parmesan cheese

Clean the wallrocket well, removing any yellowed leaves and the part close to the root. Wash repeatedly until no bits of soil remain. Pour 4 quarts (4 l) water into an 8-quart (8-l) pot, cover, and place over high heat. When the water begins to boil, add the coarse salt and the wallrocket, cover partially, and cook for 10 minutes, timing from when the water begins to boil again. Remove the wallrocket from the water with a wire skimmer, draining well, then dry thoroughly with paper towels. Using a knife, cut into pieces about ¾ inch (2 cm) long and place in a bowl. Season with the oil, ½ teaspoon (3 g) of the fine salt, and the pepper.

In a bowl, beat the eggs with a fork for about 1 minute. Add the Parmesan and the remaining ¼ teaspoon (2 g) fine salt and mix well. Put the wallrocket in an 8-inch (20-cm) nonstick skillet and place over medium heat. Pour in the beaten eggs and cook for about 10 minutes, shaking the pan every 2 minutes to keep the frittata from sticking. Remove the skillet from the heat. With a wooden spatula, check that the edges and the center of the frittata did not stick, then slide the frittata onto a plate (this frittata is not turned). The frittata may be eaten cold or hot.

STEWED WALLROCKET

Serves 4

2¼ pounds (1 kg) wallrocket
2 tablespoons (40 g) coarse salt
¼ cup (60 ml) extra-virgin olive oil
1 onion, thinly sliced
4 teaspoons (5 g) chopped fresh parsley
½ cup (50 g) grated pecorino cheese
1½ teaspoons (4 g) ground red pepper

Clean the wallrocket well, removing any yellowed leaves and the part close to the root. Wash repeatedly until no bits of soil remain. Pour 4 quarts (4 l) water into an 8-quart (8-l) pot, cover, and place over high heat. When the water begins to boil, add the salt and the wallrocket, cover, and cook for 5 minutes, timing from when the water begins to boil again. Remove the wallrocket from the water with a wire skimmer, draining well. Scoop out and reserve 1 tablespoon (15 g) of the cooking water.

Pour the oil into a pot about 9½ inches (24 cm) in diameter and 5 inches (12 cm) deep. Layer half each of the onion, parsley, wallrocket, pecorino, and red pepper in the pot. Repeat the layers with the remaining ingredients. Drizzle the reserved cooking water evenly over the top. Cover, place over very low heat, and cook for about 20 minutes, stirring a couple of times. Let rest, uncovered, for about 15 minutes before serving. This dish is usually served hot, but it is also good cold.

Wild Arugula

ERUCA VESICARIA; ITALIAN: *RUCOLA SELVATICA;*
SALENTINE DIALECT: *RAMASCIULO*

The fragrance of country herbs on the plate at Cesaretto's, rucola
anise a salad of herbs from the earth tender expansive of humours

the sky here that intervenes on people co-present horizontal
and you, and you, anyone who asks you to dance lights up
your eyes and shows his looks and grows
                              red wine
                                        capers and pillow fights[1]

ELIO PAGLIARANI, *"Physics Lesson"*

THE ENTHUSIASM THAT EMERGES from this sketch of *joie de vivre*—
from the choice of words, the emphatic repetition at the beginning of the text
(country herbs, herbs from the earth), plus the very joyful semantic "tossing
out" of the herbs that do not "exude" but "expand" the moods and the sky
that does not "threaten" but "intervenes." In essence, all the elocutionary and

syntactic refinement with which poet Elio Pagliarani captures the enduringly rustic (and exquisite) flavors in a dish served at Cesaretto's, a trattoria in Rome much visited by artists and intellectuals,[2] could lead to the idea that arugula (and the pimpernel accompanying it) has always been happily installed among the alimentary habits of Italians. Actually, although known since antiquity, arugula was always more appreciated (beyond its peasant associations) for its medicinal virtues rather than as a dish for refined palates. Even the great vinegarist and salad maker John Evelyn considers it merely a "side-kick" whose merits depend on the company it keeps "with Lettuce, Purcelain [sic], and the rest" (*Acetaria,* 60).

Pagliarani's poem is from 1964, and obviously many things have changed since then. Arugula or rocket (or *rucola,* as it is most widely known in Italy) is now cultivated feverishly. It is washed, dried, and plasticized by the preservative industry and wolfed down with illusory advantageousness by all those who are forced to put a good face on a bad joke, as well as by those who have not yet noticed that the rediscovery of arugula as an edible plant ceased being something new years ago.

We must search for the true variety, however, the kind that grows and spreads with frightening speed throughout Italy below an altitude of thirty-three hundred feet in places that are uncultivated, sandy, at the edge of roads, and along the dry beds of rivers. This wild variety is slightly tougher to the touch and taste, but ten thousand times more flavorful than the kind the "demands of the market" have popularized, with devastating and disheartening effects.

Dioscorides (*De materia medica,* II, 170) holds that arugula, if eaten raw in large quantities, is a potent aphrodisiac. He adds that the same effect is produced by the seeds, which, being "uretical and digestive," are also good for the stomach. As a final point (so to speak), Dioscorides warns that wild arugula—especially that gathered in western Iberia—has a much sharper flavor than the cultivated variety.

Michele Savonarola rages rather strongly against wild arugula. It seems to him that in order to eat it, the plant must "be grown in a garden and cooked . . . . It makes the head hurt, excites the blood. Therefore, those with cholera and the sanguinary should abstain from it. Although it increases flatulence and Galen . . . numbers it among the bad foods, its use makes milk production abundant." Nevertheless, in the end, almost sorry for the low opinion in which he holds it, he adds, "I will not omit some praise of it: its seed, ground up with wine and placed on an abscess caused by the plague, is an excellent medicine" (*Libreto,* 75–76).

Even Nicholas Culpeper holds that the edibility of wild arugula is measurable only among the cultivated variety, and he has a low opinion of its medicinal function as well. Like a responsible herbalist, however, he deals exclusively with the wild variety, forbidding its use unaccompanied by other greens: the pungent taste of arugula "fumes into the head," causing headaches. Up to this point, there is agreement with the views of Savonarola, his colleague active in the Estense court of Ferrara. In contradiction to Savonarola, however, he assures that the harms caused by arugula are minor in people of hot temperament and among those with cholera, for the simple reason that the fear of "enflaming" one's blood even more suggests that these people should eat little of it. In addition to being a physician, Culpeper is a subtle humorist.

He then confirms that arugula is highly effective in increasing sperm and, according to custom, in arousing passion. The seeds neutralize the venom of snakes and scorpions and drive out worms and other repugnant creatures that live in the intestine. The list continues relentlessly: "A decoction of its seeds takes away the ill scent of the arm-pits, increases milk in nurses, and wastes the spleen. The seed mixed with honey and used on the face cleanses the skin . . . and used with vinegar, takes away freckles and redness in the face or other parts." There's more: diluted "with the gall of an ox, it mends foul scars, black and blue spots, and the marks of the smallpox" (*Complete Herbal,* 151).

It seems useful, as well as amusing, to record what we read in a common handbook of phytotherapy regarding arugula, and *si parva licet componere magnis,* compare the assertions of today with those of the illustrious and witty English physician quoted at length above: "As food, it stimulates the repression of the organism in the case of asthenia, psychophysical weakness, and convalescence. For a diuretic diet, use it daily for periods of at least 15 days. It can be employed as a disinfectant and to cauterize wounds. Together with burdock and other garden roots, it makes a lotion useful for cleaning the scalp affected by seborrhea." The compilers are a little less certain in evaluating the specific effects of arugula in the sexual field: "It seems [precisely . . . it *seems*] that consumption of the leaves is a valid aid in the case of impotence, and since antiquity [arugula] was recommended or prohibited because of its aphrodisiac virtues" (*Erbe che curano,* 307).

Between one story and another, between rediscovery and oblivion, between the diminution of its therapeutic value and the exaltation of its gustatory fame, we could say that, today, gathering arugula and transforming it into salads or other delicacies also serves to explode the legend that ancient wisdom regarding greens (and much else) is always superior to that of the present. Rather, it is true that every rediscovery should be lived as an opportunity for new exercises for the psyche and new pleasures for the soma. Yes, for it is not at all possible that people lived better when they lived worse, as nostalgic Italians are sometimes wont to say when they think of Fascism.

The flowering and gathering period of wild arugula (the flowers are a beautiful deep yellow) runs from April and May to October and November, but the plants that have flowers need to be left in peace.

PASTA AND BEANS WITH WILD ARUGULA

Serves 4

6½ tablespoons (100 ml) extra-virgin olive oil

⅔ cup (60 g) finely chopped spring onions (white part only)

5 cherry tomatoes, seeded and finely chopped

¾ teaspoon (2 g) ground red pepper

1½ cups (300 g) dried cannellini beans, soaked overnight in water to cover, boiled until tender, drained, and half of the beans left whole and half crushed by hand

¾ teaspoon (5 g) coarse salt

5 cups (100 g) wild arugula

¾ pound (350 g) small semolina pasta such as penne or shells

Pour the oil into a 6-quart (6-l) pot and place over very low heat. Add the onions and cook until they begin to brown, about 15 minutes. Raise the heat to medium, add the tomatoes and red pepper, and cook, stirring occasionally, for 5 minutes. Add the beans and the coarse salt, reduce the heat to low, and cook for about 5 minutes to blend the flavors.

Discard any yellowed or wilted leaves, then carefully wash the arugula. Pour 6½ cups (1.5 l) water into a 3-quart (3-l) pot, cover, and place over high heat. When the water begins to boil, add the arugula and cook for 2 minutes. Then add the arugula and its cooking water to the pot holding the beans, stir well, and raise the heat to high. When everything starts to boil again, toss in the pasta, reduce the heat to medium, and cook for about 8 minutes, stirring often with a wooden spoon so that it does not stick to the bottom. Turn off the heat and let rest for 10 minutes. This dish is typically eaten hot but it is also good cold.

WILD ARUGULA RISOTTO

Serves 4

2½ cups (50 g) wild arugula
3¼ teaspoons (20 g) coarse salt, plus more for the broth
6½ cups (1.5 l) vegetable broth
½ cup (120 ml) extra-virgin olive oil
¼ cup (20 g) thinly sliced spring onions (white part only) or white onion
1¾ cups (350 g) Arborio or Vialone Nano rice
2 tablespoons (30 g) butter
⅓ cup (40 g) grated Parmesan cheese

Discard any yellowed or wilted leaves, then carefully wash the arugula. Pour 2 quarts (2 l) water into a 4-quart (4-l) pot, cover, and place over high heat. When the water begins to boil, add the 3¼ teaspoons (20 g) salt and the arugula and cook for 2 minutes. Remove the arugula from the water with a wire skimmer, draining well, then place on a flat plate. Cut the arugula leaves in half with a knife. Discard the water and reserve the pot.

Pour the broth into a 3-quart (3-l) pot, place over medium-high heat, and bring to a boil. Season to taste with the salt. The rice will be cooked in this broth, which must be kept at a simmer. Meanwhile, pour the oil into the reserved 4-quart (4-l) pot and place over very low heat. Add the onions and cook for 3 minutes. Take care that the onions do not burn. Add the arugula and cook, stirring occasionally, for about 3 minutes longer. Raise the heat to medium, add the rice, and stir for another 5 minutes to toast it.

Now begin to add the broth, a little at a time, stirring after each addition and allowing it to evaporate before adding more. After 15 to 20 minutes of cooking, turn off the heat. At this point the rice should be tender but still slightly firm at the center of each grain. Add the butter and Parmesan and stir so everything is well mixed. Let rest for 5 minutes before serving.

GARBANZO BEANS, WILD ARUGULA, AND TOMATOES

Serves 8 to 10

4 cups (1¾ pounds/800 g) dried garbanzo beans
1½ teaspoons (10 g) coarse salt
Scant 3 tablespoons (10 g) chopped fresh parsley
1 clove garlic
4 cups (80 g) wild arugula
30 cherry tomatoes, halved
1¼ teaspoons (8 g) fine salt
Chopped fresh oregano, to taste
Extra-virgin olive oil, to taste

Rinse the beans well, then place them in a pot, preferably flameproof earthenware, about 6 inches (15 cm) deep and 7 inches (18 cm) wide. They will fill the pot halfway. Add water to reach to within ¾ inch (2 cm) of the rim of the pot. Let the beans soak for 15 hours (if you cannot wait, you can use a pressure cooker to cook the beans). At the end of the soaking time, the beans will have doubled in volume.

Drain the beans, rinse them well, drain again, and then return them to the same pot. Add water to cover the beans by ¾ inch (2 cm). Place over medium heat and cover, leaving an opening of about ¼ inch (6 mm). As the beans heat, watch for foam to form on the surface and remove it with a wooden spoon. You will need to remove foam from the surface at least three times before the beans begin to boil. When the foam no longer forms, let the beans boil gently for about 2 hours, adding water as needed to keep them covered and always returning them to a boil after each addition.

After the beans have cooked for 1½ hours, add the coarse salt. After they have cooked for 2 hours, add the parsley and garlic and stir with a wooden spoon for another 30 minutes. At this point, the beans should be tender.

Just before the beans are ready, discard any yellowed or wilted leaves, then carefully wash and dry the arugula and cut into 1-inch (2.5-cm) lengths. In a bowl, combine the arugula, tomatoes, fine salt, oregano, and oil and stir well. Ladle the beans into a serving bowl, pour the arugula mixture over the top, and serve.

BEEF STRIPS WITH WILD ARUGULA

Serves 6

7 ounces (200 g) wild arugula
6½ tablespoons (100 ml) extra-virgin olive oil
1½ pounds (700 g) beef top round or other tender cut,
　　cut into thin strips (ask the butcher to cut it)
1½ teaspoons (10 g) fine salt
1 tablespoon (8 g) cornstarch
¼ cup (60 ml) balsamic vinegar

Discard any yellowed or wilted leaves, then carefully wash and dry the arugula. Pour the oil into a 16-inch (40-cm) nonstick skillet (or use 2 smaller nonstick skillets if you don't have a large one) and heat over medium-high heat for 1 minute. Add the beef and cook, turning once, until browned on both sides. Add the salt and then the arugula and stir to mix. Add the cornstarch and stir rapidly until dissolved. Finally, add the vinegar, stir briefly, and serve.

BRESAOLA WITH WILD ARUGULA

Serves 4

2½ Cups (50 g) wild arugula
7 ounces (200 g) *bresaola*, thinly sliced
½ cup (50 g) shaved Parmesan cheese
　　Fine salt
　　Ground black pepper
　　Lemon juice
　　Extra-virgin olive oil

Discard any yellowed or wilted leaves, then carefully wash and dry the arugula. Lay the *bresaola* slices on a serving plate. Put the arugula and Parmesan on another plate. Diners take the amount they want from each plate and season their portions to their own taste with salt, pepper, lemon juice, and oil.

SPAGHETTI ALLA CRUDAIOLA WITH WILD ARUGULA

Serves 4

7½ cups (150 g) wild arugula
40 cherry tomatoes, cut into pieces
2 tablespoons plus 1 teaspoon (20 g) capers in brine, rinsed
1¼ teaspoons (3 g) ground red pepper
¼ teaspoon (2 g) fine salt
6½ cup (100 ml) extra-virgin olive oil
2 tablespoons (40 g) coarse salt
¾ pound (350 g) spaghetti

Discard any yellowed or wilted leaves, then carefully wash and dry the arugula and cut the leaves in half. Place them in a large bowl and add the tomatoes, capers, red pepper, and fine salt. Stir everything together with a wooden spoon, pour in the oil, and stir again for a few minutes.

Pour 4 quarts (4 l) water into an 8-quart (8-l) pot, cover, and place over high heat. When the water begins to boil, add the coarse salt. When the water begins to boil again, toss in the spaghetti and cook for 7 minutes. Drain in a colander and add to the bowl holding the tomato mixture. Stir carefully and serve hot.

SPAGHETTI WITH WILD ARUGULA

Serves 4

⅔ pound (300 g) wild arugula
½ cup (120 ml) extra-virgin olive oil
1 clove garlic, minced
¾ teaspoon (2 g) ground red pepper
2 tablespoons (40 g) coarse salt
1 pound (450 g) spaghetti

Discard any yellowed or wilted leaves, then carefully wash the arugula. Pour the oil into a 12-inch (30-cm) skillet and place over low heat. Add the garlic and cook for 3 minutes. Turn off the heat, let cool, and then add the red pepper.

Pour 4 quarts (4 l) water into an 8-quart (8-l) pot, cover, and place over high heat. When the water begins to boil, add the salt. When the water begins to boil again, toss in the spaghetti, cook for 6 minutes, and then toss in the arugula and cook for 1 minute longer. Scoop out ¼ cup (60 ml) of the cooking water and immediately drain the spaghetti and arugula in a colander.

Add the spaghetti, arugula, and the reserved cooking water to the skillet, place over medium heat, and cook for about 3 minutes, stirring everything until well mixed. Serve hot.

ORECCHIETTE WITH WILD ARUGULA

Serves 4

7½ cups (150 g) arugula
6½ tablespoons (100 ml) extra-virgin olive oil
  1 clove garlic, minced
  6 cherry tomatoes, seeded and chopped
  ½ teaspoon (1 g) ground red pepper
  ¼ teaspoon (1.5 g) fine salt
  4 teaspoons (5 g) coarse salt
  ¾ pound (350 g) *orecchiette*

Discard any yellowed or wilted leaves, then carefully wash and dry the arugula. Pour the oil into a 12-inch (30-cm) skillet and place over low heat. Add the garlic and brown for about 1 minute. Add the tomatoes and leave them on the heat for 2 minutes, then add the red pepper and fine salt and remove from the heat.

Pour 3 quarts (3 l) water into a 5½-quart (5.5-l) pot, cover, and place over high heat. When the water begins to boil, add the coarse salt and then toss in the arugula and cook for about 2 minutes. Remove the arugula from the water with a wire skimmer, drain well, and add to the skillet holding the tomatoes. Leave the water in the pot.

Bring the water to a boil again, toss in the *orecchiette*, and cook for 10 to 11 minutes. When the pasta is ready, scoop out about 5 tablespoons (75 ml) of the cooking water and add it to the skillet holding the tomatoes. Then drain the *orecchiette*, add to the skillet, and cook everything together over medium heat for 4 to 5 minutes, stirring constantly. Remove from the heat and serve immediately.

TAGLIATELLE WITH WILD ARUGULA AND SPECK

Serves 4

7½ cups (150 g) wild arugula
5 tablespoons (80 g) butter
2 ounces (55 g) *speck* (2 or 3 slices), finely chopped
6 cherry tomatoes, seeded and chopped
1 rosemary sprig, broken into pieces
5 teaspoons (30 g) coarse salt
½ pound (250 g) egg tagliatelle

Discard any yellowed or wilted leaves, then carefully wash the arugula. Melt the butter in a 12-inch (30-cm) skillet over medium-high heat. Add the *speck* and cook, stirring, until browned. Add the tomatoes and rosemary and cook over high heat, stirring often, for 5 minutes. Remove from the heat.

Pour 3 quarts (3 l) into a 5½-quart (5.5-l) pot, cover, and place over high heat. When the water begins to boil, add the salt and arugula and cook for 1 minute. Remove the arugula with a wire skimmer, drain well, and add to the skillet holding the *speck* and tomatoes. When the water returns to a boil, add the tagliatelle and cook for about 10 minutes. Scoop out 5 tablespoons (75 ml) of the cooking water and immediately drain the pasta.

Add the tagliatelle and the reserved cooking water to the skillet, place over medium heat, and stir and toss for about 1 minute to mix everything together well. Serve hot.

RAW TUNA WITH CHERRY TOMATOES AND WILD ARUGULA

Serves 4

5 cups (100 g) wild arugula
14 ounces (400 g) cherry tomatoes, halved
2 teaspoons (2 g) chopped fresh oregano
¼ teaspoon (2 g) fine salt
14 ounces (400 g) raw tuna fillet, cut into strips

Ground black pepper
Extra-virgin olive oil, to taste

Discard any yellowed or wilted leaves, then carefully wash and dry the arugula. Put the arugula in a large bowl and place the cherry tomatoes on top. (Make sure that none of the tomatoes is too soft.) Sprinkle the oregano and salt over the tomatoes and then stir everything together gently, mixing well. Place the tuna in another large bowl, add the pepper and oil, and stir to coat the tuna. Garnish the tuna with the arugula and tomatoes and serve.

FRISELLE WITH TOMATOES AND WILD ARUGULA

Serves 4

1½ cups (30 g) wild arugula
4 *friselle* (see note)
1 clove garlic (optional)
12 cherry tomatoes, halved
2 teaspoons (2 g) chopped fresh oregano
½ teaspoon (3 g) fine salt
2 tablespoons plus 1 teaspoon (35 ml) extra-virgin olive oil

Discard any yellowed or wilted leaves, then carefully wash and dry the arugula. If you like, rub the surface of the *friselle* with the garlic. Pour 4 cups (4 l) water into a 2-quart (2-l) bowl, and immerse the *friselle*, one at a time, in the water for 1 minute each. Put the *friselle* on individual plates.

Put the tomatoes in a second bowl. Add the oregano, salt, oil, and, lastly, the arugula and mix well. Spoon the arugula mixture evenly over the *friselle*. The *friselle* must be eaten right away or they will become soft.

Note: Friselle is a dense, hard, dry bread made from semolina flour, used as a base on which other ingredients are placed. This recipe is similar to bruschetta, but made with denser and harder bread. In the absence of real *friselle,* a hard whole-grain bagel can be used.—Trans.

Wild Asparagus

ASPARAGUS OFFICINALIS;
ITALIAN: ASPARAGO SELVATICO

ALL SORTS OF ABSURDITIES have been written about asparagus, something we might not mind were it not so difficult to extricate ourselves from such a forest of unreliable information. Therefore, we will stick to talking about the two or three things regarding asparagus that are (or can pass as) certain—or that at least have the virtue of being (or seeming) interesting.

First, it is a dioecious plant, which means that there are both male and female asparagus, even if, judging by their mature shoots (the edible part), they all seem male. But today, since this neat division that was once so precise (in the soma) has become uncertain (in the psyche, and sometimes even in the soma), perhaps it is better to say that asparagus are plants of a phallic appearance and leave it at that.

Then there's the matter of the name, from the Greek *asparagos,* which in turn derives from the Persian *asparag,* meaning "spear." But don't try to order spears with eggs expecting a plate of asparagus: the combatively Persian etymology has been lost along the way.[1]

Actually, the Romans used this term to indicate cultivated asparagus, and when speaking of wild asparagus (which is more flavorful and morphologically not too distant from its cultivated cousin), they resorted to the term *corruda*. In fact, Pliny notes, "Nature has made wild asparagus such that anyone might gather it here and there, wherever it grows." He adds that the best asparagus can be found on the island of Nisida, not far from the coast of Campania, while for the cultivated varieties, nothing surpassed those that grew in the gardens of Ravenna—three of them reached the weight of a pound (XIX, 19, 54 and 42, 147–51)![2]

Martial, in his *Epigrams,* is frank in stating the difference between wild and cultivated asparagus: "The succulent stalk that has grown in watery Ravenna will not be more palatable than wild asparagus" (XIII, 21).

The controversy is not difficult to resolve, however. It is enough to follow the suggestion of Rutilius Taurus Aemilianus Palladius (fourth century A.D.), which is to transplant the best *corrudae* and cultivate them—that is, turn them into *asparagoi.* In fact, in his *Opus agriculturae* we read the following: "It seems to me likewise useful, and a proof of industry, if we get together many roots of the wild asparagus into one spot that is not cultivated, or at least stony, which may immediately yield some profit from a place where nothing was growing before" (III, 24).[3] This is instead of sowing them, an operation for which he gives detailed instructions (IV, 9).

The cultivation of asparagus is well documented in countless classics of the natural sciences and in the agricultural manuals of antiquity: Cato, Columella, and, naturally, Pliny, who repeats, word for word, what Cato had written at least two hundred years before the so-called Common Era in his *De agricultura.* It is necessary to "break up thoroughly ground that is moist, or thick. When it has been broken, lay off beds so that you may hoe and weed them in both directions without trampling the beds. . . . Plant along a line, dropping two or three seeds together in a hole made with a stick" (CLXI).[4] All of this must necessarily take place after the spring equinox. It also must be fertilized with sheep's dung, which, less than other manures, encourages the growth of weeds—these latter must be pulled up frequently, taking care to not pull up the asparagus along with them. "In the first year," continues Pliny, still following Cato (and not departing much from Columella in his *Of Husbandry,* XI, 3, 42), the plants must be protected "against winter with straw, uncovering them in spring and hoeing and stubbing the ground." This must be repeated for three years, with the additional requirement of "setting fire to the plants in the third spring. The earlier asparagus is burnt off, the better it thrives." But it doesn't end there. It is necessary to avoid "hoeing the beds before the asparagus springs up, for fear of disturbing the roots in the process of hoeing; [one must also avoid] plucking off the asparagus heads close to the root, because if the roots are broken off, the plant runs to stalk and dies off...," then "burning them off, and when the asparagus plants have appeared, hoeing them over again and fertilizing" (*Naturalis historia,* XIX, 42, 148–49). Considering that after all of this effort the asparagus plant, if attended to diligently, will last nine or ten years at most, the question comes to mind whether, instead of growing the asparagus, it might not be much more sensible (and certainly less laborious) to collect them where they grow wild—that is, in uncultivated spots, at the edges of fields near stone walls, in canebrakes, or in lands in which "pounded rams' horns are dug in as manure" (Ibid., 151).

But not everyone agrees with this business of the horns, and Dioscorides writes in his *De materia medica* (II, 152) that it is nonsense. To Pliny (and others) we also owe a long list of its beneficial effects: "Asparagus ... disperses flatulence of the stomach and colon; it improves vision also, moves the bowels gently, benefits pains in the chest and spine as well as intestinal trouble.... It is aphrodisiac and very useful as a diuretic.... as anyone who has eaten it knows."[5] The root is even more special when "pounded and taken with white wine." It "disperses stone, and relieves pains of the loin and kidneys.... Boiled down in vinegar, it is good for leprosy." Pliny specifies that the properties of wild asparagus "are more efficacious than those of the cultivated asparagus [for all of the purposes mentioned above], and those of the whiter kind are the more powerful. Both relieve jaundice." Further, with regard to its aphrodisiac effects, in order to produce any, "the water in which it has been boiled must be drunk in doses up to a hemina [9.1 ounces]" (*Naturalis historia,* XX, 42, 108–11). There are no contraindications. One should know, adds Pliny, that the boiled juice of asparagus can also be administered against snakebite.

And now, even if space is tight, here are two or three Classical and Renaissance culinary curiosities. Apicius (also assumed to be from the first century A.D.) dedicates a pair of recipes to asparagus. In the first (*Patina de asparagis frigida*), asparagus accompanies roasted warblers (*sylvia borin*). In the second (*Aliter patina de asparagis*), he suggests cooking the asparagus with eggs. Naturally, an abundant use of *garum* is also prescribed (*De re coquinaria,* IV, 11, 5 and 6). Apicius had previously (III, 111) recommended cooking the asparagus *sursum in caldam*—that is, not only in hot water but, as chance would have it, doing it in such a way that they remain erect. A real obsession!

Centuries later, in his indispensable *De honesta voluptate et valetudine*, Platina (1421–81), who, if he did not revitalize gastronomy, at least revitalized the dietetics that accompanies it, invites us to his frugal and healthy table by proposing a preparation in which "boiled asparagus is laid on a plate, and salt, oil, and vinegar are added. Some sprinkle it with aromatic seasonings. Eaten in the first course, asparagus combats flatulence of the stomach, brings clearness of the eyes, gently softens the bowels, and is good for pains of chest and spine and for ills of the intestines. Some . . . [add] wine because it is more effective that way."[6]

More than a century later, in *The Fruit, Herbs & Vegetables of Italy*, Castelvetro writes about asparagus with much more enthusiasm, suggesting that the example be followed of those who "take the plumpest spears . . . and having oiled them well, roll them on a plate in salt and pepper to season them thoroughly, and roast them on a grid. Lavishly sprinkled with bitter orange juice, this makes a most delicate dish."[7]

The natural habitat of asparagus covers a vast territory that extends from Siberia to South Africa. After the fall of the Roman Empire, asparagus also declined in Europe (but it quietly continued to grow beautiful, and turgid, in Syria, Egypt, and Spain, under the vigilant eye and expert hand of the followers of Mohammed). At the end of the sixteenth century, the renowned English herbalist John Gerard had to admit that in his country the thickness of asparagus did not exceed that of the quill of a swan's feather. It "groweth wild in Essex, in a medow adjoining to a mill, beyond a village called Thorp; and also at Singleton not far from Carbie, and in the medows neere Moulton in Lincolnshire. Likewise it groweth in great plenty neere unto Harwich, at a place called Bandamar lading, and at North Moulton in Holland, a part of Lincolnshire."[8]

Against all predictions, no great increase in asparagus consumption (cultivated or wild) was recorded after publication in 1974 of *Gli asparagi e l'immortalità dell'anima*. Achille Campanile opens the volume with this statement: "There is no relationship between asparagus and the immortality of the soul. They are a legume belonging to the family *asparagine,* I believe. Boiled well and seasoned with oil, vinegar, salt, and pepper, they are very tasty. Some prefer lemon to vinegar. Also excellent is asparagus cooked with butter and seasoned with Parmesan cheese. Some put a fried egg on top of it, and this works very well. The immortality of the soul, however, is a question that, it must be added, has wearied the minds of philosophers for centuries. Furthermore, asparagus is eaten, while the immortality of the soul is not."[9]

The best period for gathering wild asparagus is February to April.

BAKED WILD ASPARAGUS

Serves 4

1 pound (500 g) wild asparagus
5 teaspoons (30 g) coarse salt
4 tablespoons (60 ml) extra-virgin olive oil
1 clove garlic, finely chopped
½ teaspoon (1 g) ground black pepper
1 cup (100 g) grated Parmesan cheese

Use only the tender top portion of the asparagus and wash carefully. Pour 2 quarts (2 l) water into a 4-quart (4-l) pot, cover, and place over high heat. When the water begins to boil, add the salt and toss in the asparagus, cover, and cook for 5 minutes, timing from when the water begins to boil again. Remove the asparagus from the water with a wire skimmer, draining well.

Preheat the oven to 350°F (180°C). Oil the bottom and sides of a shallow 11-by-7-inch (28-by-18-cm) baking dish with 2 tablespoons (30 ml) of the oil. Arrange the asparagus on the bottom of the dish. Top them with the garlic, pepper, and the remaining 2 tablespoons (60 ml) oil, then dust the surface evenly with the Parmesan.

Bake until piping hot and the top is golden, about 15 minutes.

BAKED WILD ASPARAGUS WITH
CAPERS AND OLIVES

Serves 4

1 pound (500 g) wild asparagus
5 teaspoons (30 g) coarse salt
4 tablespoons (60 ml) extra-virgin olive oil
1 clove garlic, finely chopped

½ cup (55 g) dried bread crumbs
4 teaspoons (5 g) minced fresh parsley
2 tablespoons plus 1 teaspoon (20 g) capers in brine, rinsed
⅓ cup (50 g) pitted black olives
1¾ teaspoons (4 g) ground black pepper

Use only the tender top portion of the asparagus and wash carefully. Pour 2 quarts (2 l) water into a 4-quart pot, cover, and place over high heat. When the water begins to boil, add the salt and toss in the asparagus, cover, and cook for 5 minutes, timing from when the water begins to boil again. Remove the asparagus from the water with a wire skimmer, draining well.

Preheat the oven to 350°F (180°C). Oil the bottom and sides of a shallow 11-by-7-inch (28-by-18-cm) baking dish with 2 tablespoons (30 ml) of the oil. Arrange half of the asparagus on the bottom of the dish and sprinkle with the garlic. Dust the surface with half of the bread crumbs and scatter the parsley, capers, olives, and half of the pepper over the top. Make a second layer of asparagus and cover with the remaining bread crumbs and pepper. Sprinkle the surface with a little water and drizzle the remaining 2 tablespoons (30 ml) oil evenly over the top.

Bake until piping hot and the top is golden, about 15 minutes.

WILD ASPARAGUS WITH OIL AND LEMON

Serves 2

14 ounces (400 g) wild asparagus
1 tablespoon (20 g) coarse salt
Lemon juice, to taste
Extra-virgin olive oil, to taste

Use only the tender top portion of the asparagus and wash carefully. Pour 6½ cups (1.5 l) water into a 3-quart (3-l) pot, cover, and place over high heat. When the water begins to boil, add the salt and toss in the asparagus, cover, and cook for 5 minutes, timing from when the water begins to boil again. Remove the asparagus from the water with a wire skimmer, then rinse under cold running water and drain well. Absolutely no water should remain. Season at the table with the lemon juice and oil.

WILD ASPARAGUS WITH HARD-BOILED EGGS

Serves 2

14 ounces (400 g) wild asparagus
4 eggs
1 tablespoon (20 g) coarse salt
2 tablespoons (30 ml) extra-virgin olive oil

Use only the tender top portion of the asparagus and wash carefully. Pour 6½ cups (1.5 l) water into a 3-quart (3-l) pot, cover, and place over high heat. When the water begins to boil, add the salt and toss in the asparagus, cover, and cook for 5 minutes, timing from when the water begins to boil again. Remove the asparagus from the water with a wire skimmer, then rinse under cold running water and drain well. Absolutely no water should remain. Place on a serving plate.

Now pour 1 quart (1 l) water into a 2½-quart (2.5-l) saucepan, put the eggs in the pan, cover, and place over medium heat. From the moment the water begins to boil, cook the eggs for 5 minutes. Remove the pan from the heat, drain off the hot water, leaving the eggs in the pan, and refill the pan with cold water. When the eggs are cool, peel them and quarter each egg lengthwise.

Garnish the asparagus with the eggs, then drizzle the oil over the asparagus and eggs and serve.

WILD ASPARAGUS FRITTATA

Serves 4

14 ounces (400 g) wild asparagus
6 eggs
¾ teaspoon (5 g) fine salt
1½ teaspoons (3 g) ground black pepper
¼ cup (30 g) dried bread crumbs, moistened with water and squeezed dry
2 tablespoons (15 g) grated pecorino cheese
4 teaspoons (20 ml) extra-virgin olive oil

Use only the ends of the asparagus shoots, the last 2 to 2½ inches (5 to 6 cm), and wash carefully. Pour 1 quart (1 l) water into a 1½-quart (1.5-l) saucepan, cover, and place over medium-high heat. When the water begins to boil, add the asparagus, cover, and cook for 2 minutes, timing from when the water begins to boil again. Remove the asparagus from the water with a wire skimmer and drain well.

In a bowl, beat the eggs with a fork for about 1 minute. Add the salt, pepper, and bread crumbs and beat again, mixing thoroughly. Add the pecorino and continue to stir until everything is well combined. Add the asparagus and mix again.

Line the bottom and sides of a 9-inch (23-cm) nonstick skillet with parchment paper (which prevents the frittata from sticking to the bottom, making turning it easier). Pour in the oil and place the pan over medium-low heat for 3 minutes, swirling the pan once or twice to help distribute the oil evenly. After 3 minutes, add the contents of the bowl to the pan, taking care to spread it evenly. Cover and cook for 10 minutes. Uncover about every 3 minutes and, with a wooden spatula, check that the edges of the frittata are not sticking. After 10 minutes, uncover, invert a plate slightly larger than the skillet on top of the pan, and turn the skillet and plate together so the frittata falls onto the plate. Slide the frittata, browned side up, back into the skillet and cook, uncovered, over low heat for 10 minutes. Turn off the heat and slide the frittata onto a plate. The frittata may be eaten cold or hot.

––––––––––––

POTATOES AND WILD ASPARAGUS

Serves 4

⅔ pound (300 g) wild asparagus
⅓ cup (75 ml) extra-virgin olive oil
1 clove garlic, halved lengthwise and green sprout removed
  if necessary
2¼ pounds (1 kg) yellow-fleshed potatoes, peeled, quartered,
  and rinsed
1½ teaspoons (10 g) coarse salt

Use only the tender top portion of the asparagus and wash carefully. Pour the oil into a pot about 9 inches (23 cm) in diameter and 4 inches (10 cm) deep and add the garlic and potatoes. Pour in 1 cup (240 ml) water, add the salt, and stir to mix. Place the asparagus on top of the potatoes. Cover the pot, place over medium heat, and cook for about 15 minutes. Uncover and stir the contents carefully with a wooden spoon, or grasp the pot by its handles (but don't burn yourself!) and give it a swirling motion, so that what is on the bottom moves to the top and vice versa without breaking. Re-cover and cook for about 15 minutes longer. Check that the potatoes are cooked before turning off the heat and serving.

MEAT LOAF WITH WILD ASPARAGUS

Serves 4

⅔ pound (300 g) wild asparagus
½ pound (225 g) ground beef sirloin
1½ ounces (20 g) bread without crust (about 1½ slices, soaked in water and squeezed dry
3 tablespoons (20 g) dried bread crumbs
¼ cup (25 g) grated pecorino or Parmesan cheese
2 eggs
4 teaspoons (5 g) minced fresh parsley
1 thyme sprig, broken into pieces
1½ teaspoons (10 g) fine salt
1½ teaspoons (3 g) ground black pepper
5 slices *speck*
¼ cup (60 ml) extra-virgin olive oil
1½ tablespoons (40 ml) dry white wine

Use only the tender top portion of the asparagus and wash carefully. Pour 6½ cups (1.5 l) water into a 3-quart (3-l) pot, cover, and place over high heat. When the water begins to boil, toss in the asparagus, cover, and blanch for 2 minutes, timing from when the water begins to boil again. Remove the asparagus from the water with a wire skimmer and drain well.

In a large bowl, combine the beef, bread, bread crumbs, cheese, eggs, parsley, thyme, fine salt, and pepper. Knead everything well by hand. Place a sheet of parchment paper 16 inches (40 cm) long on a work surface. Place the meat mixture in the center and shape it into a loaf about 9 inches (23 cm) long. Lay the *speck* slices in a single layer on top. Place the asparagus in a single layer on top of the *speck*. Now roll up the meat loaf in the paper, wrapping it tightly and twisting the ends, like a wrapped caramel candy.

Pour 2 quarts (2 l) water into a 4-quart (4-l) pot, cover, and place over medium heat. When the water begins to boil, place the wrapped meat loaf in the pan, cover, and cook for 10 minutes. Uncover, turn the meatloaf over, re-cover, and cook for 10 minutes longer. Using a wire skimmer, remove the meat loaf from the pan, place it on a flat plate, and let cool inside the paper.

Unwrap the cooled meat loaf and discard the paper. If you find any residual water, dry it carefully with a paper towel. Pour the oil into a 10½-inch (26-cm) nonstick skillet and place over medium heat for about 3 minutes. Place the meat loaf in the hot oil and cook, turning as needed with a wooden spatula, until browned on all sides, about 10 minutes total. Pour the wine over the meat loaf and cook until the wine evaporates, about 3 minutes. Finally, cover the pan, reduce the heat to low, and cook for 20 minutes. Transfer the meat loaf to a plate, let cool, and slice to serve.

WILD ASPARAGUS RISOTTO

Serves 4

14 ounces (400 g) wild asparagus
2⅛ teaspoons (13 g) coarse salt
6½ tablespoons (100 ml) extra-virgin olive oil
1¾ cups (350 g) Arborio or Vialone Nano rice
⅓ cup (40 g) grated Parmesan cheese

Use only the ends of the asparagus shoots, the last 2 to 2½ inches (5 to 6 cm), and wash carefully. Pour 6½ cups (1.5 l) water into a 3-quart (3-l) pot, place over medium-high heat, bring to a boil, and add the salt. The rice will be cooked in this water, which must be kept at a simmer. Meanwhile, pour about 2 cups (500 ml) water into a 1½-quart (1.5-l) saucepan and place over high heat. When the water begins to boil, drop in the asparagus and cook for 2 minutes, timing from when the water begins to boil again. Remove the asparagus from the water with a wire skimmer and drain well.

Pour 4 tablespoons (60 ml) of the oil into a 4-quart (4-l) pot and warm over low heat for about 3 minutes. Add the asparagus and brown for about

3 minutes, stirring continuously. Raise the heat to medium, add the rice, and stir with a wooden spoon for another 5 minutes to toast it.

Now begin to add the water, a little at a time, stirring after each addition and allowing it to evaporate before adding more. After 15 to 20 minutes of cooking, turn off the heat. At this point the rice should be tender but still slightly firm at the center of each grain. Stir in the remaining 2½ tablespoons (40 ml) oil. Add the Parmesan and stir again so everything is well mixed. Let rest for 5 minutes before serving.

Wild Chicory

CICHORIUM INTYBUS; ITALIAN: *CICORIA SELVATICA*

UNLIKE BAY LEAVES AND NETTLES, chicory, which grows in all the fields of the world (with the exception, naturally, of south-central New Jersey, by now reduced to that petrochemical colander that, as Woody Allen remarks in *Sleeper,* even God does not recognize as part of his own creation), does not protect you from thunder and lightning. In fact, it attracts them—without causing damage, however, and even working true miracles. To tell the truth, it is not so much the plant itself that attracts them as it is the Italian name (*cicoria*) that represents it.

The living proof, according to what the famous neurologist Oliver Sacks relates,[1] is Mr. Tony Cicoria, a respected orthopedic surgeon who, in 1994 at the age of forty-two, after having been struck by a bolt of lightning, had, as they say, an experience of "the afterlife." He saw his own body spread out on the ground . . . in a word, dead. About a month after he returned to his senses, literally, and recovered from the shock, he began to feel an insatiable and theretofore unexpected desire to hear piano music. Not only did he learn how to play the instrument on his own, but from that moment on, music became his obsession. In addition to the case of Mr. Cicoria, Sacks relates that of Ms. Salimah M., whose musical passion manifested itself following the removal of a brain tumor, as well as other cases of sudden and unexpected musical passion. But since these have has nothing to do with the word *chicory*, we must set them aside and get back to our story. For his part, Tony Cicoria considers the lightning that he attracted to be a gift of the gods, a grace received that permitted him to access a world of unexpected pleasures: the world of music. However, I would like to reassure and remind all those whose last name is Cicoria (and there are a fair number among Italian Americans) that a name can indeed be destiny—but only once in a blue moon.

As for chicory that is herbaceous (*Cichorium intybus*) rather than human, it is a perennial plant with thick roots, a trunk as erect as it is branching, and summer-blooming flowers of a beautiful color between light blue and purplish. Although it is sometimes called wild endive, remember that true endive is a completely different plant (*C. endivia*), grown particularly in Belgium and, if it is really good, as expensive as fine cheese.

The use of chicory for medicinal ends, particularly the wild version, is as old as the hills. The plant was mentioned in the Ebers Papyrus, one of the most important medical papyri of ancient Egypt, dating to about 1550 B.C. It is named for Georg Ebers (1837–98), Egyptologist at the University of Leipzig (where the papyrus is held), who acquired it in the winter of 1873–74 from Edwin Smith, an American agriculturalist residing at Luxor. (That's what we learn from the great scholar James Henry Breasted,[2] who eventually produced a scientific edition of it and who possessed a papyrus of his own [named after him] that predates Ebers's by about fifty years.)[3]

Ebers published a facsimile of the text, endowing it with an introduction and English and Latin glossaries, but for the translation one had to wait for the work of H. Joachim in 1890. The original roll, composed of 110 sheets, contains not only magic formulas and spells for driving away evil-intentioned demons (bent on inflicting illness) but also numerous empirical observations. Most notable is the part that concerns the heart, already identified as an organism that propels blood to all parts of the body. Of great value as well are the observations regarding contraception and pregnancy; ophthalmologic, dermatologic, and dental diseases; and burns and fractures. As a final surprise, the text also speaks of depression and dementia, the care of which demonstrates that for the Egyptians, there was not much difference between illnesses of the soma and those of the psyche.

Centuries later, Pliny, referring back to the plant's "Egyptian" fame ("Certain among us have called the wild endive *ambubaïa*. In Egypt, they call the wild kind *cichorium;* the cultivated they call *seris,* which is smaller and has more veins . . ."), enters into pharmacologic details (to be honest, a little confusedly): "Their juice with rose oil and vinegar relieves headache; moreover, drunk with wine, pains of the liver and bladder. . . . " Then, after a few lines of text, "The juice of the boiled-down vegetable loosens the bowels and benefits liver, kidneys and stomach. Again, if it is boiled down in vinegar it dispels pain of urination, jaundice also if taken in honey wine, provided that there is no fever [and what if there is?]. It helps the bladder." Then, without any interruption, in a magnificent gyno-magico-lexicographical crescendo, he continues: "Boiled down in water it so helps the purgation of women as even to withdraw the dead unborn baby. The Magi [Persian priests endowed with supernatural powers] add that those who have anointed themselves with the juice of the entire plant, mixed with oil [don't forget!], become more popular and obtain their requests more easily. So great indeed are its health-giving properties that some call it *chreston* [useful] and others *pancration* [almighty]" (*Naturalis historia,* XX, 30, 74).

Aside from the trust in the curative omnipotence of chicory (*pan,* or "all"; *krátos,* or "power, strength"), it is curious that the appellation of usefulness (*krestós*) accompanies chicory even today in Salento and probably in other regions of the former Magna Graecia, where in fact this herb is known as *cicoriella cresta.*

The Roman physician Castore Durante, although delighted with some of chicory's beneficial effects ("it is very good for the stomach . . . it is the most powerful and effective remedy for purifying the liver . . . it is also excellent for the kidneys"), notes that one must pay attention to how and when it is eaten: "Boiled in water and then eaten in salad, together with greens and seasoned with oil and vinegar, or eaten raw with mint vinegar and garlic and other warm greens, it is not too bad. It is good for you in the summer, while those who are of a hot complexion[4] can eat it in any season; those who, on the other hand, have a cold stomach and are subject to catarrhal diseases should not eat it raw, but boiled in a good meat broth" (*Herbario novo,* XXXVIII).

Culpeper raises a true paean to the water in which chicory leaves and flowers have been boiled prior to distillation, noting that it "is especially good for hot stomachs, and in agues, either pestilential or of long continuance; for swoonings and passions of the heart, for the heat and head-ache in children, and for the blood and liver. The said water, or the juice, or the bruised leaves applied outwardly, allay swellings, inflammations, St. Anthony's fire, pushes, wheals, and pimples, especially used with a little vinegar." Further, the chicory water produces benefits both for tired and reddened eyes and for the breasts of nursemaids too swollen with milk (*Complete Herbal,* 177). Finally, chicory "strengthens the liver and veins, it opens obstructions, stoppings in the liver and spleen, being boiled in white wine and the decoction dr[u]nk" (Ibid., 220).

For all the perplexity that might be aroused by a combined shot of ancient and protomodern cures like those noted above, chicory's medicinal virtues are solidly certified. "As a fresh vegetable, in infusion or decoction (and the water in which it is cooked)," write the authors of *Erbe che curano,*[5] chicory is useful "for purifying the blood, kidneys, and liver; for constipation and digestive problems; baths and compresses; and for diseases of the skin. The cooked root is crushed and the juice applied to the skin of the face (or other zones) as a refreshing, softening, decongestive mask."

In the kitchen, it is much appreciated for its somewhat bitter taste and can be eaten raw in salads, boiled, and even stewed. You must remember to pick the plant before it flowers, because afterward, it becomes too hard. In a burst of enthusiasm, Massimo Vaglio speaks of table chicory this way: "It is practically the queen of wild Salentine vegetables (better than *fogghie,* a term used in the Salento to define all species of greens sought after for their rosette of edible leaves), owing both to its conspicuous diffusion and to the length of its vegetative cycle, which renders it available for a long period of the year, with the exception of the hottest months. With the first thunderstorms at the end of the summer, the chicory plants emerge and continue to sprout until late spring, when they send forth the central shoots that . . . if harvested in the first growing stage, are truly delicious."[6]

It is well known that the root, toasted and ground, can be used as a substitute for coffee or as its additive. It seems all of that began in the Napoleonic era, but it was certainly everyday practice during World War II, given the scarcity of genuine coffee in all European nations involved in the conflict.

Chicory's basal rosette, the part most desired by collectors, can easily be confused with that of other greens. This confusion ceases when the plants become adult, but as I said, we are interested in those that are young, incipient, and fresh, like the women in *Don Giovanni,* whose "predominant passion," as Leporello reveals to Donna Elvira, "is the young novice." This temporary difference matters little to John Gerard, who seems worried about the opposite—that is, the fact that in distinguishing them during their growth, "there be three sorts of plants comprehended under the title *Cichoreum* or Succorie, that is to saie Cichorie, Endive, & Dandelion, differing not so much in operation & working, as in shape and forme" (*The Herball,* II, chap. 27, 219).

Giacomo Castelvetro sets forth two reasons why "green salads" are "welcome, tasty, and healthy . . . at the beginning of this completely smiling season [spring]." One is that the cooked vegetables of winter "have become not a little regrettable"; the other is that the greens bring "a lot of pleasure to the eyes, [are] very tasty to the palate, and not a little healthy to human bodies, purging them of the melancholy and harmful humors amassed in the preceding wicked season." Even Castelvetro confuses chicory and dandelion, asserting that "the tender buds of *Cicorea salvatica* (also called dandelion) should be cooked with a little of its root, which should first be peeled then washed; and after that, in making [the salad], first rub the plate with garlic, and finally, add salt and vinegar."[7]

The dandelion—more correctly referred to by its Latin appellation, *taraxacum*—long ago entered into adulthood and was appreciated in its own right. There are many different species. Like chicory, it grows in all temperate zones, particularly in well-fertilized fields, but also in untilled lands and along paths in the countryside. It is a perennial plant with long, jagged leaves. The familiar yellow flower that forms at the summit of a central stem transforms quickly into a puffball, a white sphere that is light and filled with achenes that the wind takes upon itself to scatter.[8] As in the case of the chicory root, the *taraxacum* root, roasted and ground, can be used as a substitute for coffee. The leaves are a little too bitter to be eaten raw in salads, which is why many prefer them cooked (boiled in water, then drained).[9] Its diuretic effects are so well known that in many regions of Italy it is called *pisciainletto* (*pissenlit* in France and piss-a-beds in England). In Milan, where they prefer to highlight the toughness of the leaves that are, consequently, difficult to chew, the dandelion becomes *stracadent* (teeth pullers) and, in extreme cases, *sc'eppa piatt* (plate breakers).

The classics of medical literature also went crazy over the medicinal virtues of the dandelion, but all of them consistently refer to its effectiveness in the purification of the liver and kidneys and as an antidote to formation of kidney stones and, nowadays, cholesterol. They add that the juice of the fresh plant should clear up freckles, while a decoction might perform miracles in firming the epidermis—who needs a facelift?

Regarding the legends and fables inspired by the chicory flower (often known in Italian also as *fioraliso* or *fiordaliso*), Angelo De Gubernatis (1840–1913) goes wild in his *Mythologie des plantes*,[10] a true mine—or anthill—of information. Among the various stories he relates, it is worth transcribing one of them, told in Bavaria, which plays on the Germanic name of the plant (*wegewarte,* or "guardian of the pathways"). At first, chicory was a beautiful, young princess abandoned, naturally, by her groom (a prince who was also young and beautiful). The pain of the abandonment ends with the death of the princess, who makes this cryptic last wish before dying: "I want to die but I would also like *not* to die in order to be able to see my groom everywhere." "We wish that too," the chorus of ladies-in-waiting tells her, "so that he may see us along the roads that he must travel." The good Lord fulfills their desires and changes the princess into a flower with a white dress and her companions into flowers with blue dresses.

The best period for gathering chicory (and dandelion) is from the beginning of October to the end of March, but it depends a lot on the amount of rainfall in the preceding months.

————————

BAKED WILD CHICORY

Serves 4

2¼ pounds (1 kg) wild chicory
2 tablespoons (40 g) coarse salt
½ cup (120 ml) extra-virgin olive oil
1 cup plus 2 tablespoons (120 g) dried bread crumbs
Scant ½ cup (50 g) grated pecorino cheese
4 tomatoes, peeled, seeded, and crushed
⅓ cup (40 g) pitted black olives, chopped
¾ teaspoon (2 g) ground red pepper
½ teaspoon (1 g) ground black pepper

Clean the chicory well, removing the roots and any leaves that are not a beautiful green. If very dirty, leave the chicory immersed in water for 10 minutes to remove any remaining dirt, then rinse in several changes of fresh water. Pour 4 quarts (4 l) water into an 8-quart (8-l) pot, cover, and place over high heat. When the water begins to boil, add the salt and chicory, cover, and cook for 10 minutes, timing from when the water begins to boil again. Remove the chicory from the water with a wire skimmer and drain well. Leave the water in the pot.

Preheat the oven to 350°F (180°C). Grease a shallow 13-by-9-inch (32-by-23-cm) baking pan with 4 teaspoons (20 ml) of the oil. Create layers in this order: the chicory, half of the bread crumbs, half of the cheese, the tomatoes, the olives, the red pepper, and the remaining oil. Top with the remaining bread crumbs and cheese and finish with the black pepper. Pour 5 tablespoons (75 ml) of the chicory cooking water evenly over the surface.

Bake until piping hot, about 20 minutes. You can serve this dish either hot or cold.

————————

WILD CHICORY WITH OIL AND LEMON

Serves 4

2¼ pounds (1 kg) wild chicory
2 tablespoons (40 g) coarse salt
Lemon juice, to taste
Extra-virgin olive oil, to taste

Clean the chicory well, removing the roots and any leaves that are not a beautiful green. If very dirty, leave the chicory immersed in water for 10 minutes to remove any remaining dirt, then rinse in several changes of fresh water.

Pour 4 quarts (4 l) water into an 8-quart (8-l) pot, cover, and place over high heat. When the water begins to boil, add the salt and the chicory, cover, and cook for about 10 minutes, timing from when the water begins to boil again. Remove the chicory from the water with a wire skimmer, draining well. Dry the chicory thoroughly so that not even a drop of water remains. Season at the table with the lemon juice and oil.

————————

SAUTÉED WILD CHICORY

Serves 4

3⅓ pounds (1.5 kg) wild chicory
2 tablespoons (40 g) coarse salt
¾ cup (200 ml) extra-virgin olive oil
1 onion, finely minced
Rounded ¼ teaspoon (1 g) ground red pepper,
or ½ teaspoon (1 g) ground black pepper

Clean the chicory well, removing the roots and any leaves that are not a beautiful green. If very dirty, leave the chicory immersed in water for 10 minutes to remove any remaining dirt, then rinse in several changes of fresh water. Pour 4 quarts (4 l) water into 8-quart (8-l) pot, cover, and place over high heat. When the water begins to boil, add the salt and the chicory, cover, and cook for about 10 minutes, timing from when the water begins to boil again. Remove the chicory from the water with a wire skimmer, draining well. Not even a drop of water should remain.

Pour the oil into a 12-inch (30-cm) skillet over low heat, add the onion, and cook for about 5 minutes. Take care that the onion does not burn. Add the chicory and red pepper (or black pepper, if you prefer), cover, and continue to cook for another 15 minutes over low heat. Serve hot.

––––––––––

WILD CHICORY WITH PECORINO

Serves 4

3⅓ pounds (1.5 kg) wild chicory
     Rounded 2½ tablespoons (50 g) coarse salt
⅔ cup (150 ml) extra-virgin olive oil
1 onion, finely chopped
¾ teaspoon (2 g) ground red pepper, or ½ teaspoon (1 g) ground black pepper
1 cup (100 g) grated pecorino cheese

Clean the chicory well, removing the roots and any leaves that are not a beautiful green. If very dirty, leave the chicory immersed in water for 10 minutes to remove any remaining dirt, then rinse in several changes of fresh water. Pour 4 quarts (4 l) water into an 8-quart (8-l) pot, cover, and place over high heat. When the water begins to boil, add the salt and the chicory, cover, and cook for about 10 minutes, timing from when the water begins to boil again. Remove the chicory from the water with a wire skimmer, draining well. Leave the water in the pot. Dry the chicory thoroughly so that not even a drop of water remains.

Pour the oil into a 5-quart (5-l) pot and place over very low heat. Add the onion and cook until golden, about 10 minutes. Remove from the heat, let the oil cool, and add the red pepper (or the black pepper, if you prefer), then the chicory, and finally the cheese. Add 5 tablespoons (75 ml) of the chicory cooking water and place the pot over very low heat again. Cook, uncovered, for about 20 minutes. Serve hot.

WILD CHICORY WITH PANCETTA

Serves 4

4⅓ pounds (2 kg) wild chicory
2½ tablespoons (50 g) coarse salt
1 pound (450 g) pancetta, cut into 1-inch (2.5-cm) cubes
Scant ¼ cup (50 ml) extra-virgin olive oil
1 onion, finely chopped
4 tablespoons (15 g) chopped fresh parsley
1 celery stalk, finely chopped
3 tomatoes, peeled, seeded, and chopped
1½ teaspoons (4 g) ground red pepper
1 teaspoon (2 g) ground black pepper
2 bay leaves
¼ teaspoon (2 g) fine salt
½ cup (50 g) grated pecorino cheese

Clean the chicory well, removing the roots and any leaves that are not a beautiful green. If very dirty, leave the chicory immersed in water for 10 minutes to remove any remaining dirt, then rinse in several changes of fresh water. Pour 4 quarts (4 l) water into an 8-quart (8-l) pot, cover, and place over high heat. When the water begins to boil, add the coarse salt and chicory, cover, and cook for 7 minutes, timing from when the water begins to boil again. Remove the chicory from the water with a wire skimmer and drain well.

Pour ¼ cup (60 ml) water into a 4-quart (4-l) pot and add the pancetta, oil, onion, parsley, celery, tomatoes, red pepper, black pepper, bay leaves, and fine salt. Cover the pot, place over medium heat, and bring to a boil. Reduce the heat to low and cook for 1 hour. Add the chicory and stir everything together well with a spoon and fork. Finally, add the pecorino and continue to cook and stir over low heat for another 30 minutes. Serve hot.

WILD CHICORY PIE
Serves 6

FOR THE DOUGH

2 tablespoons (25 g) brewer's yeast

1 tablespoon whole milk, warmed

2 cups plus 2 tablespoons (350 g) semolina flour, plus more
for sprinkling

6½ tablespoons (100 ml) extra-virgin olive oil

¾ teaspoon (5 g) fine salt

⅔ cup (150 ml) warm water

FOR THE FILLING

2¼ pounds (1 kg) wild chicory

2 tablespoons (40 g) coarse salt

⅔ cup (150 ml) extra-virgin olive oil

2 or 3 large onions, finely chopped

¾ teaspoon (2 g) ground red pepper

6 small tomatoes, seeded and chopped

⅓ cup (50 g) pitted black olives

6 small tomatoes

1¾ teaspoons (4 g) ground black pepper

½ teaspoon (3 g) fine salt

2 tablespoons plus 1 teaspoon (20 g) capers in brine, rinsed
Extra-virgin olive oil and all-purpose flour for preparing
the pan

To prepare the dough: Dissolve the yeast in the warm milk. Place the flour in a bowl and add the oil, fine salt, and dissolved yeast. Mix everything together with a wooden spoon, then gradually pour in the warm water while continuing to stir until everything comes together in a rough mass. Work the dough with your hands until it becomes soft and compact. Cover with a bowl or kitchen towel and let rest for about 1 hour.

To prepare the filling: Clean the chicory well, removing the roots and any leaves that are not a beautiful green. If very dirty, leave the chicory immersed in water for 10 minutes to remove any remaining dirt, then rinse in several changes of fresh water. Pour 4 quarts (4 l) water into an 8-quart (8-l) pot, cover, and place over high heat. When the water begins to boil, add the salt and the chicory, cover, and cook for about 10 minutes, timing from when the water begins to boil again. Remove the chicory from the water with a wire skimmer and drain well. Cut the chicory into pieces about 1¼ inches (3 cm) long.

Pour the oil into a pan 11 or 12 inches (28 or 30 cm) in diameter and 2¾ inches (7 cm) deep and place over low heat. Add the onions and red pepper and cook until the onions are golden, about 15 minutes. Raise the heat to medium and add the chicory, tomatoes, pepper, and fine salt. Let everything cook, stirring occasionally with a wooden spoon to prevent sticking, for about 10 minutes to blend the flavors. Finally, add the capers. At this point, there should be no water at the bottom of the pan; only a little bit of oil should remain. Remove from the heat and let cool.

To assemble: Sprinkle a little flour on a marble or wood work surface. Divide the dough in half and shape each half into a ball. Place a ball on the work surface and flatten with your palm. With a rolling pin, roll out the dough into a circle about 13 inches (32 cm) in diameter. Repeat with the second ball of dough.

Preheat the oven to 350°F (180°C). Grease the bottom and sides of a pan 12 inches (30 cm) in diameter and 1½ inches (4 cm) deep with oil, then dust the pan with flour. Line the pan with a dough circle, pressing it against the bottom and sides and allowing it to extend slightly beyond the rim of the pan. Spoon the filling into the pan, spreading it evenly over the crust. Top the filling with the second dough circle and press along the edge of the pan with a fork to join the top and bottom crusts together well. With the fork, make some deep holes in the surface to vent the steam as the pie bakes.

Bake the pie until the crust is golden, about 45 minutes. The pie may be served hot or cold.

FAVA BEAN PURÉE WITH WILD CHICORY

Serves 6

3⅓ cups (500 g) dried fava beans
1 white onion, finely chopped
1 sweet potato, peeled and finely diced
2 cloves garlic, 1 whole and 1 minced
½ teaspoon (2 g) ground red pepper

¼ cup (60 g) coarse salt
2¼ pounds (1 kg) wild chicory
½ cup (120 ml) extra-virgin olive oil, plus more for drizzling
½ teaspoon (3 g) fine salt

To prepare the beans: Rinse the beans well. Place them in a 4-quart (4-l) pot, pour in 2½ quarts (2.5 l) water, and let the beans soak for 12 hours. Then place the pot over medium heat without changing the water and cover, leaving only a small opening to let the air out. As the beans heat, check them often, removing any foam that forms on the top with a wooden spoon. When no more foam forms, add the onion, sweet potato, whole garlic clove, and ¼ teaspoon (1 g) of the red pepper. As soon as the water starts to boil, add 1½ tablespoons (25 g) of the coarse salt, reduce the heat to the lowest setting, and cook the beans for 1½ hours, never forgetting to stir often and vigorously so that the beans become mushy and do not stick to the bottom. The final result must have a creamy consistency. Turn off the heat and let the covered pan rest for about 15 minutes so the purée thickens.

To prepare the chicory: Clean the chicory well, removing the roots and any leaves that are not a beautiful green. If very dirty, leave the chicory immersed in water for 10 minutes to remove any remaining dirt, then rinse in several changes of fresh water. Pour 4 quarts (4 l) water into an 8-quart (8-l) pot, cover, and place over high heat. When the water begins to boil, add the remaining 2½ tablespoons (35 g) coarse salt and the chicory, cover, and cook for about 10 minutes, timing from when the water begins to boil again. Remove the chicory from the water with a wire skimmer and drain well.

Pour the oil into a 12-inch (30-cm) skillet over low heat, add the minced garlic (it must not burn, so make sure the heat is at a minimum for a good minute), the remaining ¼ teaspoon (1 g) red pepper, the chicory, and the fine salt. Stir repeatedly with a fork so the salt is evenly distributed. Continue in this manner for about 15 minutes, then turn off the heat.

Transfer the fava bean purée to a deep serving plate and serve the chicory alongside it. Drizzle the purée with olive oil.

Wild Fennel

FOENICULUM VULGARE;
ITALIAN: *FINOCHIETTO SELVATICO*

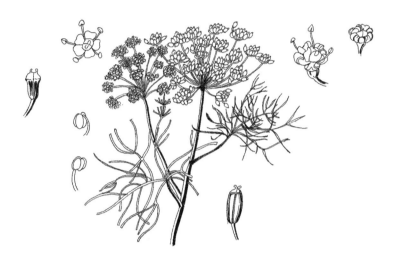

AMONG WILD PLANTS, wild fennel is perhaps the most easily identifiable. It is a perennial Mediterranean herbaceous plant with a thin stalk that rises to six feet in height and sometimes even higher. It seems that its scientific name, *Foeniculum vulgare,* comes from the Latin *fenum,* which is of uncertain etymology but means "hay," and whose leaves resemble those of wild fennel. But how similar is it to hay, really? Who can swear to have the shape of hay leaves clearly in his or her mind? With fennel flowers, on the other hand, there is no problem: they are yellow and bunched in small umbrellas with ten or twelve medullary rays each.

The difference between wild and cultivated fennel is insurmountable. It is useless to uproot the wild species in the hope of finding even the most rudimentary basal sheath (the edible part of sweet fennel that you buy from the greengrocer). First of all, that sheath is not the root (it rests above ground), and if it remains white, it is because growers cover it with dirt to prevent light from getting to it. The taste of anise, however, is shared between the wild and cultivated varieties. It is enough to bite down on a sprig of wild fennel or put one of its flowers in your mouth to convince yourself that it tastes like fennel.

It grows everywhere but prefers the edges of dirt roads. It grows easily, and there are some places, overwhelmed by its presence, that ended up adopting its name. In Rome, for example, Finocchio is the name of the district that extends along the eighteenth kilometer of via Casilina, not far from ancient Gabi (see the chapter on red poppy). But historically, the most famous wild fennel grows in Greece and gave its name to Marathon (a name that means, in fact, fennel), whose plain, which has also been mentioned with respect to sow thistle in this volume, must have been completely covered with it. At Marathon, around 490 B.C., the Greeks (the Athenians, to be exact) under the command of Miltiades, inflicted a lesson on the barbarian Persians, whose king, Darius I, was dying to subjugate them. He had been induced to do so by some overbearing Greeks in exile who had taken refuge at his court. According to Herodotus, the Spartans—to whom the Athenians had turned for help—responded that they would happily lend their assistance but that "it was out of their power to do so immediately, as they were unwilling to violate the law: for it was the ninth day of the current month; and they said they could not march out on the ninth day, the moon's circle not being full. They, therefore, waited for the full moon. Meanwhile Hippias, son of Pisistratus, had led the barbarians to Marathon."[1]

Herodotus also tells of Pheidippides, but he does not connect him in the least with his nice little run from Marathon to Athens (a bit more than forty kilometers, the distance of the modern athletic competition),[2] which left him just enough strength to announce to his fellow citizens "*Níke níke*" ("Victory, victory") and kick the bucket. Rather, Herodotus says that Pheidippides was chosen to go to Sparta to ask for help, and not only because he was, by profession, a herald capable of covering enormous distances on foot in a single day (something unimaginable today even with a Lambretta), but also because "This man, as Pheidippides himself said and reported to the Athenians, met Pan near Mount Parthenion, above Tegea; and Pan, calling out the name of Pheidippides, bade him ask fellow citizens why they paid no attention to him, who was well inclined to the Athenians, and had often been useful to them, and would be so hereafter."[3]

The vox populi (although not necessarily the *vox dei*) prevailed on the authority of Herodotus, permitting the modern-day administrators of the city of Athens to construct a monument to Pheidippides that is of rare ugliness. Whoever enters the city from Marathon, or from the new Venizelos airport, cannot avoid coming across it: plates of glass superimposed and cut in all their grayness and all their disgusting heaviness (it seems that Pheidippides, or whoever did it for him, ran the entire distance without removing his armor) to vaguely represent a running man.

Other than as a toponym, the word *finocchio* (sadly, as is well known) has come to be used with impunity in Italy as a perjorative term for a homosexual. How that came to be remains a mystery, and of the hypotheses that have been formulated, almost none bears up in the face of common sense. Moreover, the expression is Florentine and entered into general circulation only recently. The first to record it was Pietro Fanfani in the *Vocabolario dell'uso toscano*.[4] Older attestations of the term record it as the equivalent of *babbeo* (idiot), as can be read, for example, in the writing of Meo de' Tolomei of Siena, whose records date from 1250 to 1310. Describing his own brother, Mino del Zeppa, as someone so clumsy that he would stick his finger in his eye when making the sign of the cross and so vulgar that he would address God by saying, "May God grant you a good day, Lord God," de' Tolomei concludes by asserting that, because of such foolishness, the least one could do is call him *finocchio*.[5]

We must reject the hypothesis that because fennel has a hollow stem, the noun *finocchio* might be an analogical euphemism for "hole."[6] Also to be discarded is the conjecture that the appellation derives from the fact that bundles of wild fennel (the English term *faggot* means, literally, "bundle of sticks") were burned in the fires of the Middle Ages, to render less unpleasant the odor of the flesh of sodomites burned at the stake. Not only are there no attestations supporting this, but the word *faggot* is of French derivation and dates from the nineteenth century.[7]

We confess to nurturing some sympathy, however, for the hypothesis advanced by Alberto Menarini, according to whom, "the figurative appellation of *finocchio* may derive from the popular mask [that is, the stock figure of the commedia dell'arte] of the same name, which, even if is almost unknown today, played a secondary but hardly irrelevant role in those theatrical repertoires that knew moments of great fortune in the past . . . . It's plausible to suppose that the figure of Finocchio, with his activity as a swindler and a middleman for hire, and particularly with his affected and effeminate ways, may have lent itself to a similarity that corresponded fully with the tastes and mentality of the popular audience."[8] Similarly plausible is the hypothesis suggested by the authors of the *Dizionario etimologico*, whereby the metaphor may have been born of the saying *il finocchio fra le mele* (fennel among apples), an adage innocent in and of itself but susceptible to malicious interpretation, when fennel is seen as a stand-in for the male member.

Undoubtedly linked to the name *finocchio* is the verb *infinocchiare*, which, in Italian, has come to mean "deceive, cheat, swindle," and so on. The association of all these reprehensible actions with fennel probably derives from the fact that the taste of fennel has been used to cover unpleasant flavors, be they of medicines or of spoiled foods.

Because cross-dressing is often a form of deception in the world of show business, the name Finocchio's, which was long attached to a famous San Francisco nightclub, certainly alluded to the homosexuality of many of the female impersonators who performed there. But the name actually came from the simple fact that one Joe Finocchio was the club's founder and owner. The venue, which closed its doors on November 27, 1999, after more than sixty years of history and stories that only a liberal city like San Francisco could welcome self-assuredly, had opened its doors in the 1920s during Prohibition, at the end of which (1933) it left its original catacomb on Stockton Street and moved to the fashionable district of North Beach.

Those who might be asking what all of this has to do with wild fennel *tout court* (the gathering and use of which should be our primary focus here) should know that its medicinal fame dates to antiquity (Egyptian papyri and the like). But so that we do not lose ourselves in the mists of time, let us halt our backward run at the indispensable Pliny, who lets us know that "fennel has been made famous ... by serpents, which [eat] it to cast off their old skin and with its juice improve their eyesight. Consequently, it has been inferred that ... fennel juice [can remove] the dimness of human vision." Forget carrots! "There is in this class of plant," continues Pliny, "a wild variety called *hippomarathum,* by some *myrsineum* ... ." While the latter term sounds like a complete stranger, something can be remarked about the Greek origin of the former in which the prefix *hippo-,* which normally means "horse," assumes an augmentative function of the term that accompanies it, the already-encountered *marathon.* Following this is the string of (numerous) benefits and (almost no) contraindications from which we have come to understand that for Pliny (like for Culpeper, centuries later), if a plant is good for you, it is good for nearly everything—but particularly for snakebite (*Naturalis historia,* XX, 95, 254 and 96, 256).

Michele Savonarola, usually so reluctant to sing the praises of anything, after having promised us observations regarding fennel from the garden, which "digests slowly and gives poor nourishment," mixes the advantages for man and for snakes together, making the surprising assertion that "it comforts sight in every type of administration, such that it is said that snakes that have been in caves (that being their way to pass the winter) rub their eyes with fennel for the restoration of their sight. It is also very effective in the operation of the liver and of the urinary tract" (*Libreto*, 76).

Culpeper writes about snakes, too, but to tell us that fennel is a good antidote against the venom of their bite and against poisons in general. What especially arouse our curiosity, however, are the praises he sings to the old habit of "boil[ing] Fennel with fish; for it consumes that phlegmatic humour, which fish most plentifully afford and annoy the body with, though few that use it know wherefore they do it" (*Complete Herbal*, 73).

The tips and flowers (called *caruselle* in the Salento), if gathered when they are very tender, can be savored in small doses (because of their strong taste) in spring salads and, if preserved in jars with acidulated water, can be used year-round. Stems and flowers, in turn, are used to flavor preserves and the brines in which black olives are pickled in the traditional Salentine way.

The gathering period for the end of the stem with the buds is February to September (from the end of April, in rainy years). For the flowers, on the other hand, the period runs from the beginning of June to the end of August.

PICKLED WILD FENNEL FLOWERS

Makes 1 small jar

1½ cups (50 g) wild fennel flowers
2 cups (500 ml) white wine vinegar

Gather only the most tender flowers. Wash and dry them well. Then let them "bruise" for 2 days—that is, let them dry on a tray (even better if it is perforated) placed in an airy and cool place.

Place the flowers in a jar about 3¾ inches (8 cm) in diameter and 4 inches (10 cm) deep with an airtight cap. Pour in the vinegar, then press on the flowers with a wooden spoon until they are completely submerged in the vinegar. Cap tightly, place in a cool, dark place, and let 40 days pass before eating. The pickled flowers are an excellent substitute for capers in focaccia and in salads.

GROUPER CARPACCIO WITH
WILD FENNEL AND OLIVES

Serves 4

2 grouper or other white fish fillets, 6 to 7 ounces (170 to 200 g) each

6½ tablespoons (100 ml) extra-virgin olive oil

1 clove garlic, crushed

1 small dried chile, halved

3½ teaspoons (10 g) salt-packed capers, brushed to remove salt

2 tablespoons (20 g) green olives, pitted and finely chopped

3 tablespoons (15 g) finely chopped wild fennel, tender tips only

Lay the grouper fillets on a cutting board and cut them into thin strips, removing any errant bones. Arrange the strips on a serving plate. Pour the oil into a small skillet and place over medium heat. When the oil just begins to smoke, add the garlic and chile and let them brown for about 2 minutes. Add the capers and olives, heat for 3 minutes, then remove from the heat and remove and discard the garlic and chile.

Pour the hot oil with the capers and olives over the fish strips and let stand for about 10 minutes. Stir together the fish and seasoned oil, scatter the fennel over the top, and serve.

GROUPER CARPACCIO WITH
WILD FENNEL AND LEMON

Serves 4

2 grouper or other white fish fillets, 6 to 7 ounces (170 to 200 g) each

10 ice cubes

1½ teaspoons (10 g) fine salt

Extra-virgin olive oil, to taste

Juice of 1 lemon

2 tablespoons (10 g) finely chopped wild fennel, tender tips only

Lay the grouper fillets on a cutting board and cut them into thin strips, removing any errant bones. Put the ice cubes and salt in a bowl and lay the fish strips on the ice. Pour in water to cover the fish and let soak for about 2 hours.

Drain the fish strips well. Arrange the strips on a serving plate and season them with the lemon juice and oil. Scatter the fennel over the top and serve.

———————————

MULLET WITH WILD FENNEL

Serves 4

4 mullet or other small, white-fleshed fish
2½ ounces (70 g) wild fennel, tender tops and stems only
3½ tablespoons (30 g) capers in brine
1 clove garlic, chopped
5 tablespoons (75 ml) extra-virgin olive oil
½ teaspoon (1 g) ground black pepper
6½ cup (100 ml) dry white wine

Wearing rubber kitchen gloves, clean the mullet as follows: open the belly with kitchen shears, carefully remove the guts, and wash the fish carefully inside and out. Dry them well with paper towels. Wash the fennel carefully and dry well. Place it on a cutting board with the capers and garlic. (Do not rinse the capers; you will not be using any other salt in the dish). Chop the fennel, capers, and garlic together well. Sprinkle the mixture with 5 teaspoons (25 ml) of the oil, add the pepper, and mix well. Stuff this mixture into the belly of the fish, dividing it evenly.

Preheat the oven to 400°F (200°C). Line the bottom of a 13-by-9-inch (32-by-23-cm) baking pan with parchment paper. Sprinkle about 5 teaspoons (25 ml) of the oil over the bottom of the lined pan. Arrange the mullet in the pan in a single layer, pour the wine over the fish, and then drizzle the remaining 5 teaspoons (25 ml) oil over the top.

Bake for 8 minutes. Remove the pan from the oven, turn the mullet over, return the pan to the oven, and bake for about 5 minutes longer. To test if the fish are done, insert a knife tip between the backbone and the top fillet of a fish; the fish is ready if fillet lifts easily away from the bone. Remove from the oven and serve.

WILD FENNEL PIE
Serves 6

FOR THE DOUGH

2 cups plus 2 tablespoons (350 g) semolina flour, plus more
for sprinkling

6½ tablespoons (100 ml) extra-virgin olive oil

1¼ teaspoons (8 g) fine salt

⅔ cup (150 ml) warm water

FOR THE FILLING

2¼ pounds (1 kg) wild fennel, tender tops and stems only

3½ tablespoons (50 g) coarse salt

Scant 1 cup (220 ml) extra-virgin olive oil

2 onions, finely chopped

2 teaspoons (5 g) ground red pepper

1½ teaspoons (3 g) ground black pepper

6 tomatoes, seeded and chopped

2 teaspoons (12 g) fine salt

2 tablespoons (20 g) capers in brine, rinsed

½ cup (60 g) pitted black olives

Extra-virgin olive oil for preparing the pan and brushing
the crust

To prepare the dough: Place the flour in a bowl. In a small pan, heat the oil over low heat for about 1 minute. Pour the warm oil onto the flour, add the fine salt, and stir with a wooden spoon until well mixed. Gradually pour in the warm water while continuing to stir until everything comes together in a rough mass. Work the dough with your hands until it becomes soft and compact. Cover with a bowl or kitchen towel and let rest for about 1 hour.

To prepare the filling: Wash the fennel carefully. Pour 4 quarts (4 l) water into an 8-quart (8-l) pot, cover, and place over high heat. When the water begins to boil, add the coarse salt and fennel, cover, and cook for 10 minutes, timing from when the water begins to boil again. Remove the fennel from the water with a wire skimmer and drain well.

Pour the oil into a deep 12-inch (30-cm) skillet and place over low heat. Add the onions and red pepper and cook, stirring occasionally, until golden, 10 to 15 minutes. Add the fennel and black pepper and cook for 10 minutes.

Add the tomatoes, fine salt, and capers and cook for a few minutes. Stir occasionally with a wooden spoon to ensure that nothing sticks. There should be no water on the pan bottom; only a little oil should remain. If any water remains, raise the heat and stir to evaporate it. Turn off the heat and let the filling cool.

To assemble: Sprinkle a little flour on a marble or wood work surface. Divide the dough in half and shape each half into a ball. Place a ball on the work surface and flatten with your palm. With a rolling pin, roll out the dough into a circle about 13 inches (32 cm) in diameter. Repeat with the second ball of dough.

Preheat the oven to 350° to 400°F (180° to 200°C). Grease the bottom and sides of a 12-inch (30-cm) round baking pan with 1½-inch (4-cm) sides with the oil. Line the pan with a dough circle, pressing it against the bottom and sides and allowing it to extend slightly beyond the rim of the pan. Spoon the filling into the pan, spreading it evenly over the crust. Sprinkle the olives evenly over the top. Top the filling with the second dough circle and press along the edge of the pan with a fork to join the top and bottom crusts together well. Brush the top surface and the edges of the crust with the oil. With the fork, make some deep holes in the surface (say, as deep as the tines of a table fork) to vent the steam as it bakes.

Bake until the crust is golden, about 45 minutes. The pie may be served hot or cold.

WILD FENNEL FLOWER GRAPPA

Makes 1 pint (500 ml)

1½ cups (50 g) wild fennel flowers
2 cups (500 ml) unflavored grappa

Gather only the most tender flowers. Wash and dry them well. Then let them "bruise" for 2 days—that is, let them dry on a tray (even better if it is perforated) placed in an airy and cool place.

Put the flowers in a 1-quart (1-l) glass container with an airtight cap. Pour in the grappa, cap, and leave in the open for 8 days (and nights). Filter through a tight-weave strainer and store in a capped bottle.

WILD FENNEL WITH OIL AND LEMON

Serves 4

2¼ pounds (1 kg) wild fennel, tender tops and stems only

2 tablespoons (40 g) coarse salt

Lemon juice, to taste

Extra-virgin olive oil, to taste

Wash the fennel carefully. Pour 4 quarts (4 l) water into an 8-quart (8-l) pot, cover, and place over high heat. When the water begins to boil, add the salt and fennel, cover, and cook for 10 minutes, timing from when the water begins to boil again. Remove the fennel from the water with a wire skimmer and drain well. Absolutely no water should remain. Season at the table with the lemon juice and oil.

BRAISED WILD FENNEL

Serves 4

3⅓ pounds (1.5 kg) wild fennel, tender tops and stems only

3½ tablespoons (50 g) coarse salt

⅔ cup (150 ml) extra-virgin olive oil

1 to 2 onions, finely chopped

2 teaspoons (5 g) ground red pepper

1 teaspoon (2 g) ground black pepper

Wash the fennel carefully. Pour 4 quarts (4 l) water into an 8-quart (8-l) pot, cover, and place over high heat. When the water begins to boil, add the salt and fennel, cover, and cook for 10 minutes, timing from when the water begins to boil again. Remove the fennel from the water with a wire skimmer and drain well.

Pour the oil into a 5-quart (5-l) pot and place over very low heat. Add the onions and cook for about 10 minutes. Remove the pot from the heat and let the oil cool slightly to avoid splattering when the fennel is added. Then add the fennel, red pepper, and black pepper, mix well, cover, and cook over very low heat for about 45 minutes.

WILD FENNEL FLATBREAD (SCHIACCIATINE)

Serves 4

⅔ cup (20 g) wild fennel flowers

1 pound (500 g) boneless veal chops, ground twice (this allows the meat to mix better with the other ingredients)

2 slices (50 g) stale bread, soaked in water and wrung out lightly

½ cup (50 g) grated pecorino cheese

1 egg

1 teaspoon (6 g) fine salt

1 tablespoon (15 ml) extra-virgin olive oil

Wash and finely chop the fennel flowers. In a 4-quart (4-l) bowl, combine the fennel flowers, veal, bread, cheese, egg, and salt. Carefully mix with your hands for a long time until everything is well combined. Divide the mixture into 8 equal portions and shape each portion into a ball. Using your palms, press each ball into a "flatbread" about 3½ inches (9 cm) long, 2 inches (5 cm) wide, and ⅓ inch (1 cm) thick.

Grease the bottom and sides of a 12-inch (30-cm) nonstick skillet with the oil. Lay the flatbreads in the pan, cover, place over medium heat, and cook for 12 minutes. Move the pan back and forth occasionally (or in a swirling motion) to keep the flatbreads from sticking to the bottom. Uncover, turn the flatbreads over with the help of a wooden spatula, re-cover, and cook for another 8 minutes. At this point, the flatbreads should be nicely browned on both sides and cooked through. Remove from the heat and serve immediately. This recipe can also be made with wild fennel seeds in place of the flowers.

Wild Raspberries

RUBUS IDAEUS; ITALIAN: *LAMPONE SELVATICO*

WITH HIS CUSTOMARY PRECISION—which a psychoanalyst today would not hesitate to classify as a symptom of obsession—Henry David Thoreau lets us know that raspberries began to mature where he lived on June 25. He remained silent, however, as to the day of the week and the hour. He further added that raspberry season, although lasting through all of August, begins to decline after July 15. As with blueberries, American raspberries prefer swampy land. But unlike blueberries, although they grow relatively peacefully, they never produce an abundant harvest, unless, continues the champion of civil disobedience (that is, the right of the individual to peacefully oppose the unjust laws of the state), it rains as terribly as it did in the summers "of 1859 and 1860" (*Wild Fruits,* 28).

But the most surprising piece of information that Thoreau passes on to us, beyond these details (meaningful, perhaps, for the profile of his psychic apparatus, but sterile with regard to the history of raspberries), is what the American philosopher drew from the writings of the English botanist John Lindley (1799–1865), the soundness of which Thoreau openly confesses to doubt. "I have before me," he wrote to Lindley, "three plants of raspberries raised from seeds which were taken from the stomach of a man whose skeleton was found thirty feet below the surface of the earth [in England]. He had been buried with some coins of emperor Hadrian, and it is therefore probable that the seeds were 600 to 1,700 years old" (Ibid.). What is surprising nowadays, even more than the tenacious procreativity of the raspberry seed, is the skepticism with which Thoreau talks about it. Those of us who now live in the expectation of getting dinosaurs back by extracting them from molecules fossilized millions of years ago might also greet thousand-year-old raspberry seeds with indifference.

If Thoreau shows himself to be meticulous in temporal annotation, John Gerard is unsurpassed in specification of place. After having assured us that the raspberry does not grow wild (something that, among other things, contrasts with the invasive nature of the brambles, which propagate rapidly by means of subterranean rhizomes), the English herbalist introduces a couple of exceptions to the rule of cultivation. There are some wild ones "in a field by a village in Lancashire called Harwood, not far from Blackburne" (*The Herball,* II, 1, 273). And he admits to having found some "among the bushes of a causey, neere unto a village called Wisterson, where I went to schoole, two miles from the Nantwich in Cheshire," a county in which some have even found cats perched in the trees who, laughing, make themselves disappear.[1]

Nevertheless, the fact that the raspberry—both cultivated and wild—has been a desired plant since the time of ancient Rome (and since time immemorial, truth be told), is an affirmation we find in Pliny, who lists it under the rubric of brambles ("Not even brambles did Nature create for harmful purposes only") and assures us that the Latin name of the raspberry (*Rubus idaeus*) derives from the fact that "no other [type] grows on Mount Ida.[2] It is, however, more delicate than other brambles and smaller," continues Pliny, "with canes farther apart and less prickly; it grows under the shade of trees. The blossom of it with honey is applied to the fluxes of the eyes [excessive tear production] and to erysipelas [Saint Anthony's fire, or herpes zoster], and mixed with water, it is given as a drink to patients with disordered stomachs" (*Naturalis historia,* XXIV, 73, 117 and 75, 123).[3] And this is in addition to hundreds of other virtues that brambles have in general.

Among the general uncertainty regarding the origin of the English term *raspberry,* it makes sense to console ourselves with the ascendant *raspis* (that's what Gerard calls both the plant and the fruit), which *The Oxford English Dictionary* "decries" as having an obscure origin (rendered even more obscure if you are trying to read the microscopic print in the *Compact Edition*). Not to be excluded is an initial Neo-Latin and Pan-Romance source, which can be glimpsed in the Old French *rasper* (today *râper*), the Spanish *raspar,* and the

Italian *raspare* (to rasp, to scrape). This, however, introduces very unpleasant connotations for such a delicate fruit (yet there are those who, when faced with roses, always think of thorns).

In France, the raspberry becomes *framboise,* after having been *frambeise,* in turn descended, through the influence of *fraise* (strawberry), from the Frankish *brambasia,* which bears a close relationship to the English *bramble.* Thank goodness that at the end of this very long tunnel of peculiar etymons and connotational camouflage, you might succeed in getting yourself a small glass of framboise—that is, a brandy in which fermentation of the raspberry plays a principal role. Beyond this brandy, the raspberry is used, alone or in combination, in a thousand syrups and antioxidant juices. There are even those who use raspberries to alter the taste of tap water that they then sell in small plastic bottles—a notoriously disgusting thing!

Raspberries, like strawberries, can be associated with birthmarks. One very famous raspberry birthmark in Italian literature concludes a wonderful and proverbial section of Alessandro Manzoni's *The Betrothed.* To try to remedy the disaster caused by the refusal of Don Abbondio to perform the marriage of Renzo and Lucia, Agnese (Lucia's mother) suggests "resorting to legal avenues" and Manzoni takes advantage of the opportunity to make us understand how benevolent (and paternalistic) his view of the poor and outcast is. Agnese says to Renzo, "Poor folk like us see our troubles as more tangled than they really are because we haven't got the key to them; but then sometimes the advice of a man who knows his books, just a couple of words from him . . . . Take my advice, Renzo, go to Lecco, find Dr. Quibbler, and tell him about it—but don't call him that, for heaven's sake, it's only a nickname. You'll have to ask for Dr.—oh, dear, I've forgotten his real name, everyone calls him that. Anyway, look for a tall, thin lawyer with a bald head, a red nose, and a raspberry[4] mark on his cheek." A veritable Adonis! Today, a celebrated attorney like Quibbler would try to have that birthmark removed, perhaps subjecting himself to a dermatologic peel at some renowned institute of cosmetic surgery.

The raspberry that one eats (or drinks) grows in all regions of the world and, in Italy, particularly in the types of landscapes that cover the national territory: clearings, woods, and stony places between 350 and 6,500 feet in elevation. When you find them in an unexpected place, you can be sure that they were carried there by birds through the oldest known method of dissemination, described scientifically as "avian excretion." The raspberry has astringent, diuretic, and anti-inflammatory therapeutic properties. With the leaves dried in a cool and ventilated place, decoctions can be made that are effective against rhagades and hemorrhoids.

Raspberries are gathered in the summer, when the fruit detaches very easily from the supporting stalk.

WILD RASPBERRY RISOTTO

Serves 4

1 cup (120 g) wild raspberries
6½ cups (1.5 l) beef broth
    Coarse salt
¼ cup (60 ml) extra-virgin olive oil
1 onion, finely chopped
1¾ cups (350 g) Arborio or Vialone Nano rice
3 tablespoons (40 g) butter
⅓ cup (40 g) grated Parmesan cheese

Wash the raspberries, let them drain well in a colander, and then place them on paper towels to dry. Pour the broth into a 3-quart (3-l) pot, place over medium-high heat, and bring to a boil. Season to taste with the salt. The rice will be cooked in this broth, which must be kept at a simmer. Meanwhile, pour the oil into a 4-quart (4-l) pot and place over very low heat. Add the onion and cook for about 3 minutes. Take care that the onion does not to burn. Raise the heat to medium, add the rice, and stir with a wooden spoon for another 5 minutes to toast it. Pour in the wine and continue to stir until it has evaporated.

Now begin to add the broth, a little at a time, stirring after each addition and allowing it to evaporate before adding more. After 15 minutes of cooking, add the raspberries and stir for 5 another minutes. At this point the rice should be tender but still slightly firm at the center of each grain. Turn off the heat, add the butter and Parmesan, and stir until everything is well mixed. Let rest for 5 minutes before serving.

Wild Strawberries

FRAGARIA VESCA; ITALIAN: *FRAGOLINA DI BOSCO*

IN *THE FRUIT, HERBS & VEGETABLES OF ITALY,* Castelvetro addresses his English readers, noting that, "you happy mortals" do not get "these fragrant and health-giving berries" early in the year (as in Italy, where he could find them in the spring), "[but you] have them twice a year, in mid-June and in October. Last year I was in Cambridge on October 28 [1613] and was amazed to be eating strawberries by the plateful, not just one or two. They were exquisite" (p. 71).

Castelvetro's enthusiasm for strawberries finds confirmation in a sentence attributed to a doctor William Butler (d. 1621)—a new Asclepius, according to his contemporaries—by the great trout fisherman and notable writer Izaak Walton (1593–1683) in *The Compleat Angler* (1655):[1] "Doubtless God could have made a better berry, bout doubtless God never did!" Walton used this for establishing a comparison between strawberries and his preferred sport. Just as among wild berries there is none better than the strawberry, so too among all types of recreation there is none more calm, quiet, and innocent than fly-fishing. It must have immediately become a phrase used by everyone: on the other side of the Atlantic, the liberal (and therefore disliked by the Puritans) theologian, Robert Williams (1603–83), one year before establishing what would become the State of Rhode Island (1644), had already referred to it on page 98 of his *Key into the Language of America,* one of the first studies of the language of the Narragansett Indians, with whom Williams had managed to establish excellent relations.

We find a lexicographic excursus regarding the word *strawberry* in the native languages of North America in Thoreau's *Wild Fruits:* "[The *Oteagh-minick* of the Indians is so-called because it in some measure resembles a heart].... According to Sir John Franklin, the Cree name is *Oteimeena,* and Tanner says that the Chippeway name is *O-da-e-min*—all evidently the same word, as they have the same meaning."[2] Thoreau adds that they grew in such numbers that one could gather enough to fill a ship in the space of a few miles.

The esteem in which the Indians of the Five Nations held the strawberry can also be deduced by a "festival" dedicated to the fruit, a ceremony with ritual dances, recently revived by the Algonquin and by the Iroquois and first called for by Handsome Lake (Ga-Nyah-Di-Yoh), a Seneca prophet who lived from 1735 to 1815. In his "Code" (which the Indians recited during the three-day celebrations at the beginning of their year) we read, among other things: "Verily the servants of the Creator (Hadio^{n}yă"geono^n) said this. Now, moreover, they commanded that henceforth dances of this same kind [like those they performed to celebrate the autumn harvest of corn] would be held and thanksgiving offered whenever the strawberries were ripe." It was the third festival in their calendar, following the maple and the seed festivals. The strawberries were the first fruits of the year and their juice was drunk mixed with maple sugar and diluted with water.[3]

But good though they may be, strawberries can also be dangerous, especially if they end up embroidered on silk handkerchiefs, like the one that perfidious Iago takes away from Desdemona, accusing her, to her credulous husband, of having given it to Cassio, her imagined suitor—which, as every one-year-old knows, sends Othello into a fury (*Othello,* III, III, vv. 435–436):

IAGO: Have you not sometimes seen a handkerchief
    Spotted with strawberries in your wife's hand?
OTHELLO: I gave her such a one: 't was my first gift.

And Othello himself threateningly explains its provenance and the evil consequences of its possible disappearance (Ibid., IV, vv. 52–71):

OTHELLO: That handkerchief
    Did an Egyptian to my mother give:
    She was a charmer, and could almost read

The thoughts of people. She told her, while she kept it,
'T would make her amiable and subdue my father
Entirely to her love; but if she lost it.
Or made a gift of it, my father's eye
Should hold her loathèd and his spirits should hunt
After new fancies. She dying gave it me,
And bid me when my fate would have me wive,
To give it her. I did so, and take heed on 't;
Make it a darling, like your precious eye.
To lose 't or give 't away were such perdition
As nothing else could match.

DESDEMONA: Is 't possible?

OTHELLO: 'Tis true: there's magic in the web of it:
A sibyl, that had numbered in the world
The sun to course two hundred compasses,
In her prophetic fury sewed the work;
The worms were hallowed that did breed the silk,
And it was dyed in mummy, which the skilful
Conserved of maidens' hearts.

Will the exclamations that we would traditionally use to exorcise such a crescendo (Wow!, Imagine that!, Golly!, Did you ever?!, My goodness!, Holy cow!, Damn!, Good grief!) be enough to loosen the limbs of the gentle reader stiffened by fear? Will they relax the reader enough to cross over into the serene flower beds of the "strawberry fields" that are easier to reach and, by now, even more famous than the well-watered Platonic meadows that teem with essential ideas, and the dryness, phobia, and boringness of the Elysian Fields? Anyone who wants to can find them in Central Park in New York, not far from the entrance of the home where the most tragic of the Beatles ceased to say (with insight?) that love is all we need. But not to stray too far, here is the beginning of his lofty (or spaced out) words: "Let me take you down, 'cause I'm going to / Strawberry Fields. / Nothing is real / and nothing to get hung about / Strawberry Fields forever"—that is, *in saecula saeculorum.*[4]

We will take advantage of this vaguely liturgical allusion to segue into the strawberry's symbolism, which Angelo De Gubernatis (*Mythologie,* vol. II, 146–48) has spoken of with an abundance of detail. Among the various Germanic legends that he recalls is one he extracts from *Germanische Mythen* (1858) by Johann Wilhelm Mannhardt (1831–80), in which mothers who have lost a child avoid eating strawberries because the little ones rise to heaven hidden in strawberries. If the mothers were to eat them, they would be doing a wrong to the Virgin Mary (to whom the strawberries are bound), which could prevent those children whose mothers had stolen fruit destined for her from entering Paradise. De Gubernatis also records that, according to a popular English song, robins wrap their stillborn baby birds in strawberry leaves and bury them in the forest. Whatever their true symbolic function might be, strawberries are also part of the iconographic wealth that frames the central image of many books of hours, the medieval illuminated manuscripts in which devotional texts are distributed according to the seven canonical hours.

At the dietetic-gastronomic-medical level, it is good to note the epochal contrast between a prominent exponent of medieval medicine, Hildegard von Bingen, and Nicholas Culpeper, the "enlightened" representative of seventeenth-century English medicine. The former paints strawberries in very dark colors: "The wild strawberries . . . make a kind of mucus in the person who eats them. They are beneficial as food for neither a sick nor a healthy person because they grow near the ground and, indeed, in putrid air" (*Physica,* CLXX). The latter includes a long list of the benefits of which the roots and leaves of the fruit[5] are capable: a bona fide remedy for every season.[6] It is good for the liver, the blood, the kidneys, and the bladder. It cures ulcers, slows menstruation, is good for gargling, and so on. (*Complete Herbal,* 175–76).

Culpeper, after all, knew very well that even with the best of ingredients, medicine can be hard to pin down. In his *English Physician* (1652), he rails often and with irony against the College of Physicians, which tyrannized the practice of the medical profession. His preferred stratagem was to relate the opinion of the college and then demolish it. For example, regarding *Tinctura Fragroram,* he writes (p. 290):

> *College.* Take of ripe Wood-strawberries two pounds, put them in a phial, and put so much small spirits of Wine to them that it may overtop them the thickness of four fingers, stop the vessel close, and set it in the sun two days, then strain it and press it but gently; pour this spirit to as many fresh Strawberries, repeat this six times, at last keep the clear liquor for your use.

> *Culpeper.* A fine thing for Gentlemen that have nothing else to do with their money, and it will have a lovely look to please their eyes.

The Roman physician Castore Durante, in chapter XCIII of his *Herbario novo,* notes that strawberries, although worth little as nourishment and harmful to paralytics and to whomever might be a victim of trembling and convulsions, are nonetheless good (when it is very hot) for young men, the quick-tempered, and for full-blooded types in general. They must be eaten before ingesting other food (the same is true for cherries, blackberries, and fruit of that sort), after having been separated from the leaves, cleaned well, immersed in white wine, and sprinkled with sugar. Be careful, however (concludes Durante), because if you eat too many, you run the risk of getting a nasty fever.

Just as raspberries can be associated with birthmarks, so too can strawberries. In Italian, the word *voglia* means both "craving" and "birthmark." The two meanings, and their association with strawberries, come together in an old superstition. There was a time in which a pregnant woman, craving a nice strawberry gelato, tried not to touch any part of her body before having that desire satisfied, in order to avoid having the unborn child develop a red birthmark at the same spot on his or her body. The *voglia* for strawberries, together with that for chocolate, might be among the most widespread. A classic story about pregnancies had attentive husbands searching desperately for strawberry ice cream, even at three o'clock in the morning.

In fairy tales, the presence or absence of a strawberry birthmark could betray the true identity of a character and allow the discovery of a princess under false clothing (scullery maid, orphan, shepherdess, and the like). The most famous strawberry birthmark, however, may the one on the neck of Anne Boleyn, second wife of Henry VIII and mother of Elizabeth I, who, despite this minor defect (and an incipient sixth finger on one of her hands) passed as an irresistible woman. But even a woman who could make a king lose his head could end up losing her own. Nonetheless, she showed herself as having a lot of class up to the last moment. Her response to the notice that the type of execution had been changed (from strangulation on the gallows to cutting off of her head) seems to be historically accurate: "I have heard it said that the executioner is very good, and I have a small neck."

The gathering period for strawberries is all summer—unless you live in England (see above).

WILD STRAWBERRY CREAM PIE

Serves 6

FOR THE CRUST

2 cups plus 2 tablespoons (265 g) all-purpose flour
¼ cup (50 g) sugar
⅛ teaspoon (1 g) fine salt

⅔ cup (135 g) cold butter, cut into cubes

1 egg

2 tablespoons (30 ml) sparkling mineral water, ice-cold

¾ cup (150 g) dried cannellini beans

FOR THE CREAM

3 egg yolks

½ cup (100 g) sugar

½ cup (70 g) all-purpose flour

2 cups (500 ml) whole milk

Zest of 1 untreated (unwaxed) lemon, in strips

FOR THE TOPPING

2 cups (300 g) wild strawberries, washed, hulled, and well dried

To prepare the crust: In a bowl, combine 2 cups (250 g) of the flour, the sugar, the salt, the butter, and the egg. Mix everything while gradually adding the sparkling water, mixing just until the ingredients come together in a rough mass. Shape the dough into a ball, flatten it into a disk, put it in a covered bowl, and then in the refrigerator for 2 hours.

Preheat the oven to 350°F (180°C). Remove the dough from the refrigerator. Sprinkle some of the remaining 2 tablespoons (15 g) flour on a marble or wood work surface and set the dough on the surface. Sprinkle the remaining flour on top of the dough. With a rolling pin, roll out the dough into a circle 11 inches (28 cm) in diameter. If the dough begins to tear, press it together with your hands. Butter a 9-inch (23-cm) round pan with 1¼-inch (3-cm) sides. Then, with a swirling motion, add the remaining flour to the pan so that it sticks well everywhere, tapping out the excess. Line the pan with the dough circle, pressing it against the bottom and sides of the pan. Cut a sheet of parchment paper into a 9-inch (23-cm) circle, place it on top of the dough, and spill the beans onto the paper. This will keep the dough from swelling in the oven.

Bake the crust until you see that it has a nice golden color, about 30 minutes. At this point, remove from the oven, scoop out the beans and lift out the parchment, and let the crust cool on a wire rack. Now invert a flat 10-inch (25-cm) plate on top of the pan and turn the pan and plate together so the crust falls onto the plate. Turn the crust over again onto a second plate of the same size.

To prepare the cream: Place the egg yolks and sugar in a bowl and stir with a wooden spoon to combine. Add the flour little by little while stirring constantly to prevent lumps from forming. Add the milk, always pouring it slowly and without ever ceasing to stir. Pass the mixture through a tight-weave strainer, return it to the saucepan, and add the lemon zest. Place the pan over medium heat and continue to stir, always in the same direction, for 30 minutes (be careful not to let the mixture start to boil). Then reduce the heat to very low and cook for another 5 minutes, never forgetting to stir (otherwise the cream will stick to the bottom). Remove from the heat, remove and discard the lemon zest, and continue to stir the cream often as it cools.

Pour the cooled cream into the crust and arrange the strawberries on top.

WILD STRAWBERRY RISOTTO

Serves 4

⅔ cup (100 g) wild strawberries
6½ cups (1.5 l) vegetable broth
Coarse salt
¼ cup (60 ml) extra-virgin olive oil
1 onion, finely chopped
1¾ cups (350 g) Arborio or Vialone Nano rice
¼ cup (60 ml) strawberry wine
2 tablespoons (30 g) butter
⅓ cup (40 g) grated Parmesan cheese

Hull the strawberries, wash them, let them drip well in a tight-weave strainer, and then arrange them on paper towels to dry. Pour the broth into a 3-quart (3-l) pot, place over medium-high heat, and bring to a boil. Season to taste with the salt. The rice will be cooked in this broth, which must be kept at a simmer. Meanwhile, pour the oil into a 4-quart (4-l) pot and place over very low heat. Add the onion and cook for about 3 minutes. Take care that the onion does not burn. Raise the heat to medium, add the rice, and stir with a wooden spoon for a good 5 minutes to toast it. Pour in the wine and continue to stir until it has evaporated.

Now begin to add the broth, a little at a time, stirring after each addition and allowing it to evaporate before adding more. After 15 minutes of cooking, add the strawberries and stir for another 5 minutes. At this point the rice should be tender but still slightly firm at the center of each grain. Turn off the heat, add the butter and Parmesan, and stir until everything is well mixed. Let rest for 5 minutes before serving.

NOTES

PREFACE

1. Massimo Vaglio offers this advice in his book *Cicorielle e lampascioni* [Chicory and cipollini] (Nardò, Lecce: Besa, 2000), 96. The profession of the gatherer is nearly extinct in the area of Puglia known as the Salentine peninsula, thus you must learn quickly from the few remaining expert gatherers before their secrets are lost forever. It is best to rely on someone who specializes in gathering a particular food, such as mushrooms, chicory, or raspberries.

INTRODUCTION

1. The quote translated here is from the 1543 Venetian edition of *Commentario delle più notabili e mostruose cose d'Italia, e altri luoghi, di lingua Aramea in Italiana tradotto, nel qual s'impara, e prendesi istremo piacere. Vi si è poi aggionto un breve* CATALOGO *delli inventori delle cose, che si mangiano, e che si bevono, novamente ritrovato, e di M. Anonimo de Utopia, composto MDXVIII*, ed. G. and P. Salvadori (Bologna: Pendragon, 1994), 140. According to the *vocabolario* of the Accademia della Crusca (fifth printing, 1886), "eringio" is counted among the plants whose small young leaves are used in foods seasoned with salt. It is said that when a goat takes the small herb called *eringio* into its mouth, it stops and makes the whole herd stop until the goatherd has taken it from him." *Fiadoni* are casings of rolled dough that contain a sweet or salty filling. *Enula* comes from the Latin *inula:* an herbaceous plant also called *enula campana* (bell enula) with a rhizome endowed with refreshing and antiseptic properties. *Salviata* is a type of cake made of eggs, cheese, and sage.

2. The words that Shakespeare employs to delineate the prospect of such pleasure are, however, "a real trip": "Within this limit is relief enough, / Sweet bottom-grass and high delightful plain, / Round rising hillocks, brakes obscure and rough, / To

shelter thee from tempest and from rain: / Then be my deer since I am such a park; / No dog shall rouse thee, though a thousand bark."

3. The biblical quotations herein are from the New Revised Standard Version (NRSV).

4. Bulaq Papyrus 117 (Egyptian Museum), Age of Amenhotep II, stanza IV. See *Ancient Near Eastern Texts Relating to the Old Testament,* ed. J. Pritchard (Princeton: Princeton University Press, 1955), 366. This clean separation is taken up again in Psalm 104 (v. 14): "You [Lord] cause the grass to grow for the cattle, / and plants for people to use, / to bring forth food from the earth, / and wine to gladden the human heart, / oil to make the face shine, / and bread to strengthen the human heart." Apart from the allusion to the use of olive oil as a cosmetic, particularly valuable here is the distinction between grass and plants, which would come to weigh heavily on those "plants" that grow *among* the grasses and whose fruits, maturing close to the earth, participate in its putrid dullness (when compared to the luminosity of tree fruit, which matures suspended in air). Even forest strawberries, so precious to us in all senses of the word, remained for a long time wrapped in scorn. Only the poor, with the courage of desperation, would have dared to feed on them.

5. Plutarch, "Of Eating of Flesh," in *Plutarch's Morals,* ed. W. W. Goodwin (Boston: Little, Brown, 1874), 3–5.

6. Homer, *Iliad,* trans. Robert Fagles (New York: Viking, 1990), 225.

7. See *The Notebooks of Leonardo da Vinci,* trans. Edward McCurdy, vol. 1 (New York: Reynal, 1938), 90. For Platina, see *On Right Pleasure and Good Health: A Critical Edition and Translation of De honesta voluptate et valetudine,* trans. and ed. Mary Ella Milham (Tempe, AZ.: Medieval and Renaissance Texts and Studies, 1998).

8. John Ray, *Historia Plantarum* (London: Maria Clark, 1686).

9. John Evelyn, *Acetaria, a Discourse of Sallets,* 2nd ed. (London: B. Tooke, 1706), 171–72.

10. Representing verses 3–6 in Ovid's original, this is the sixteenth-century translation of John Dryden. We cannot exclude the fact that this enthusiasm may also be due, first, to the richness and popularity of Latin literature of an agronomic sort and/or, second, to knowledge of Cato's *De re rustica* [On agriculture], and particularly to the fact that his work dedicates much attention to the domestication of plants. See also, for example, the Wild Asparagus chapter.

11. For the full text of the *Capitulare de Villis* in English, see *Introduction to Contemporary Civilization in the West: A Source Book* (New York: Columbia University Press, 1960), 326–334.

12. Walafrid (ca. 808–49), known as Strabo or Strabus (that is, the Squint-eyed), lived in various monasteries, including one at Fulda (where he studied under the guidance of Rabanus Maurus) and one at Reichenau. *Hortulus* was composed, in all probability, in 842, but the oldest (and non autographic) manuscript dates to twenty-five years after his death and was published for the first time in Vienna in 1510. The text opens with sage and ends with the rose, which "surpasses every other plant in virtue and scent and therefore merits being called the flower of flowers."

13. For the cookbook of Maestro Martino, see Maestro Martino, *The Art of*

Cooking: The First Modern Cookery Book, ed. L. Ballerini and J. Parzen (Berkeley: University of California Press, 2005).

14. Giacomo Castelvetro, *The Fruit, Herbs & Vegetables of Italy,* trans. Gillian Riley (New York: Viking, 1989), 49. Most references to Castelvetro's work in this book are to this edition. Citations to the Italian title, *Brieve racconto di tutte le radici, di tutte l'erbe e di tutti i frutti, che crudi o cotti in Italia si mangiano* [Brief account of all the roots, all the herbs and all the fruits that are eaten in Italy, whether raw or cooked], indicate passages of the original Italian text not present in the English edition.

15. Ibid., 133.

16. Ibid., 65.

17. For the original Middle English orthography, see *The Forme of Cury* (London: J. Nichols, 1780), 41–42.

18. From the pages of the *Grand Dictionnaire de Cuisine* by Alexandre Dumas (Paris: Tchou, 1965), it emerges as a rather French passion. The author of *The Three Musketeers* dedicates some of his best pages to salad. Among other things, we read that salad is not at all a natural food for man (who should not turn his gaze toward the ground but rather toward the sky, even though holding his nose up will feed him even more poorly than eating greens will) and that, in any case, the fruit of intelligence and refinement cannot be lowered to the rank of a side dish. This is gastronomic heresy, intones Dumas, and it is a culinary impiety to entrust its care to the servants. "Therefore, the duty of seasoning this revolutionary course falls to the master or mistress of the house, provided of course that they are worthy of such ministry" (pp. XLVI et seq.).

19. See "La favola delle erbe" in Giacomo Castelvetro, *Brieve racconto di tutte le radici, di tutte l'erbe e di tutti i frutti che crudi e cotti in Italia si mangiano* (Mantua: Gianluigi Arcari Editore, 1988), 7.

BAY LEAVES

1. We can remain silent here regarding all of these except Gian Lorenzo Bernini, who succeeded in modeling the marble of his sculpture (on view at the Galleria Borghese in Rome, which is occasionally also open at night) in such a way that whoever looks at it seems to feel the hardening of the skin that is becoming bark, the laziness of the feet that are becoming roots, and that of the arms that are becoming branches. In short, it's beautiful.

2. A debased echo of the symbolic virtues inherent in the crown of laurel is perpetuated up to our time in the term *laurea* (conferred on those in Italy who are victorious in their studies) and, with the addition of the berries (*bacche*), in *baccalaureato, baccelliere* (*bachelier* in France), and bachelor of arts in the United States, where the Apollonian ancestry of the recognition is completely unknown. On the other hand, demonstrating his familiarity with mythology and the evolution of its chain of meanings, Baron Münchhausen recounts (at the end of the fifth chapter

of his wonderful adventures) how a veterinary officer successfully used young laurel branches to sew together the two halves of the horse he was riding (cut in half by a portcullis that suddenly fell on his back while he was entering a walled city at full speed): "The wound healed and, what could not have happened but to so glorious a horse, the sprigs took root in his body, grew up, and formed a bower over me; so that afterward I could go upon many other expeditions in the shade of my own and my horse's laurels." Rudolph Erich Raspe, *The Surprising Adventures of Baron Münchhausen* (New York: Thomas Y. Crowell, 1902), 30.

3. K. Kerèny, *Gli dei e gli eroi della Grecia* [*The gods and heroes of the Greeks*], trans. V. Tedeschi (Milan: Il Saggiatore, 1962). For a partial English translation by N. Cameron, see *The Gods of the Greeks* (London: Thames, 1951). See also Jacques Brosse, *Mythologie des arbre* [The mythology of trees] (Paris: Plon, 1989).

4. But here we are already stealing words from Petrarch, distinguished son of Ser Petraccolo of Ser Parenzo, cited earlier and about whom we will say more later.

5. Tibullus, *The Elegies of Tibullus,* trans. T. C. Williams (Boston: Gorham Press, 1905), 80–81.

6. Elémire Zolla, *Le meraviglie della natura* [The wonders of nature] (Milan: Bompiani, 1975), 44–45. The verses at the end of this quote open poem 246 of Petrarch's *Canzoniere:* "The aura sighing gently as it moves / the verdant laurel and her golden hair, / turns, with its aspects new and delicate, / souls into pilgrims wandering from their bodies." Petrarch, *Canzoniere,* trans. Mark Musa (Bloomington: Indiana University Press, 1996).

7. Alain Denis, *Erbe spezie condimenti* [Herbs, spices, seasonings] (Rome: Gambero Rosso, 2005), 28–30.

8. Nicholas Culpeper, *The Complete Herbal* (1653; repr., London: Thomas Kelly, 1843), 18.

BLACKBERRIES

1. For decades in Italy, the devastating inanity of *Che dice la pioggerellina di marzo* (What the March shower says) was inflicted pitilessly on generations of young innocents and still obsessively infests their organs dedicated to memory.

2. Ovid, *Metamorphoses,* trans. M. M. Innes (London: Penguin, 1955), 97–98.

3. Of the many species of blackberry found in the United States, the most common include *R. allegheniensis* (Allegheny blackberry), *R. argutus* (sawtooth blackberry), the nonnative *R. armeniacus* (Himalayan blackberry), *R. frondosus* (Yankee blackberry), and *R. laudatus* (plains blackberry).

4. This description is from the Region of Piedmont's Web site devoted to its parklands and protected areas: www.regione.piemonte.it/parchi/ppweb/rubriche/angoli/archivio/2007/01.htm.

5. Hildegard von Bingen, *Hildegard von Bingen's Physica,* trans. Priscilla Throop

(Rochester, Vermont: Healing Arts Press, 1998), 78. All quotations from Hildegard in the present volume follow this translation.

6. Michele Savonarola, *Libreto de lo excellentissimo physico maistro Michele Savonarola: de tutte le cose che se manzano comunamente* (1515; repr, Jane Nystedt, ed., Stockholm: Almqvist & Wiksell, 1988), 94.

7. A decoction results from boiling plant matter such as herbs and leaves in water. Conversely, an infusion involves placing the vegetation in water that has already been heated (or pouring the liquid over it) and allowing it to steep. –Trans.

8. Translations of Pliny throughout this volume are taken from the Loeb Classical Library translation of Pliny's *Natural History,* trans. W. H. S. Jones (Cambridge: Harvard University Press, 1951–56).

BLUEBERRIES

1. Born in 1928, his real name is Antoine Dominique. His first success, *"The Fat Man"* (1949), is about him personally. Mr. Domino weighed more than 220 pounds. In 2005, when Hurricane Katrina smashed New Orleans, his hometown and place of residence, word spread that he had died. He had decided not to abandon his home, but then someone forced him to, and he and his family were rescued by the Coast Guard.

2. Henry David Thoreau, *Wild Fruits* (New York and London: W. W. Norton, 2000).

BORAGE

1. Denis, *Erbe spezie condimenti,* 45.

2. To add to the confusion, Nicholas Culpeper holds that since borage is known to everyone, it is not at all necessary to describe either borage or *buglossa*. However, he adds that there is a third green called *langue de boeuf* that causes some taxonomic perplexity, given that *buglossa* means in Greek what *langue de boeuf* means in French, as he himself admits.

3. Homer, *Odyssey,* trans. Robert Fagles (New York: Viking Penguin, 1996), 131.

4. The information available regarding nepenthe is less than crystal clear. Culpeper gives a precise recipe where neither borage nor *buglossa* nor ox tongue appears. In their place, one must use "tincture of Opium made first with distilled Vinegar, then with spirit of Wine, Saffron extracted in spirit of Wine, of each an ounce, salt of Pearl and Coral, of each half an ounce, tincture of species Diambræ seven drams, Ambergris one dram: bring them into the form of Pills by the gentle heat of a bath" (*Complete Herbal,* 344). It is not surprising that for some time, the word *nepenthe* is found only in the mouths of certain nineteenth-century Gothic and Late Romantic poets—Edgar Allan Poe, to name one. Although he probably knows nothing of the

drink's chemical composition, Poe recommends it highly in *The Raven* to anyone wanting to forget a certain Lenore, lost forever: "Quaff, oh quaff this kind nepenthe and forget this lost Lenore!"

5. For a recent edition, see Robert Burton, *The Anatomy of Melancholy* (New York: New York Review of Books, 2001).

6. Jacques Ferrand, *De la maladie d'amour ou mélancolie érotique,* ed. Donald Beecher and Massimo Ciavolella (Paris: Garnier, 2010). An English version of the Beecher and Ciavolella edition was published by Syracuse University Press in 1990.

7. Or, precisely, "happy." Pliny speaks specifically of a green "like the tongue of an ox [*boum linguae*]. The most conspicuous quality of this is that thrown into wine it increases the exhilarating effect and so it is also called euphrosynum, the plant that cheers" (*Naturalis historia,* XXV, 40, 81).

8. "I, borage, always bring joy." John Gerard, *The Herball or General Historie of Plantes gathered by John Gerarde of London Master in Chirurgerie very much Enlarged and Amended by Thomas Johnson Citizen and Apothecarye* (London: Adam Islip Joice Norton and Richard Whitakers, 1636), 797.

9. The scene recorded here is not from the book by L. F. Baum, but from the 1939 screenplay by Noel Langley (1911–80), Florence Ryerson (1892–1965), and Edgar Allan Woolf (1889–1948). As you might imagine, there is no critical edition of this screenplay, and the text published by Delta Press in 1989 records *courage* as the final word of this scene. The word *borage* that concludes our excerpt must be considered a variant—in truth, quite rare—of the more common *courage,* with which it rhymes and which is the Cowardly Lion's ultimate object of desire. If the report of a *borage* variant ultimately proves erroneous, it makes nonetheless for a good story.

10. Dickens speaks explicitly about borage in his "Cupboard Papers," published in his 1872 almanac *All the Year Round* (see November 30, p. 66): "Now the tea you drink is dedestable [sic], adulterated, and very dear stuff. It does you no good: now take my advice, grow borage, which will cost you nothing, and drink borage tea. It helps digestion, is a sudorific, has a delightful aroma, and will have no bad effects on your nerves, or the nerves of your wife."

CAPERS

1. *Itinerari didattici. La Rocca di Lugo, il giardino pensile e le vecchie mura* [Educational tours: The Fortress of Lugo, the hanging garden, and the old walls] (Lugo, 1987), 69.

2. *Enquiry into Plants,* III, 11, 2.

3. Ibid., I, 111, 6.

4. Ibid., VI, v, 2.

5. Columella, *Of Husbandry* [De re rustica] (London: A. Millar, 1745), 496 (XI, 111, 54). The text and punctuation of this translation have been somewhat modernized.

6. Athenaeus, *The Deipnosophists or Banquet of the Learned,* trans. C. D. Yonge, vol. 3 (London: H. G. Bohn, 1854), 908.

7. Pellegrino Artusi, *Science in the Kitchen and the Art of Eating Well,* trans. M. Baca and S. Sartarelli (Toronto: University of Toronto Press, 2003), 118.

CHAMOMILE

1. There are also many types of chamomile. Beyond *Matricaria,* we must at least note *Anthemis nobilis,* also called noble or Roman chamomile: noble perhaps because it scorns growing wild and prefers by far to be cultivated. Those who care to plant it should use recently collected seeds and choose soil that is well drained and exposed to as much sun as possible.

2. In Italian, *matrice* is a literary term for "uterus."—Trans.

3. See *Erbe,* ed. M. T. della Beffa (Novara: De Agostini, 2001), 153.

4. Maria Treben, *Health Through God's Pharmacy,* trans. from the German (Steyr, Austria: Wilhelm Ennsthaler, 1980), 17. By 2005, this book was in its twenty-sixth edition.

5. The compress also needs to be pressed against the painful area.

6. In the linen strips used to wrap the mummy of the Ramses II, "traces of chamomile pollen were found inserted, with the probable intention of instilling in him the strength and the calm necessary to face the journey to the afterlife." Alfredo Cattabiani, *Florario* (Milan: Mondadori, 1998), 555.

7. Angelo De Gubernatis, *La mythologie des plantes; ou, Les légendes du règne végétal* (Paris: C. Reinwald, 1879), 4.

CIPOLLINI

1. It is entertaining to imagine, in this nascent period of botany, the intense traffic of bulbs and seeds traveling from one point to another in Europe, and of the "novelties" that arrived from the Americas and the countries of the Near East.

2. Massimo Vaglio, *La cucina del Salento* [The cuisine of the Salento] (Nardò, Lecce: Besa, 1999), 56.

3. Ibid., 57.

4. I was able to drink some of this water (thinking as little as possible about the eel) several years ago at Port Badisco, a few kilometers to the south of Otranto (and where legend would have it that Aeneas landed, veteran and survivor of several storms and chased by Dido's curses). It had been iced—having passed from the cement of the Neolithic cistern to the postmodern plastic of a Sub-Zero refrigerator.

5. Apicius, *De re coquinaria,* 175.

6. *Varro si quid de bulbis dixit.* There is, however, no trace of this discussion in Varro.

7. Ovid, *The Amours, Art of Love, Remedy of Love,* trans. H. T. Riley (London: Bell & Daldy, 1869), 423.

CRESTED WARTYCABBAGE

1. Antonio Costantini and Marosa Marcucci, *I rimedi della nonna. Le erbe, le pietre, gli animali nella medicina popolare del Salento* [Grandmother's remedies: herbs, stones, and animals in the popular medicine of the Salento] (Galantina: Congedo, 1992), 113.

2. See Ada Nucita, *Un grappolo di modi di dire* [A cluster of sayings] (Banca Popolare Pugliese, 1984), www.bpp.it/apulia/html/archivio/1984/I/art/R84I012. html.

3. The noun *vaiasse* reappears in the name of one of the most popular Neapolitan musical instruments, the *scetavaiasse,* or "servant-waker," because of the sound produced when its "bow" of notched wood is rubbed against a second rod propped against one's shoulder, like a violin.

DAISY

1. Dante Alighieri, *The Banquet,* trans. Christopher Ryan (Saratoga, CA.: ANMA Libri, 1989; repr., Charleston: BiblioBazaar, 2006), 159.

2. See Franco Sacchetti, "Pietre preziose e loro virtù" [Precious stones and their qualities] in *I sermoni evangelici, le lettere e altri scritti inediti e rari,* ed. O. Gigli (Florence: Le Monnier, 1857), 264–65. For Boccaccio and the story of Calandrino, see *Decameron* (VIII.3).

3. *Prediche sopra l'Esodo* [Sermons on Exodus], ed. P. G. Ricci (Rome: Bardetti, 1956), vol. II, 3.

4. Luigi Pulci, *Morgante,* trans. J. Tusiani (Bloomington: Indiana University Press, 1998), 667. Perhaps the knights and leaders (sovereigns) of France might sing better of the poor wretches to whom they thought themselves capable of teaching to write chivalric novels (the French being masters of that art). At most, they would succeed in teaching them the same old story of torture with rope, a certain foreshadowing of their imminent death.

5. The daisy's corolla is made up of petals that are white as milk. It may, however, also present tones of red, purple, and violet.

6. John Evelyn suggests also *Bellis major* and *Buphtalmum,* that is, ox eye, which the daisy resembles (though it takes a little imagination). According to this author, "The young Roots are frequently eaten by the Spaniards and Italians all the Spring until June" (*Acetaria,* 22–23).

7. Francesco De Bourchard had already spoken about a not dissimilar pizza in *Usi e costumi di Napoli* [Habits and customs of Naples], 1866, vol. II, 124.

1. Jacques Brosse, *Les arbres de France: Histoire et légendes* [The trees of France: History and legends] (Paris: Plon, 1987).

2. Luigi Castiglioni, *Viaggio negli Stati Uniti dell'America settentrionale, fatto negli anni 1785, 1786 e 1787* [Travels in the United States of North America, made in the years 1785, 1786 and 1787] (Milan: Giuseppe Marelli, 1790), 367–69. Among other things, Castiglioni was one of the first botanists to note the existing floral relationship between the easternmost regions of Asia and those of North America.

3. Harriet Keeler, *Our Native Trees and How to Identify Them* (New York: Scribner's Sons, 1902), 102.

4. In his *Enquiry into Plants* (IV, 11, 8), Theophrastus (ca. 371–287 B.C.) speaks of a thorny plant not unlike our own called *ákantha* because of its thorns (*ákanthodes*).

MALLOW

1. Although none of them are native, mallow species can be found throughout the United States. The most common include *Malva moschata* (musk mallow), *M. neglecta* (common mallow), *M. parviflora* (cheeseweed mallow), *M. pusilla* (low mallow), *M. sylvestris* (high mallow), and *M. verticillata* (cluster or Chinese mallow).

2. The original term used in Job is *mallûah*—and may the god of transliterations help us. There is complete uncertainty regarding the origin of the word *mallow*. Some (the desperate) have suggested the Greek verb *malásso,* which means "render soft" (particularly metals), but also "sweeten," "calm," "mitigate," and "bring relief."

3. Among the "Poets" listed by Evelyn, we find Pythagoras, Epimenides, and Galen (*Acetaria,* 35–36), although these individuals are not poets in the current sense of the term.

4. As a boy, he went in search of a "lost sheep" and fell asleep in a grotto on Mount Ida, some say for forty years, others say fifty-seven.

5. Being from Crete himself, he appears to have said that all Cretans lie, thus giving rise to the liar's paradox (is he who says, "I'm lying," lying or telling the truth?) that was so dear to the Welsh philosopher Bertrand Russell (and to the painter from Piacenza, William Xerra).

6. In reality, Hesiod limits himself to asserting that those who trust the judgment of the king during strife are foolish in that "they know not, in their selfish soul, / How far the half is better than the whole; / The good which asphodel and mallows yield" (Hesiod, *Works and Days,* trans. C. A. Elton [London: A.J. Valpy, 1832], 5, vv. 53–55).

7. See "The Banquet of the Seven Wise Men," in *Plutarch's Miscellanies and Essays,* vol. 2, 6th ed. (Boston: Little, Brown, 1889), 27.

8. A Latin adjective used to describe foods that provoked belching. –Trans.

9. One Roman *cyathus* was equal to about forty-five milliliters, or about three tablespoons. –Trans.

10. In Patricia Telesco, *A Kitchen Witch's Cookbook* (St. Paul, Minn.: Llewellyn Publications, 1994).

MILK THISTLE

1. In the Salento, however, the holy thistle is more docile (and less thorny), with violet buds. Exquisite king oyster mushrooms grow at its base.

2. In confirming the source (*Commentarii,* IX, 2), Alfredo Cattabiani completes the quotation: "It is said that Charlemagne, during a journey to Rome, passed by here [Mount Amiata] with an army struck by the plague. . . . While he was sleeping, he was visited by an angel who said this to him: 'Rise and climb this mountain, and when you have reached the peak, throw a javelin. Then pick the herb whose root will have been pierced by the point of the weapon. Then roast it, and when it has been reduced to a powder, mix it into wine and have those who are ill drink it. It will chase away every poisonous contagion and will restore the health of your army.'" (*Florario,* 290).

3. The analogical connection to milk is evidenced by the popular conviction that the thistle can be an excellent stimulator of milk flow and, as such, a primary food in the diet of the puerperal.

4. The donkey also gets the best of it in Greece. There, the term is *gaidurangatho,* formed from *gaidáron* (donkey) and *ákantha* (thorn).

5. A physician from Taranto in the second century A.D. and author of a lexicon, in alphabetical order, of the works by, or attributed to, Hippocrates.

6. One gram of milk thistle seeds crushed and reduced to powder and boiled in water for about ten minutes. It should be drunk once a day during the week before departure. The problem is that nowadays it is difficult to determine precise dates of departure.

7. Alan Davidson, *The Oxford Companion to Food,* 2nd ed. (Oxford: Oxford University Press, 2006).

8. Removal of the thorns is also strongly recommended by Culpeper, who adds, "unless you have a mind to choak yourself." Beyond all the other benefits of thistles that Culpeper lists (they strengthen the stomach, renew the blood in the spring, expel kidney stones, and on and on), they also, according to him, work wonderfully as deodorants. He writes: "All these thistles are good to provoke urine, and to mend the stinking smell thereof; as also the rank smell of the arm-pits, or the whole body; being boiled in wine and drank, and are said to help a stinking breath" (*Complete Herbal,* 180). It is curious that a single remedy may be used both to refresh your breath and to drive out melancholy.

9. Nonetheless, exactly one hundred years before James III, Louis, Duke of

Bourgogne, had established a chivalric order, Our Lady of the Thistle, that used the plant as its symbol and as its tutelary deity, so to speak.

MINT

1. Robert Graves, *The Greek Myths* (New York: George Braziller, 1957), 1:121.

2. See verse 273 of the *Homeric Hymn to Demeter* in *The Homeric Hymns and Homerica,* ed. Hugh G. Evelyn-White (Cambridge: Harvard University Press, 1914). "The term for rite is *òrgia,* which has, however, a different meaning in ancient Greek than *orgy* has in our language. It designated an intense interior state in which the initiate felt immersed and, therefore, propelled to an opening of consciousness near the dimension of the sacred" (S. Arcella, *Hera* 69, October 2005). As for the *kykeon* that Demeter prepares with her own hands in the *Hymn* (vv. 208–209), the goddess uses only "meal and water with soft mint." The *kykeon,* in its simplest form, is presented as a mixture of a liquid and a solid. The name *kykeon* derives from the fact that, before being drunk, the beverage must be stirred (from *kykao,* which means "to move, to mix, to stir"—like 007's martinis that must be served "stirred not shaken").

3. Despite the presumed recurrence of several ingredients in both potions, *kykeon* should probably not be identified with the beverage administered by Circe to Ulysses's unfortunate companions in Book X of the *Odyssey:* "then she mixed them a potion—cheese, barley / and pale honey mulled in Pramnian wine—/ but into the brew she stirred her wicked drugs / to wipe from their memories any thought of home" (trans. Robert Fagles [New York: Penguin, 1996], 237). All of this, naturally, occurs before turning them into swine.

4. Martial, *Epigrams,* trans. W. Ker, vol. 2 (London: Heinemann, 1920), 343.

5. Actually, the author of the *Problemata* (its attribution to Aristotle is at least doubtful) asks himself, "What is the reason of the saying, Mint should neither be eaten nor planted in season of warfare? Is it because mint has a cooling effect upon the body, as is shown by the corruption it causes in the semen? This is opposed to courage and spirit [which are required for fighting], being the same in nature" (XX, 2, 923a). Does that clear it up? For the *Problemata,* see *The Works of Aristotle,* trans. E. S. Forster, vol. 7 (Oxford: Clarendon Press, 1927).

6. Castore Durante, *Il tesoro della sanità* [Treasure Trove of Health] (Rome: Zanetti, 1586), 96.

7. A. Costantini and M. Marcucci, *I rimedi della nonna* [Remedies of a grandmother], (Galatina: Congedo, 1992), 110.

MYRTLE BERRIES

1. He was invested with the title by Victor Emanuel III (on the proposal of Benito Mussolini) on March 15, 1924, to celebrate the annexation of Fiume to Italy, which he had briefly occupied, years earlier, *manu militari. La pioggia del pineto* [Rain in the pine forest] is part of the collection *Alcyone,* published in 1903.

2. Pausanias, *Description of Greece,* trans. J.G. Frazer (London: Macmillan, 1913), 392.

3. *Metamorphoses,* IV, 538.

4. K. Kerényi, *Gli dei e gli eroi della Grecia,* vol. II, 237.

5. Ibid., 238–39.

6. Dante, *Purgatorio,* trans. Robert Durling (New York: Oxford University Press, 2003), 351.

7. To discover the native city of Statius, it was necessary for the Humanist bloodhound, Poggio Bracciolini, to find (in 1417) a manuscript of the *Silvae* (and therefore, a work unknown to Dante) in which Statius reveals his own origins (III, v).

8. This is certainly not the same Herostratus who, in order to become famous, burned and destroyed the temple to Artemis at Ephesus in 356 B.C.

9. Athenaeus, *The Deipnosophists,* vol. 3 [XV, 18], 1079.

10. Translation of Robert Fagles (New York: Penguin, 1996), 247.

11. "To this unanimous interpretation" says the dictionary of Cortelazzo and Zolli, "V. Valente (LN, XLIX, 1998, 15) counters with the idea that it comes from the Old French *morterel,* from the Latin *mortariu(m),* the mortar in which meat was crushed" (1009).

NETTLES

1. See vv. 117–118. Supposedly written between 1070 and 1112 and published in 1477, this work describes the medicinal properties of seventy-seven herbs.

2. In the previous book (XXI, 55, 92), however, Pliny had noted that the "stinging quality . . . does not come at once with the plant itself, but only when this has grown strong through sun exposure. When young indeed in the spring nettles make a not unpleasant food, which many eat in the further devout belief that it will keep diseases away throughout the whole year." The claim is not unlike that for today's apple, which, according to the proverb, keeps the doctor away if eaten once a day. During the Cold War, Americans substituted "the doctor" with "the Communists:" *An apple a day keeps the Commies away.* Everyone's an expert!

3. Maria and Nikos Psilakis, *Herbs in Cooking: Dietary Choices from Nature's Supply of Seasonings and Drugs* (Heraklion: Karmanor, 2003), 92.

4. A. Cattabiani, *Florario,* 292.

5. In the Salento, however, even the poor used nettles as turkey feed until not very long ago. They also did this with *pilusi*—that is, the leftovers from making cheese.

6. *Urtica dioica* is the most commonly found species native to North America. *U. urens,* the species described by the ancient sources mentioned in this chapter, can also be found in many parts of the United States and Canada, though it is not native.

1. One of the most famous books for children, Collodi's *Pinocchio* was translated into Latin not once, but twice. The first time was by Enrico Maffacini (1902–56) and was published by the Florentine publisher Marzocco in 1951. *Pinoculus* was so successful that two years later it was printed in New York, with an introduction in English and notes by O. Ragusa, by the publisher S. F. Vanni. It was translated a second time by the noted Latinist and Hellenist U. E. Paoli, *Pinoculus latinus* (Zurich: Artemis, 1982).

2. See "Antroponimia letteraria," *Rivista italiana di Onomastica,* vol. II, anno II, no. 2, 356–68.

3. *The Forme of Cury,* 31. Alkenet is a plant related to borage from which henna, used as a cosmetic, is extracted.

4. Denis, *Erbe spezie condimenti,* 146.

5. Apicius, 173. We present these brief quotes as a means of documenting the learned persistence of the term *pinocchio.* See also the Italian version of the Milanese futurist Paolo Buzzi (*La cucina di Roma* [Milan: Veronelli, 1957], 167 and 169). Not bad for a futurist of the first hour who promoted the destruction of museums and of traditional libraries.

1. This was, among other things, exactly what Satan had promised (Genesis 3:4–5): "But the serpent said to the woman, 'You will not die; for God knows that when you eat of it your eyes will be opened, and you will be like God, knowing good and evil.'"

2. Origen (A.D. 185–254) transforms everything into an anagogic metaphor and holds that even in the "cheeks like those of a turtledove" of a woman who had arrived at the threshold of marriage, "the beauty of the soul is represented."

3. See p. IX of the Italian edition produced by M. Simonetti, Fondazione Valla (Milan: Mondadori, 1998).

4. *Homeric Hymn to Demeter,* trans. H. G. Evelyn-White.

5. Friezes of pomegranates also decorated the capitals of Solomon's temple.

6. It is also a wonderful product for coloring hair (best to use the skin of the unripe fruit).

7. A gastropod that emits a stinking and burning liquid when frightened.

PRICKLY PEAR

1. See, respectively, pp. 265–267 of Book I and pp. 8–9 of Book II in the edition edited by Juan Pérez de Tudela Bueso for the Biblioteca de Autores Españoles (Madrid: Ediciones Atlas, 1959).
2. He accompanied the expedition of Cortéz, which he relates in his book *Historia verdadera de la conquista de la Nueva España*.
3. These were decidedly above-average pirates. Since 1659, the codex has been held by the Bodleian Library at the University of Oxford.
4. *Vita napoletana*, in *Le opere*, ed. P. Pancrazi, vol. 1 (Milan: Garzanti, 1944), 1099.
5. A. Costantini and M. Marcucci, *I rimedi della nonna*, 82–83.

PURSLANE

1. To the eternal damnation of those who compile linguistic atlases, *portulaca* is noted in different regions with different denominations: in Italian as *porcellana, procaccia, procacchia, perchiazza, sportellaccio, andraca;* in English as *purslane, purslave, pursely, pusley;* in Spanish and Catalan as *verdolaga, verdalaga, bulosa, hierba grasa, porcelana, tarfela, peplide* (Spain only), *colchón de niño* (El Salvador), *flor de las once* (Colombia), *flor de un día, lega* (Argentina); in Portuguese and Galician as *beldroega bredo-femea, baldroaga;* in Basque as *ketozki, ketorki, getozca;* in French as *pourpier, portulache;* in Chinese as *ma-chi-xian;* in Arabic-speaking countries as *baqla hamqa* (which means "crazy plant").
2. Sandra Mason, "If you can't beat it; eat it!" *The Homeowner's Column*, University of Illinois Extension, August 4, 2005, http://web.extension.illinois.edu/champaign/homeowners/050804.html.
3. But purslane lacks cholesterol.
4. Vaglio, *La cucina del Salento*, 80.
5. See Cicero's oration *In Verrem* (II, 1, 19). In Greece, one of the first to speak of purslane was inevitably Theophrastus in his *Enquiry into Plants* (VII, 1, 2), where he describes it as cultivatable and suggests seeding it in April.

RED POPPY

1. The record sold more than seven hundred thousand copies, twenty-five thousand more than the winning song of the festival that year, "Vola colomba" (Fly, dove). The lyrics of the winning song address a dove (traditional symbol of peace) in a very patriotic tearjerker calling for the return of Trieste to Italy, which would ultimately occur in 1954.
2. See "DC, PCI e una morale 'che dirvi non so,'" www.galleriadellacanzone.it/canzoni/anni50/schede/papaveri/dc.htm.

3. Gianni Borgna, *Storia della canzone italiana* [A History of Italian Songs] (Milan: Mondadori, 1992), 136.

4. Tommaseo's dictionary adds that *papavero* is used for a man who is foolish and has an unrefined mind.

5. "Tagliare le spighe più alte: ambizione individuale e interesse collettivo nella Polis," *Athenaeum* XCV, 2007, 745–53.

6. The text of *Hortulus,* originally included in Migne's *Patrologia Latina,* is now also available online.

SAMPHIRE

1. To be sure, it is unlikely that North American foragers will ever come across *Crithmum maritimum,* as it is not native to this continent and extremely rare. In its place, native edible succulents of the genus *Salicornia,* such as *S. bigelovii* and *S. pacifica,* also known as pickleweed, marsh samphire, or dwarf saltwort, can be used.

SOW THISTLE

1. Salvatore Presicce, *Piante medicinali spontanee del Salento* (LiberaArs editrice-multimedia, s.l., 2004), 50.

2. An obvious trace remains in the scientific name, *Sonchus oleraceus.* Another common name in Italian for this plant is *crespigno.*

3. Evelyn asserts that he was not speaking of sow thistles but of *taraxacum* (a.k.a. dandelion or piss-a-beds), which he defines as a healthful, slightly bitter green and inferior with respect to taste (but just a little) when compared to chicory (*succory*) and lettuce (*endive*); *Acetaria,* 15.

4. That is, samphire or *finocchio di mare*; see page 167.

5. This meeting, though brief (the protagonist dies before the victorious Theseus returns), overshadows even the actual capture of the bull and the triumphant return to Athens.

6. Ultimately, we may also want to consider what it means for there to have been so many bulls and minotaurs in Theseus's life.

7. This differs substantially from the meaning that Culpeper assigns to it, wherein the walking is not the cause but the effect.

STRAWBERRY TREE / ARBUTUS

1. But its habitat includes all of southern Europe and the Atlantic coasts as far north as Ireland. The terrain just needs to be right: noncalcareous, exposed to the sun, and not subject to cold winds. The strawberry tree tolerates drought, and in forests devastated by fire, it is one of the first plants to get itself back on track.

2. The Greek terms do not refer to two different kinds of arbutus. Rather, the first refers to the tree and the second to the fruit, which (according to Theophrastus) takes a year to mature and for this reason is found on the branches of the plant along with the flowers (*Enquiry into Plants,* III, XVI, 4). Juba II (52 B.C.– A.D. 23), King of Numidia and Mauritania, was raised in Rome by Octavian Augustus, with whom he became allied against Antony. A very cultured man, his (lost) work served as a guide to Pliny in the fields of zoology and botany.

3. Lucretius, *The Way Things Are* (*De rerum natura*), trans. Rolfe Humphries (Bloomington: Indiana University Press, 1968), 186–187.

4. *The Georgics and Eclogues of Virgil,* trans. T. C. Williams (Cambridge: Harvard University Press, 1915), 83.

5. Virgil, *The Aeneid,* trans. Robert Fagles (New York: Viking, 2006), 326.

6. In the body of the text, the poet designates the fruit with a very Tuscan name, *àlbatro.*

THYME

1. That is how Italian author and literary critic Giorgio Manganelli (1922–90) defined those of his acquaintances who, feeling the urgent need to read the classics in the original (and having reached a mature age) would dream of reestablishing familiarity with the Greek and Latin learned at school and "painfully" forgotten over the years. Useful to the appearance of being a reborn aficionado of ancient literature is leafing through a Greek or Latin grammar in such places as waiting rooms of railway stations, at airport gates, on public buses, and the like.

2. A "characteristic [that] is to be found only in the wild kind, mostly in rocky districts; the cultivated does not creep, but grows up to be a palm in height." It is also found more than frequently in soils that are dry, sunny, and (preferably) rich in silicon. If it does not creep, it forms magnificent pillows as a result of the wind's action. Speaking of pillows, it was a widespread opinion in the Middle Ages that a bunch of thyme placed under your pillow would keep nightmares away.

3. *The Georgics and Eclogues of Virgil,* 129–132.

4. Born in Perugia in the middle of the sixteenth century and died in Rome in 1622, Ripa was in the service of Cardinal Anton Maria Salviati, to whom *Iconologia* (1593) is dedicated, and he was a member of important academies like the Filomati, the Incitati, and, in particular, the Intronati (those seated on the throne) of Siena.

5. Plutarch, *Moralia,* trans. W. C. Helmbold (Cambridge: Harvard University Press, 1939), 6.

6. It was also believed in the distant past that the scent of thyme was welcome to the gods and that it would render the journey to the other world more enjoyable. We are not in a position to affirm whether this corresponds to the truth, but it is known that a sprig of thyme was found in the tomb of the pharaoh Tutankhamen.

7. In truth, there would also be oregano, which sometimes goes by the name *T. pulegioides,* and which may be substituted at any time for *serpyllum,* or common thyme, to which it is very close in both taste and qualities. Nonetheless, there are two good reasons for omitting it. First, it is well known to anyone who has ever set foot in a Chinese, Indian, or even Neapolitan pizzeria. Second, it is not an herb that figures in the present volume.

8. Davidson, *The Oxford Companion to Food,* 794.

9. The bouquet garni was created by François Pierre de la Varenne and described for the first time in his masterpiece, *Le cuisinier françois* (1651).

WALLROCKET

1. *Diplotaxis tenuifolia* (a perennial) and *D. muralis* (an annual) are the predominant species in North America. The former is, itself, sometimes called wild rocket or wild arugula. —Trans.

2. "Ragusano [cheese]," writes Antonio Casa at the site www.press.sicilia.it/formaggio_ragusano.cfm, "is born in an atmosphere from another time, among wooden tools with old names and slow gestures. As soon as the milk is drawn it is brought into the cheese-making shop. Smooth and rich in cream, the fresh milk here gives off the flavors of Hyblaean plateau grasses." "It has the form of a parallelepiped, it can reach a weight of thirty-five pounds, and it is marked by a Mediterranean scent. In six hundred years of history, assert the "card carrying" members of Slow Food, no industry has succeeded in reproducing such a richness of aromas. The hand of the dairyman and the nose of the cheese-ager are irreplaceable" (see Guglielmo Nardocci, *"Il cacio del picciriddu"* [The children's cheese], Famiglia cristiana online, no. 32, August 11, 2002, www.stpauls.it/fc02/0232fc58.htm).

3. Readers are advised not to consume cheese products made from the milk of cows that graze on slopes that become ski runs in winter and where, lacking natural snow, artificial snow saturated with poisonous chemical substances is sprayed. The poisonous substances melt into the ground and from the ground sprout poisoned grasses with which ignorant cows produce poisoned milk with which, in turn, those with few scruples make poisoned cheese. The end of this poisoned chain is, naturally, man.

4. Soon to be published is the *Dizionario botanico del Salento* [The botanical dictionary of the Salento], edited by Domenico Nardone et al., a work that will put an end (we hope) to this distress that we might define as Edenic, given that even Adam was one of its victims, charged by the Almighty with giving names to the things that he found himself surrounded by (only the animals, really).

5. Instead of *ramasciulo,* you sometimes come across the name *ruchetta violacea,* or "purple arugula."

1. Elio Pagliarani, *The Girl Carla and Other Poems,* trans. Patrick Rumble (New York: Agincourt Press, 2009) 111.

2. Cesaretto's was not a trattoria "like those you read about in novels"; it really existed, in the heart of Rome. The clients (almost always famous, such as painters Mino Maccari and Giulio Turcato, writers Goffredo Parise and Enzo Siciliano, actress Laura Betti, filmmaker Federico Fellini, photographer Mario Dondero, and so on) would sit wherever there was room and would more or less eat whatever was offered by the owner. Pagliarani ate there for years, almost daily.

WILD ASPARAGUS

1. Interesting, but absolutely fantastic, is the etymology proposed by John Evelyn in his *Acetaria,* in which he ascribes the name to the consequence of its roughness ("*ab asperitate,*" he writes). But then again, "next to Flesh [meat]," adds Evelyn "[there is] nothing more nourishing" (*Acetaria,* 66).

2. It seems that the Greeks were not lovers of asparagus as much as the Romans were. Theophrastus is more attracted by its prickliness ("these have no leaves except their spines") than by its comestibility ("the stalk comes up from the plant in spring and is edible") (*Enquiry into Plants,* VI, I, 3 and VI, IV, 2). If the weight and dimensions mentioned by Pliny seem exaggerated, then what can we say about Athenaeus (*The Deipnosophists,* II, 62), according to whom specimens can be found in Getulia (corresponding to present-day Mauritania and to the coastal territories of Tunisia and Algeria) that are thirty cubits high (about forty-five feet)?

3. Palladius, *The Fourteen Books of Palladius Rutilius Taurus Aemilianus on Agriculture,* trans. T. Owen (London: J. White, 1807), 130.

4. Cato, *On Agriculture,* trans. W. D. Hooper (Cambridge: Harvard University Press, 1934), 155.

5. In the *Guardian* of September 23, 2005, Peter Barhan refutes the opinion that there may be consumers of asparagus who produce odorless urine, arguing that the sulfuric molecules of asparagus acid end up in the liquid excretions of everyone who eats it. It's just that some people do not have an olfactory system sufficiently developed to notice it. We should be so lucky.

6. Platina, *On Right Pleasure and Good Health,* trans. and ed. Mary Ella Milham, 223.

7. Castelvetro, *The Fruit, Herbs &Vegetables of Italy,* 50.

8. See the entry "Of Sperage, or Asparagus" in J. Gerard, *The Herball.*

9. Achille Campanile, *Gli asparagi e l'immortalità dell'anima* [Asparagus and the immortality of the soul] (Milan: Rizzoli, 1999), 63.

1. See "A Neurologist's Notebook: A Bolt from the Blue," *New Yorker,* July 23, 2007, 38.

2. *The Edwin Smith Surgical Papyrus,* ed. J. H. Breasted (Chicago: University of Chicago Press), 1930.

3. This papyrus, which is said to have been found between the legs of a mummy in the Theban necropolis, can be seen today at the New York Historical Society.

4. According to the Hippocratic-Galenic classification of moods: hot or cold or dry or wet.

5. Various authors, *Erbe che curano* [Herbs that heal] (Florence: Giunti, 2004), 129.

6. M. Vaglio, *Cicorielle e lampascioni* (Nardò, Lecce: Besa, 1999), 34–35. Luigi Rizzo, a kind gentleman from Tricase (in the province of Lecce) notes that the crests of chicory plants are an essential ingredient in the so-called *paparotta,* a homemade dish that field workers traditionally consume midmorning (after having already worked for many hours). The other ingredients are stale bread, peas or beans, oil, garlic, salt, and chiles. If stale bread is not available, you can use the pasta left over from the previous evening.

7. *Brieve racconto,* 138. Castelvetro concludes his instructions for the preparation of a good salad ("and whoever does this and does not find it good, can complain to me") with what he defines as the [sacred] text of the "Salad Law . . . : Salad well salted, / a little vinegar and well oiled" (Ibid., 140). The confusion (or better yet, the habit) of grouping these greens into a broader family dates to antiquity. Among the first was Theophrastus, who holds the dandelion is "unfit for food and bitter" (*Enquiry into Plants,* VII, XI, 4).

8. Lovers also do this by blowing on them. In fact, it is widely believed that if the puffball falls apart completely at the first blow, the lover can be certain of being loved in return (either in the present or in the not-too-distant future).

9. Cleaned well, the entire rosette may be eaten either boiled or fried in a skillet. The flower heads, when they are still closed, are edible and can be pickled like capers.

10. De Gubernatis, *Mythologie des plantes,* vol. II, 86–92.

WILD FENNEL

1. Herodotus, *Histories,* trans. Henry Cary, book VI, 106–107 (London: George Bell, 1885), 393.

2. In 1921, the distance was fixed at exactly 42.195 kilometers.

3. Herodotus, *Histories,* book VI, 106.

4. Pietro Fanfani, *Vocabolario dell'uso toscano* (Florence: G. Barbera, 1863).

5. This example is noted by Cortellazzo-Zolli.

6. *Finocchio* is also used in the sense of "straw," and thus as a sign of weakness and fragility. Luigi Pulci draws on this connotation when, in *Morgante,* he writes of his character Rinaldo that he "still was making all the hostile spears / look like soft stalks of fennel all about" (XI, 39, 5–6). He also makes Orlando say that he wants to reduce the powers of Marcovaldo, the giant: "'You're talking out of shame: / you've labored hard to break a stalk of fennel'" (XII, 57, 1–2). And again Bianca says to her sister Brunetta, in order to humiliate her, "'No one breaks / a stump of fennel in your honor here; / my lover breaks all lances with his spear'"—that is, no one would fight for you, even with lances that would break easily, like those made of straw (XXII, 225, 6–8). Pulci, 196, 226, 521.

7. And in any case, they burned juniper to counter the bad smells. For some of these observations, we are indebted to *La gaya scienza,* the home page of Giovanni Dall'Orto.

8. *Lingua nostra* [Our language], XXIV, 1963, 57–58. The prolific eighteenth-century playwright Carlo Goldoni also recalls this character in his *Memoires* (part II, chap. 24): "[The character] Brighella represents a scheming, crafty, and under-handed servant. Dressed in a sort of servant's livery, his swarthy mask exaggerates the color of the inhabitants of those tall mountains burned by the scorching sun. Some actors who specialized in that part took the name of Finocchio, Fichetto, or Scappino, but all of them are the same servant, originating from Bergamo."

WILD RASPBERRIES

1. The Cheshire Cat is a character with the form of an animal in *Alice in Wonderland.* Alice meets him for the first time in the house of the duchess and then outside, in a tree. An entertaining conversation ensues between the protagonist of Lewis Carroll's book and the cat—one that, nonetheless, is not without its moments of irritation.

2. *R. idaeus* is also the most common raspberry species found in the United States and Canada and is often referred to as the American red raspberry. Other North American species include *R. occidentalis* (black raspberry) and, on the Pacific coast, *R. leucodermis* (whitebark raspberry) and *R. nivalis* (snow raspberry), all of which were used by Native American tribes for medicinal and nutritional purposes.

3. Pliny had previously said the same thing, almost word for word (Ibid., XVI, 71, 180).

4. Alessandro Manzoni, *The Betrothed,* trans. Bruce Penman (London: Penguin, 1972), 61. Penman's translation actually describes the mark as "strawberry," but in the original novel (*I promessi sposi*), Manzoni clearly uses the Italian *lampone,* or "raspberry," which has been substituted here.

1. Part I, chap. V.

2. *Wild Fruits,* 15–16. The Italian word *fragola,* on the other hand, has olfactory origins and derives from *fragranza,* or "fragrance." Even Thoreau, with innocent wonder, notes this peculiarity of the fruit.

3. See *The Code of Handsome Lake* in *Parker* [Arthur C.] *on the Iroquois,* ed. W. N. Fenton (Syracuse: Syracuse University Press, 1968), 25. The exact species to which these terms referred remains unknown. Both *Fragaria vesca* (or woodland strawberry, which is the equivalent of the *fragolina di bosco* found in Italy) and *F. virginiana* (Virginia strawberry) are found throughout New England and, in fact, across North America. A third common species, *F. chiloensis* (beach strawberry), is found along the Pacific coast.

4. On March 26, 1981, the New York City Council decided that the area of Central Park from Seventy-First to Seventy-Fourth Streets, inclusive, would be rebaptized Strawberry Fields. John Lennon's widow, the artist Yoko Ono, donated one million dollars for the area's modernization and maintenance. The zone covers an area of six acres. At the center is a mosaic donated by the city of Naples. Beyond all the psychedelic implications that have come to be attributed to "Strawberry Fields Forever," it appears that the title of the song takes its name from an orphanage in Liverpool, not far from Lennon's childhood home. The strawberry and its juice have shown themselves irresistible for quite a number of rock and country singers and groups, including "Strawberry Wine" by Matraga Berg and Gay Harrison, recorded by Deana Carter. Another song of the same title is counted among the repertory of the Bloody Valentines, and yet another vibrated the vocal cords of Ryan Adams. Finally, we cannot forget "Baby Fragola" by the Italian reggae group Pitura Freska: "When I see her, I go off the deep end, she who is so sweet and beautiful as a strawberry . . . Oh Baby Fragola—moments that seem like a fairy tale, Oh Baby Fragola."

5. Strictly speaking, the strawberry that we eat is not the fruit but its packaging. The fruits are the golden achenes visible on the surface.

6. Not without a word of caution, however: "it is not amiss to refrain from them in a fever, lest by their putrifying in the stomach they increase the fits."

INDEX OF RECIPES

CALIFORNIA STUDIES IN FOOD AND CULTURE

Darra Goldstein, Editor